SOPHIA'S RETURN

SOPHIA'S RETURN

Uncovering My Mother's Past

SOPHIA KOUIDOU-GILES

Published 2021
Printed in the United States of America
Print ISBN: 978-1-64742-171-7
E-ISBN: 978-1-64742-172-4
Library of Congress Control Number: 2021907028

For information, address:
She Writes Press
1569 Solano Ave #546
Berkeley, CA 94707

She Writes Press is a division of SparkPoint Studio, LLC.

Dedicated to my mother, Eleni,
and to all moms and their daughters.

Life's hurdles are surmountable,
and the future is full of promise. Claim it.

CONTENTS

PROLOGUE: THESSALONIKI, GREECE
October 2015

"I need to find my mother's grave," my voice rang with urgency, "before I leave Greece!" The woman behind the desk sat unwavering at her computer. She didn't seem to understand. I had just days to locate and visit my mother's burial site before returning to my home in America. Couldn't she see the necessity? How important this was? That, after a lifetime of wrestling with the loss of my mother, I'd just gotten a hint that she might not have meant it—that it might not have been her fault. I had to follow whatever paper trail might lead to her grave and trace whatever other clues might still survive along the way.

The clerk, a short, pudgy woman who worked on the second floor of Thessaloniki's City Hall, did not seem to understand. None of this mattered to her: who we'd been as a family, or who we were today—or who I might be, if I could finally put these pieces of the past back together again. She didn't even blink as she blithely checked her computer screen once more.

That morning, just as the shops were opening, I had walked again along the familiar, picturesque waterfront and through the park to the modern complex of municipal services that took up a whole city block. Like any other casual visitor, I'd entered through the lobby showered in daylight streaming in from glass walls and climbed up the stairs to an interior balcony that wrapped around an atrium lined with workstations. My heart seemed to press against my throat as I waited through that slow shuffle—the uncaring pace of bureaucracy, new or old.

1

Watching the woman search through her computer screens, not once but several times, I'd nearly left. Still, I'd waited, breathing as calmly as I could. What cemetery would my enigmatic mother be resting in? What grounds would she be roaming, waiting for her daughter to find her among silent companions and tall cypress trees?

"Sorry." The woman lifted her head and spoke fast. "There's no birth or death certificate for Eleni Hadjimichael."

No certificates? But that was impossible! "My mother lived in this city for nearly sixty-eight years." My voice came in a rush. My mother had been someone—someone who mattered, at least to me. How could there be no record of her, a whole life erased? "There must be some trace of her here somewhere." I had lost her in many ways in life, and I was not about to give up on her in death.

My gaze flitted desperately around those sterile offices, but the clerk just shrugged and sent me to another station around the corner. There, a bespectacled man sat at a similar-looking machine. He looked at me blankly as I insisted that my mother's death certificate must be found. He nodded, though not very convincingly, and I watched his hands press the keys on his keyboard until he finally stopped at one screen. "Here." He pointed at a document that my father had filed when he'd married my stepmother, declaring that his first wife had no rights to his estate. I took a quick breath, leaning back onto my heels. There it was, a signal of the yet undefined money disputes between them.

"Thank you," I said, though still it told me nothing of my mother's burial site, or the rest of the story—so very many years of it. But what if that was it? What if, after all these decades, all this grief, this was all that remained of my mother: just these financial records involving her dowry and divorce? Something in my gut shuddered at the ugly, high stakes of my parents' divorce that marked the end of the family I had known, the beginning of a second family—and, somehow, the eventual eclipse of the woman who was my mother.

"She was born here," I told the man. "I know that for a fact." But he returned a passive look and assured me that there was nothing more he could do. Now I was coming unhinged. It was time either to turn disagreeable or to give up. Filled with burning anger and the iron will that stemmed from frustration and past failures, I demanded, "I would like to talk to the supervisor."

The wiry man hesitated, but he finally got up, and I followed him down the hall where he stopped to knock on the supervisor's door. A woman's voice answered, "Come in."

"The lady wants to speak to you," he said once we were inside a well-lit office dominated by an organized desk with documents piled in a couple of trays and a blonde woman sitting behind it. The man turned toward me and waited.

Persistence has its benefits because the supervisor, a responsive matronly lady, looked at me expectantly. She was short, nearly lost behind the huge desk, a sharp dresser in a light blue suit, and she listened to my explanation sympathetically. When I finished, she nodded, and then she asked the waiting clerk to give me access and time to examine original documents stored somewhere in the complex. I thanked her gratefully, and she returned a warm smile. Then the man escorted me to a room with long wooden tables filled with attorneys peering over papers that they would return to city staff before leaving the room. Another clerk hurriedly carried in and handed me enormous logs, bound in black covers, a series of recorded deaths covering a couple of decades. Entries were handwritten in ink, each line dedicated to one deceased person after another. I ran my trembling finger down the page, tracking names and dates recorded in the customary Greek sequence: day, month, and year. October had been the month of her passing: Iasonidis, Gavriil, Loumis, Mavridou . . . Nothing there. Just in case, I decided that I should check over a period of three, four years to be sure; maybe I had the wrong month. September, October, and November. I took my time. No, still nothing. I shook my head, shut the last tome, and got up, weaving my way disappointedly out of the room, leaving all those useless logs with a clerk. That long morning had ended with copies of my maternal grandparents' death certificates—but nothing at all about my mother.

Until that warm October morning, I had been confident—blindly, optimistically, and perhaps now, I could see, foolishly confident— that I would finally accomplish my goal of visiting Mother's grave. After all, she *had* lived her whole life in Thessaloniki. Had married, given birth, divorced, and finally died here. How could it be possible that nothing was left to remember her? But somehow, nothing was. Disheartened, I trudged along the shops and morning traffic on Egnatia Street, carrying the only precious documents I could find, not of my mother's life, but her parents'. Still, I couldn't believe that this was the end of the line. Time endured; people endured. I was still here, and I was still questioning. *There had to be something, something else that I could do. How could my mother have disappeared entirely?* Blaming the bureaucracy was easy enough, but perhaps some of the fault was my own. Perhaps I'd gone too far afield, waited too long, and now the past—my family's and my own—was escaping me. Having lived abroad all these years, I was truly unfamiliar with the bureaucratic processes of my natal home. How did I know, anymore, how history was kept? What was Greece? And who was I? "I need help," I admitted to myself finally, speaking the words aloud so they hung in the air to witness my decision, not at all in my nature, to ask for help—beginning with my first cousin who, as far as I knew, had always lived here.

In the past, I had come back to Greece, my sunny, ancient country of a thousand temples to the Olympians, to spend most of my vacation in Thessaloniki, my birthplace, nestled on the northern shores of the Aegean Sea. North of Athens and an hour from the border with Bulgaria, a large metropolis, famous for its Roman and Byzantine monuments, it is the keeper of my story and home to several members of the Kouidis family. Although I had traveled here many times as an adult, this was my longest journey yet, one that I hoped would shed light on significant questions that still lingered in the shadows of my childhood. Now in my late sixties, I kept coming back, roaming its familiar wide streets, the narrow cobblestone alleys, knocking on doors of family and friends, visiting libraries and offices, and being met with smiles or frowns, all along searching out answers.

Why had my mother left me with my father when I was nearly seven years old? Why had she left at all? From what I had been able to deduce, I knew that my parents' story had been, in truth, an ordinary one in today's terms, even in Greece, though the simple facts of the case had been almost unheard of when I was young: divorce; a second marriage; a cheating husband passing time with women willing to pluck the low-hanging fruit of a failed marriage; and my mother moving back in with her parents, lost in the shuffle. Then as now, it's a sad story—but at least I had escaped such a stressful destiny, scaffolding a future in America, my new country, where I'd launched into a career in social services after completing studies in psychology and social work. Because of my occupation, I had encountered and understood well the plight of children lost in the mix of broken families and custody battles. Time and again, I had witnessed the children's sense of helplessness and confusion.

The loss of daily contact with the parent who leaves the household often weakens the bond between that parent and their child while the relationship with the custodial parent also suffers. This distancing from parents, the primary people in a child's life, often results in acting-out behaviors or withdrawal for children because they feel insecure, and their world seems chaotic and unpredictable. School performance may suffer too, as the child is grieving and has a hard time focusing on their assignments. The impact on me was to resent the loss, the distance from my mother, and become an introverted child, observant and careful in the world. Although I displayed few acting-out behaviors in my teens, it was evident that I had turned inward, often escaping to the world of literature.

So what, then, was missing? I'd launched my life forward, so why was I still gazing back at the past? Whatever held me there remained nameless, shapeless; I couldn't even tell what it was that was haunting me, but whatever it was, something still eluded me—and I had to sort it out.

So here I was, now, inside the soaring ceilings and stone walls of our family's Egypt Street loft, glancing up at the pale moon mocking me as it peered down from the skylight. On a dark, rainy evening, alone in the stillness of the old Kouidis Coffee warehouse, I replayed old reels of my childhood years. After six Septembers of seeking out answers about what had caused their divorce, all I knew was that my father had had affairs, and my mother's ineptness in the kitchen had caused my grandmother, Yiayia Sophia, to criticize her brutally. These weren't pleasant conflicts between brides and their mothers-in-law, but neither were they unique.

So, what was it? Were there more shameful stories, nasty family secrets, and scavengers hiding on the sidelines? Had that tension and mystery been caused by clashing cultures, incompatible personalities, alluring women, or life circumstances that I simply did not know? What, in the end, had sent my mother away? And what else might have played a role in my parents' break-up? Maybe I had done something to cause their separation? Thumbing through those bureaucratic files in Thessaloniki, I was no longer a naïve youngster, having raised a son and divorced my own husband after a twenty-five-year marriage, but some days still made me gasp with uncertainty about my inability to figure it all out, to force that past to reveal itself entirely. Ironic though it was, even someone like me, with forty years of professional experience in child welfare, couldn't seem to unravel the skein of my own story.

Through the unlatched roof window, sunlight peeked over the brow of Mt. Hortiatis and washed the room. A cruise ship's horn signaled its departure from the port, waking me up before the alarm went off. That morning, I would return to the Pacific Northwest, and my cousin was giving me a ride to the airport. He had been my father's favorite nephew, a boy he loved and teased, and a constant support to me who for many years had pummeled me with invitations to his family home whenever I vacationed in Thessaloniki.

We were traveling along the bay, on a dusky sunrise. After a three-month stay, my search in the past had netted me very little. Was it possible he had some answers? He had been kind and helpful to me in the past. He would be honest if he decided to share information. I checked his profile—thinning white hair and Roman nose—and decided to finally ask him. "The courts gave my custody to my father instead of my mother—why would they have done that?" He was, after all, older than me by three or so years and might have known more.

His deep brown eyes, a proud mark of the Kouidis clan, shifted to a far point on the road, as his fingers clutched the wheel firmly. Before he even spoke, I knew what he was going to say: "My parents were careful. They did not have such discussions in front of us kids."

Perhaps not, but I was sure he knew more, even though he was also right: My family held tightly onto secrets. He was one who had always been careful and measured with his words. I had done my homework in order to prepare for this quest and had interviewed several family members, taking notes, sharing what I knew, and confirming my own recollections against theirs. It was gratifying to revisit our younger years as it sometimes led us to tearful musings, rolling laughter, and even pregnant silences. I had missed opportunities that time affords those who stay put to pan more gold about circumstances and their roots because I left Greece right after high school on a Fulbright scholarship for post-secondary studies.

Reviewing the history of Greece in the early twentieth century— besieged by two world wars and a civil war, reeling from the influx of Greeks displaced from Turkey—gave me the historical backdrop of the era my family lived through. Visiting libraries to read old news-paper articles and contacting organizations that had genealogical information about Greeks from Turkey yielded results about the loca-tions where my people had resided. That led me to travel in distant parts of the Middle East, where my father had been born and lived. The stark reality was that records were scarce, since many had been destroyed or were inaccessible because of wars, fires, and the general lackadaisical record-keeping practices of that era. When I sought my own records, in order to establish a passport and Greek identity card, I witnessed how contemporary Greek bureaucracy was just begin-ning to enter the age of computers and tracking of documentation. The country was in a state of "reconstruction," attempting to fill in lost and destroyed records of people and landholdings. I also gained a sense of the socioeconomic and social issues of the time and an appreciation of the obstacles and struggles people had to overcome.

What mattered more at this juncture was the fact that I was leav-ing Greece again, empty-handed. I had not answered my main ques-tion about how the custody had been settled. Recently retired from social services, my oversized suitcase filled with research notes about family history loaded into the belly of an airplane, I had no infor-mation about the custody question. Divorced and single, I had been struck by how living on two continents and all the years of settling into the United States had made my childhood story impervious to penetration. Sometimes, I wondered why I had not given up the search.

After bidding my cousin goodbye, I walked on Macedonia Airport's asphalt tarmac and climbed up the passenger loading stairs. On the plane, following the lineup to the economy class section, I stored my carry-on and coat in the overhead compartment and settled into an aisle seat. Clasping the seat belt, I placed my laptop in the seat pocket in front of me, reached for a magazine, and smiled quickly at the old woman next to me, unwilling to start a conversation.

The crew started broadcasting "Welcome aboard" announcements, and the whirl of jet engines signaled that we would be on our way shortly. I was about to leave Thessaloniki, my multicultural birthplace that sprawls around lazily in an arched coastline at the top of the Thermaikos Gulf of Northern Greece. Leaning into the drone of the plane, I shut my eyes, preparing to cross worlds, and eventually reached for my laptop to begin studying the scanned documents I had collected on this trip. How could I penetrate more deeply into all the available information, the public records and documents held by family and friends? Undoubtedly, there was resistance from certain people when it came to answering all my questions. If the people I knew wouldn't help me, I needed another approach. Perhaps what I needed was to hire a neutral party, someone outside my family. Yes, that was it. Next time, when I returned in the fall, I would seek a local expert, someone who could finally help me sort out the mysteries of the past.

PART I

1 SIGNS OF TROUBLE
Fall 1952–Spring 1953

The gray October sky drizzled a melancholy rain for a few days over Thessaloniki. Pools formed in the chuck holes of the wide *alana*, the open space we played in, and heavy drops hung on the doorways and windowsills of our homes. Children stayed inside, deserting the neighborhood streets. It was time to dig out our wool dresses, long sleeves, and sweaters in Thessaloniki.

On a quiet Sunday morning, Mother and I swept around the rugs we'd laid on the floor for the winter and spring at our 25th of March Street home, a street named after a national Greek holiday. I tried to bargain for permission to play in the yard but soon resigned myself to our life indoors as my mother brought in a gunny sack with clothes-pins from the laundry room and dumped them on the living room carpet. I knelt next to her, a tall, spindly, restless six-year-old girl, wishing to be outside at play.

"Help me sort out these pins," my mother instructed, taking off her apron and settling cross-legged on the floor. Then we sat together for some time, collecting dismantled pins and searching for loose metal springs. I returned the good pins to the gunny sack and watched Mother assemble springs back into limbs and toss out the leftovers. She had always overseen the entire litany of washing, hanging, and ironing clothes and was good at finding projects for both of us, even on the rainiest of days.

In the other room, Yiayia Sophia, my paternal grandmother, began working on dinner, chopping lettuce for the salad, while my parents went to their bedroom for an afternoon nap. Even without my mother's watchful eye, I knew I couldn't go outdoors because of the chill, and everyone said it was still too early in the season to fire up the new stove. From the living room window, I watched a flock of crows perched on tawny brown branches holding on brittle, lingering leaves of the plane tree in our backyard, scouting for food. Then I heard Yiayia's voice from the kitchen.

"Come *yiavri mou*," my "little bird," she called to me in her own colorful Turkish dialect. "Come here for just a minute." When I arrived, she asked me to open a can of tomato paste. "Here," she handed me the can, her fingers refusing to bend because of her rheumatism. I did her bidding and handed back the open can, watching as she spooned the contents into a pan that was heating over the Primus stove, stirring it for a while, then pausing to taste the sauce. "Mmmm!" She smacked her lips in satisfaction, turning off the burner. "If your father asks, tell him I'll have dinner ready at the usual time. I'm going next door to your aunt Eleni's." Taking an unopened can along with her umbrella, she headed out the back door to her daughter's house. "Back soon," she called out.

Time was dutifully marching along, as it does—until, that is, some incident or other suspends it dead in its tracks. But for the time being, I had no idea about the tricks of time, and I settled carelessly into playing my familiar, solitary games. An only child, I was used to alone time, waiting for adults and devising ways to fill the quiet hours of the day. That particular day of my seventh year was one of those quiet afternoons when, setting my shoes by my bed, I picked up the box of wooden cubes and tiptoed in my stocking feet under the black living room table to play with them.

That sleek living room table had three spindles supporting its center, which were decorated with shiny brass rings that fascinated me. I liked to turn the cool, looped rings and pretend I was driving a car, imitating the sounds of an engine as I changed gears. Up the hill, I imagined, the gear floundered at the top, and I stopped to look around, shading my eyes, expecting something and nothing at the same time. I was a girl alone, content, living in my imaginary world where nothing much happened, and it seemed it never would. But that day, inexplicably, turned out to be unlike the others. Suddenly, amid my play—long before I'd expected my solitary revelry to be interrupted—my father appeared in his pajamas. Indeed, like some crazy satyr I'd summoned in a dream, he sprung out of my parents' bedroom chasing my mother, who was a few steps ahead of him. As though in a horror movie, they reached the table, oblivious to my presence there hunched over underneath it. Instead, in a strange, spontaneous choreography—too quick, too certain—he kept after her, stretching to grab her—growing closer and larger than life. I held my breath; I didn't dare move.

"Stop it!" my mother cried in a distorted, high-pitched voice, sounding afraid and helpless. She was moving fast in her bare feet, alarm in her voice. I felt myself shrinking into nothing, moving close to the center of the table to stay out of sight. Shaken, hidden, and unseen, I watched their rushing footsteps, willing them to stop.

But they didn't stop. Instead, my father's leather slippers whirled by me with the speed of lightning. "You're a bitch!" he seethed and lunged, reaching for my mother.

What?! Stunned by his anger, I followed their voices, tracking them back to their bedroom, as their door thundered shut. A moment later, their stormy explosion quieted down, though I stayed frozen under the table for a long time. Time in its trickery stood still, as it does now and then, whenever I relive that scene. How was it possible? Still like a terrible dream, that brief interlude was the only time that I saw my father being physical with anyone, and it telegraphed that something was terribly wrong in our home, colored with a tinge of violence.

When I could finally move, I ran out the back door without an umbrella and found Yiayia in Aunt Eleni's living room. The pelting rain had penetrated my bones, and muddied socks chilled my feet. "I'm cold!" I shouted, running inside, with Aunt Eleni following behind me, protesting the mud prints on her floor.

"Look at this mess. I just mopped!" She was piqued.

"Are you okay?" From the living room couch, Yiayia straightened. "Are you okay, Sophoula?" She was holding a demitasse cup of Turkish coffee and motioned me to sit next to her.

"I am," I mumbled, "but Father is angry with Mother." She flinched, and I thought for a moment that my words had stung Yiayia, but she answered reassuringly.

"Come here," she said, turning toward me. "It's nothing," she promised, setting her coffee on the table and stripping off my wet socks. "Why did you leave the house without shoes, *zevzekiko*?" she scolded lightly in her own brand of Turkish, rubbing my feet with vigorous affection. After a while, she turned toward her daughter. "Eleni, bring a pair of dry socks and slippers for Sophoula." Her voice was light, but she was wringing her hands. "She must have upset him," she muttered to herself. But how could Yiayia say that it was nothing? Even Aunt Eleni was acting out of sorts. She forgot to bring back socks.

"Come on, Eleni," Yiayia called, annoyed, and Eleni rushed out of the room. My grandmother was always taking care of things, keeping busy in the kitchen, offering me treats, toys, and enduring love, but she avoided dealing with trouble. It certainly would have been worth having a talk with her son about this matter. She could have helped them get along; he would listen to her. But would she? Did she? There certainly were enough Turkish conversations in our household that I knew my father and grandmother had matters they kept to themselves. Secrets, I supposed, but I told myself I didn't care. All I wanted was for both of my parents to be home when we got back for dinner, calm and peaceful; but my father was gone, and already I sensed that I wouldn't be getting any explanations—because, of course, my yiayia believed that what I didn't know would not hurt me.

Sure enough, I didn't see any other incidents for quite a while; whatever was going on was kept from me, though it wasn't entirely true that it didn't affect me. After that day, I had reasons to be watchful, realizing that adults had secrets; and whatever their trouble was, it was as hateful as it was frightening. It was as if the landscape had shifted: A sudden wind had blown and filled the yard with fallen leaves, and naked trees were piercing a graying sky. What was certain was that my parents were burdened. That day, alarms had gone off, whistling in my ears.

The cold winter months rolled on without incident, and then spring set in with its blossoms, sunny days, and blue skies. My days returned to their ordinary rhythm. By then, I was used to morning school and adored my kindergarten teacher, a gray-haired, motherly woman with limpid blue eyes. Each day, I walked the few blocks to the classroom by myself. When school was over, I returned home to look for my neighborhood playmates.

On one such day in the middle of a still gray March sky, during an afternoon of ordinary play, my world turned upside down again. My pals and I were playing hide-and-go-seek out in the *alana*. The whole neighborhood gang had gathered that day, a gaggle of boys and girls passing the time in a game of speed and hiding. I was a fast runner, but the older boys were especially good at catching up with the younger set, and I paid the price of being "it" a lot, although I could find them easily because they always used the same hiding places.

Careful and persistent, I checked for signs of shoes, ankles, anything that would give them away. Crouching to look under cars, I tracked shadows inside yards and movement behind fences. We sped around the dirt floor of the *alana*, dust covering our shoes and socks, and occasionally scraping our knees from sudden collisions. The game had gone on awhile, and I was getting short of breath, sweat trickling down my back. My throat felt dry, and near our neighbor's lumber shed, I decided to take a break from the game, long enough to get a drink.

"I'm out," I shouted, crossing the expanse of the *alana* to get a glass of water. Then I noticed a truck parked in front of our house, but it wasn't our jalopy, my father's business truck. I stopped and squinted to be sure, but no, the truck wasn't like anything I knew. Stranger still, our front door was wide open, and men were moving a trunk and boxes out to the parked vehicle. The cab was nearly full, and I thought I saw Mother's nightstand loaded in. The men were muscular hamals (porters), but not anyone I knew from Father's warehouse in the Ladadika district. They were moving quickly, hardly speaking to each other. Who had let them in? And where was my father?

A man came out then, sat behind the wheel, and started the engine, waiting for it to warm up. Just as quickly, my mother walked out of the house, her gait unsteady, and took the passenger seat. I tried to get her attention, but she was looking away from me, so far off into the distance that I couldn't imagine exactly what she was thinking. Then, with a snap, she pulled the door shut. If she cried, I couldn't see it, though I imagine now, all these years later, that same image of my mother, hunched forward, contemplating her life, forlorn as a loon.

And then, just as soon as I'd noticed them, they were gone. A couple of hamals slammed the cab doors and climbed on the back, riding on the truck bumper, likely getting a lift to the next bus stop. Slowly, the truck disappeared on an elbow turn of the road, but still no one came out of the house. Nothing moved as that truck rolled away with my mother in the cab. I watched it, motionless, a chill coursing through my body and a vague sense of fear seizing my heart.

Maybe she would return soon, I thought, as the truck wound its way out of sight. Maybe she would bring back new things for the house and call me in for supper. Even then, I knew that couldn't be right—but neither was it right, what was happening. Even all these years later, I wonder how she could have left me, her only daughter, without a word. Perhaps it was too painful just then to seek me out and tell me that she was going away. Still, she could have said something—that she would be gone for a while, maybe even making up some excuse so I wouldn't be waiting for her to return. Or Yiayia could have told me, "Your mom doesn't get along with your father. She is moving in with her parents." Any message would have signaled that I had permission to ask more and been better than silence. But there was none. My mother was gone, and my father said nothing. In their day, it would never have occurred to them to tell me together that they were splitting up. That kind of communication was definitely not the realm of fathers. Children were assigned to women.

And I? What did I do? Did I call out to my mother, watching her disappear, feeling the cold sweat begin dripping down my collar, giving me a little shiver? If I did, I don't remember it now—not a single sound coming from my lips.

After some time—who knows how long—Yiayia came to the door. "Come inside. Your soft-boiled egg is ready."

When I walked inside, I wasn't hungry. I was thirsty for an explanation. Yiayia's wrinkles seemed deeper, her mouth tighter, her eyes a little darker.

"Where did Mother go?" I asked, gulping down the glass of milk she handed me.

But she just calmly cleared her throat. "She took some stuff away, Sophoula." Then she asked if I wanted more milk.

My grandmother was a master at redirecting my attention, but that day it didn't work. I shook my head and, not reassured with her answer, I decided to wait and see. My mother would tell me when she returned. But she did not come back by my bedtime, and my father was late again.

In bed, I began counting sheep. Darkness, nourished by Yiayia's silence, crept into my dreams and stirred up worries, but I managed to keep hope alive that dawn would bring my mother back.

2 REUNION
October 2013

I have always maintained contact with my father's siblings and their children in Greece. In recent years, whenever my family and I came to Greece for summer vacations, it would be my first order of business to call and alert my Kouidis relatives that I had landed.

"I am in town. How are you? When will I see you?" It was the first blush, my greeting phone call to invite them to meet us. Often calling from my father's home, for that is where I based my stays in Thessaloniki, this was my outreach to my Kouidis cousins.

We had grown up together, sometimes crowding into Father's jalopy on family outings, and other times spending afternoons watching weekend backgammon tournaments between my uncles in our backyard and playing hide-and-go-seek or soccer. When my relatives gathered, it was an opportune time to eavesdrop on their conversations and get casual news and updates on family gossip.

Gathering around Aunt Eleni's veranda, we would watch a couple of backgammon games—or three if there was a tie—unfold. Often it was my father with Uncle Chris, Aunt Eleni's husband, or Uncle Yiannis who accepted the challenge. Two chairs and a table were set up on the veranda or in the yard, by the round daisy flower bed. The wooden game board would be set on the table, and the dice would be tossed with gusto, hitting the wooden surface loudly, all eyes fixed on the dots of the dice. These games were taken seriously; they were competitive events, dotted with war cries announcing good rolls, poor moves, and victories.

"Another game lost! Get ready to lose again," the winner would provoke.

Women usually sat nearby and carried on their own conversation, and that was the best gossip of all.

"Did you know so and so's wife is pregnant? Is this going to be a boy or a girl?" someone would ask.

"I think a girl, judging from the way she is carrying the baby," Yiayia Sophia might guess.

"Pears are in season. Go to the Modiano Market to pick some up. Real good!"

Later, while I was attending university in the US, I would receive an occasional letter from my cousins with updates about their plans, studies, engagements, and the like, and I would write back.

They too kept track of me through the years, and I found them welcoming me with open arms to their homes, meeting places, family dinners, and gatherings in cafés and restaurants during my Greek vacations. My first cousins were like brothers and sisters to me, sibs I had grown up with as an only child until age ten, sharing family vacations and weekend activities. But there were those that I lost track of who were acquaintances and relatives on my mother's side.

My cousin Stella had never visited our 25th of March Street home when we were youngsters. I always met her at my maternal grandparents' home, but it had been over forty years since our last get-together. She was younger than me by three or four years, and the daughter of my mother's brother. At one point, my mother had given me the only photograph that I have of the two of us. Back then, I was a tall youngster in elementary school, while Stella hadn't yet started kindergarten. In that old photograph, we're posing in front of a statue in a park, holding hands and looking serious. She wore a dainty organza dress, and I sported mid-calf slacks, two perfect images of girlhood.

After all those years, it had taken quite a lot of effort to find my first cousin because she was now married and settled in another city.

Over most of an entire fall of that year, I focused on searching the internet, tracking potential addresses, knocking on neighborhood doors, ignoring barking dogs, asking past neighbors for clues, leaving notes in mailboxes. Weeks passed, hope waned, and then my phone rang. It was Stella! After a friendly exchange I made my request. Stella was enthusiastic. "Meet? Back in Thessaloniki? Of course!" In her gravelly smoker's voice, she suggested, "How about Aristotle Square, near the Olympion movie theater?"

So there I was, waiting at an outdoor café in the main city square of downtown Thessaloniki. It was the right place to meet, a well-known square that had been used for auspicious and everyday gatherings, rallies, festivals, and celebrations.

In my Sunday best—a light green, short-sleeved pant suit and sandals matching my purse—I stood there, just as auspiciously, having run just like a schoolgirl down the steps to the cobblestone street to meet her. During the ten minutes it took to walk from the loft to the square, I wondered if she'd be waiting there already—and if she would recognize me. Would she look the same? Would she remember our childhood years as fondly as I did? And, most importantly, would she share information about my mother?

As usual, the square was teeming with people. A young crowd filled tables set under shading umbrellas, hovering at cafés for long hours with friends, placing orders for coffee, soft drinks, and toasted sandwiches, carrying on animated conversations. I glanced around. Where was she? Had she come? My heart beat faster as I searched through the faces spread around tables at the café, next to the movie theater. But then, with a sigh of relief, I spotted her. Not only that, but her face was astonishingly recognizable: high cheeks, light brown eyes, long hair with blond highlights, and tan skin. Her smile was warm and wide. "Oh, Stella," I cried. "I would recognize you anywhere!"

My cousin stood up to greet me, and we hugged. "Sophia," she smiled wider, "what a joy to see you. All those years—I feel like not a day has gone by!"

Her family had come along, too, and one of Stella's sons, a tall and lanky young man, dropped by to meet me and soon left to find his friends.

"They enjoy the company of people their own age." Stella laughed.

I guessed that he must have been younger than my son. "He is, but my second son is older, married with a daughter and settled in Romania."

"You must pay him visits, just to watch that grandbaby growing," I replied. "I have two grandsons too." And we both reached for our cell phones to share photographs of our sons' families.

"So, where do you live and what do you do?" The town she lived in was a good size, and her husband was in electronics manufacturing. We exchanged updates about ourselves and bragged about our grandkids.

That afternoon, what stood out were some long forgotten moments. Stella had a knack that Mother had loved. Even when my mother's eyes were shut in momentary consternation, a smile would blossom on her lips when Stella offered to fix her hair. She took pleasure modeling new hairdos. "Don't you love this curl!" she would tell the mirror, admiring her coiffed style. It was no surprise when Stella told me that she and her sister were engaged in merchandising creams and skin products.

During my college years in America, my cousin had joined Mother on some excursions in the countryside and had pictures to show that she promised to send me. "I wish I could have been there too," I told her. "Sometimes, I still feel guilty about the way I abandoned everyone here to settle in America, even though I tried to bring my mother to stay with me."

"But you are here now," she beamed. "And what do you think? When will you come back to Thessaloniki again?"

Whenever we spoke on the phone, her voice would lift up a tone or two, and I would insist, "Let me know when you visit Thessaloniki. I would love to see you next time." When she did, I treated us to dinner in the Ladadika district.

"Do you have any old family pictures of Mother, your aunt Nitsa, to share with me?" She did. Later, after I'd returned home, I found a handful of black and white photographs in my email. Thanks to Stella, I got a glimpse of my mother in her high school days, with her parents and siblings, in the countryside in front of a grove of trees, all lined up in two rows. "Just look at them." I smiled, tracing the edges of the photograph. They wore city clothes, my grandfather and Stella's father, a very tall and thin teen, in suits and vests, the women in long dresses, and everyone looking serious. Mother wore a white collar over a simple, dark dress and sat next to my grandmother Athena in the back row. Her hair was short, and her eyes were fixed dreamily in the distance. My aunt Marika was lying on the ground right up front, looking at the photographer, relaxed. It seemed that she and my mother enjoyed family outings in their early days. The photograph, I thought, must have been taken a handful of years before World War II had broken out, in the days when the family was still thriving.

After that initial visit, there were more conversations, occasional phone calls when we painted in small and large canvases as we chatted about the past. Stella spoke of my mother's devotion to her sister, our aunt Marika, who continued to need hospitalizations because of mental health problems. "But I came to the apartment often to see her and Marika when she was home," Stella explained to me by phone. "We even took a couple of day trips to other parts of Greece together." Cousin Stella knew, too, that my dream to bring my mother to America had finally taken place—though only for a few months. "She talked about how glad she was to see you in a good marriage in America. She liked your husband." My mother apparently also liked to highlight the comforts we had—the car, the dishwasher—but she also spoke about the long hours and hard work that our jobs required.

"That sounds like hard work," my cousin sympathized, referring to the forty years I had worked in child welfare—practicing, researching, teaching, administering, and learning about human nature, dysfunctional families, and the potential to strengthen and improve when people are willing to commit to change. Although my cousin did not know much about the demands and tasks of each workday, she understood that "interfering" in families' lives because of concerns that children might be abused or neglected had to be challenging. She was kind, though our communication faltered in time because of distance, dwindling mostly to phone calls and Facebook exchanges. All the same, I remain grateful to Stella for giving me a lead that I hoped would take me to Mother's grave. Out on the plaza that day, she named the church where my mother's funeral services had been held.

Later that week, I found myself walking up the steps through the central arched colonnade of Panagia Dexia, an imposing Orthodox church dedicated to the Virgin Mary on Egnatia Street. My hope was that a record of my mother's burial site was kept in the church office. In the shadows of the narthex, I lit a candle to the icon of the Virgin Mary and looked around, but the only person there was an overweight church caretaker who had finished sweeping. She set her broom aside and began collecting the melting candles that were set in sand, burning next to mine. She dropped them in a box for recycling and turned toward me as I explained my mission.

"The priest will be back soon. He just left to run an errand," she assured me sympathetically—but he never turned up. Once it was time to leave, as I got up, a yearning came over me and, surrounded as I'd been with icons of ascetic saints and scenes of Christ's burial and resurrection, a vision came over me of descending the church steps to the depths of Nitsa's grave. There in her coffin she lay, peaceful and resting; her lifeless, gaunt face, her hollowed cheeks, a bitter mask of absence. Drawn to her bony hand, I remembered how once she had combed my hair and held me tight in endearment, and I wept.

That evening, after my unsuccessful trip to the church, I climbed up the circular staircase to my Egypt Street loft. Impulsively, and almost in spite of myself, I dialed my oldest cousin's phone number in Athens, resolved to prod hard for answers. He picked up the phone, that boy who had once lived next door to our 25th of March Street house. He'd been tall and skinny then, an avid cyclist who appreciated the neighborhood bakery treats. Now, after a few pleasantries, I steeled my voice and ventured a guess: "I heard that they tried to make my mother out to be crazy." Even as I spoke, I could feel anger seeping from my pores, my spine erect. "And I had to hear it from people outside the family. That is wrong, you know. You should have told me." Shifting in my chair, I waited for his response, stewing over an intuition that my aunt's mental health problems could have been used to smear my mother's reputation.

I imagined my cousin's bushy eyebrows moving up to his hairline. "They *had* to exaggerate their accusations to be heard by a family court," he answered hesitantly, embarrassed and almost apologetic. "Divorce was unheard of back then."

"Yiayia, she was part of the trouble," I added, compelled to lay out all my suspicions, but then paused.

"They didn't get along," his voice sounding gentle and conciliatory this time.

"They must have had paid witnesses who lied in court," I continued, rushing to expose all my suspicions. "Do you know who it was?" Again, he was silent. There was no more he could or would give out. *There must be something awful he is not sharing*, I decided, *but I am not giving up*, and I laid the handset in its cradle.

3 THE AFTERMATH
March 1953

The house on 25th of March Street was not the same with Mother gone. I missed her voice, her touch, and the presence that filled our home. Where was she? When would she be back? And why would no one answer my questions? It was the heart of fall, the day promised to be warm, bright, and clear, and our front door was wide open. A whole week had gone by, and early in the day, I sat in the doorway to wait for the milkman. Father had already left for work, and I was waiting for Mother. Maybe she would turn up in time to get the milk? Each day, I hoped that she would.

Our home was early on the delivery route. A tall man and his docile gray donkey came around the bend. On either side of the saddle hung large, galvanized jugs of milk, and several small measuring containers clanked rhythmically against each other each time the animal took a step. Hearing the racket of metal containers, Yiayia Sophia rushed out of the kitchen, drying her hands on her apron, her forehead dripping with sweat from cooking over the stove, and she met him with a deep pot in hand.

"Good morning, Mrs. Sophia. What will it be? The usual? Do you need some cream?" he called out.

"The usual," she answered.

Under Yiayia's watchful eye, the milkman measured out the ivory liquid and walked to our door to pour it in her pot.

Then he asked, curious, "Is Mrs. Nitsa sick?"

My ears perked, listening for her answer. Yiayia had to know where my mother was.

"I will get the milk from now on," she answered curtly. And that was all.

A sinking feeling awoke in my stomach. Usually, I enjoyed gazing at the donkey—his large, shiny eyes and twitching ears—and I would linger to watch his milk deliveries throughout the neighborhood; but that day was different. Shutting the door behind us, I let my shoulders slump and made fists with my hands as I followed Yiayia to the kitchen, troubled.

Yiayia had her routines about everything. She fired up the stove to heat the liquid and stood close by to make sure that it did not boil over. "Get your sweater on," she told me. "Time to walk to school."

Stung by her abruptness, I was overcome with a sense of foreboding and instead simply looked down at my shoes.

"Here," she handed me a square piece of chocolate that she had wrapped in foil. "Put this in your pocket for the school break."

I stuck it in my pocket.

The milk had cooled down some when she poured it in a pitcher, not quite ready for the icebox.

Where was Mother? Was she coming back?

"Go on. You will be late for school," she said, avoiding my eyes. I did not move. Yiayia dried her hands on her apron again, set the pitcher on the counter, took me by my hand, and firmly walked me to the door. My sweater hung limp on the doorknob. Slipping my arms into the sleeves, I turned to plead with her for an answer one last time—but her hard, steely eyes stopped me.

Outside, I shivered in the morning chill and crossed to the sunny side of the street. The milkman and his donkey were long gone. From the sidewalk, I could almost see our schoolyard and hear the children chirping like starlings as they gathered. I never did find out where my mother was that morning. Maybe she would come to pick me up from kindergarten as it let out. Sometimes she did.

When I arrived home from school, I found only Yiayia at home, and I settled sullenly in the living room. My neighbor Soula, sister of the same milk—for her mother had breastfed me because I was the baby of a wealthy family—knocked on the kitchen door ready to play. As ever, I ran to answer it, following her to the backyard—but then stopped in my tracks.

"What was going on at your house?" she asked right away.

"Don't know." I scowled and looked away, realizing that the whole neighborhood must have witnessed that scene. "Hamals loaded a truck, and Mother left with them."

Soula of the wide forehead and the short, straight hair fiddled with a hair pin and said, "I know, but why?"

Fretting, I replied, "How do I know?" How could I explain to her what I did not understand myself, let alone find words to describe my fears? Grabbing her wrist, I pulled her toward the *alana*, looking away toward a blurry 25th of March Street, quickly wiping scalding tears from my cheeks with the back of my hand.

Gradually, we walked to our marked hopscotch spot outside of Aunt Eleni's fence, and Soula started playing. Taking my turn, too, I did my best to get into the familiar rhythm of that game. *Watch where my feet land, jump a bit higher, time to split and land*, I plotted, and then kicked the pebble. Success, I got to keep playing. Drawn into the game with my friend, I felt relief and detachment from my recent troubled days.

That spring afternoon, filled with the fragrance of honeysuckle under a lapis sky, rolled by in play. Hop and jump and kick the pebble, over and over again. Then I heard Yiayia calling me from the kitchen. "It's lunchtime. Come in." Soula heard her, too, and we each returned to our homes.

I was watching Yiayia like a hawk these days for any clues about

Mother's whereabouts; she shared her sandwich with me, layered with salami and thin slices of tomatoes. She was her usual busy self, attending to our meal that we finished in silence, sharing slices of a red apple she had quartered, keeping the peel. "Good vitamins," she said, taking a bite.

Father, who was accustomed to shopping for seasonal fruit and vegetables, always insisted, "Fruit is our natural food. Have some." She never had to press me, so I gobbled down my share but I did not feel like hanging around her or going out to play. Although I usually resisted naps, I felt tired today and told her that I would lie down for a while.

"I'll wake you up for your afternoon snack if you aren't up soon," she answered, a little surprised and examining my face, but I headed off for my nightgown and my soft bed. Hypnos, the ancient god of sleep, came easily, sending his sons and daughters to awaken my dreams. In this hazy, dreamy stage, an unfamiliar, smoky shadow lingered outside a large dark house. The ghostly shape began to move toward me. I could see it from my bedroom window and somehow knew that walls would not stop it from seeping in. Alarmed, I rushed to lock the front door and ran down the stairs to the basement. The cement floor felt hard under my bare feet, and, for a moment, I felt safe.

But the apparition reappeared outside the basement window and slithered inside. It began taking the vague shape of a woman. I looked away, only to feel the warmth of breath on my cheek. Turning, I came face to face with my mother's dark eyes. Watching her lips move, I strained to understand her whispers, but couldn't make out any words. I reached to touch her, but almost as soon as she had appeared, she faded away.

Waking up in terror, I sat up at the edge of my bed. Dripping with sweat, I remained still and silent in my dark room with the shutters closed. Even though I knew this was a dream, in a moment of panic I called for my mother—but no one answered.

"Yiayia Sophia!" I called, worried, but there was no answer. "Yiayia . . . where are you?" Where could she be? Still no response. Heart pounding, I crept out of my bedroom, thinking that she, too, had abandoned me.

She had not. She was a stone's throw away, visiting with her daughter, my aunt Eleni, in our backyard. I heard their voices and, still in my nightgown, ran outside and nestled in my grandmother's lap. She made room and held me gently on her chest.

"You were tired, Sophoula," she said. "You've been sleeping for a couple of hours. Let me feel your forehead. It's sweaty."

Sitting on her warm lap was soothing. "Here, let's get you a glass of cold milk with coffee. That will wake you up," she said, settling me in her chair. Then she headed to our kitchen; and in that moment, barely awake, I was overtaken by a force of fear and alienation. Mother was gone, missing—I was really alone.

I kept that dream a secret from Yiayia, sensing her discomfort with anything that had to do with Mother. But the next day, when the apparition returned, I couldn't hold it in any longer, so I told my friend Soula.

"I have nightmares too," she confided, even though I hadn't thought of my dream as a nightmare—but she was right.

"It scares me," I admitted. "I don't know where Mother is."

"My mom says that she left suddenly," Soula answered. "But I don't know any more." I frowned and remained silent.

"If I hear anything, I'll tell you," she promised. I knew she would. What I did not know was how Father had managed to make Mother go away. No longer interested in play, I turned my back on my friend and walked toward my own house.

Yiayia was preparing dinner. The two of us were waiting for my father once more. Some of the time, I was upset with my mother, and other times, I was angry with Yiayia's silence, but I missed my mother all the time. The landscape of my days was murky, and my questions suppressed.

A few days later, I decided to tell her about my dream, because I couldn't stand not knowing any longer. "Is my mother still alive, Yiayia?"

I held my breath. Frowning, she stopped chopping the lightly boiled greens that had been gathered on the hills of nearby Mt. Hortiatis. Bent over her pot and staring at her knife, she replied, "She is fine," and resumed chopping. After a moment, she paused again and finished her thought: "You won't be seeing her for a while."

There was a brazen tone to her voice that I did not care for. *She is not coming home?* In utter confusion, I asked her, "For how long? Why?"

Yiayia answered calmly, "We will be all right, Sophoula."

Did she mean herself and me? What about my mother? Did she not have the real words to tell me what was happening? I left the room without looking at her and sat on the kitchen stoop for a while. Then, reaching into my pocket, I took out my four good marbles. I began twirling them in my hands and then looked in the yard to find a stick that I used to draw a triangle in the dirt, and I set my marbles one on each corner. Taking aim, I knocked them out over and over again and hovered in the same spot until dark. *Why had Father sent Mother away?*

Eventually, Yiayia called me in again with "Sophoula, dinner," but I ignored her. It gave me pleasure to pretend I didn't hear her, to make her come out to coax me in. She called me several times. I knew I would catch a sound scolding for it later, but so what?

In the kitchen, she went on, "Were you playing deaf? What is the matter with you? My throat is sore from calling." She placed the salad greens in a bowl, added chopped olives, and dressed it all with oil and lemon. Then she asked me to take it to the table and, to appease me, she started peeling potatoes to make the French fries I so loved.

Yiayia certainly did not seem to care about Mother, nor did she seem to care for my apparitions and phantoms. When I brought it up again, she outright snubbed me: "You are too old to worry about it. It's just a nightmare. Cross yourself before you go to sleep, and it will go away."

Frustrated, I decided not to mention Mother again and walked away, turning on my heels. Sulking, I left the kitchen wondering if what she knew was "not for kids' ears." After all, I was a precocious seven-year-old, anyway, and I certainly wanted to understand what had happened to my mother.

As I think about Yiayia now, I recognize how well she kept her thoughts locked away. They were her company all day long, and she kept them private. Whispers, questions, dreams, and to-do lists formed and whirled around her busy days when she took over fixing my breakfast, when she sat in the empty house once my father and I had left for the day, when she cooked and baked, and when she made my bed. They were always with her—but she kept them to herself. Always, from that point onward, she was an impenetrable wall of silence. But why? My own young mind worried, *Was she hiding something truly terrible?*

Whatever it was, I still think she must have held mountains of resentment toward my mother that never explicitly escaped her lips around me—but which, I later learned, she shared with her own adult children. Surely, she wished for a peaceful, happy family life for her successful son—and for herself in her old age, expecting the household to live by the values that she had grown up with. But perhaps she didn't realize that her silences, however natural they felt to her, and however aimed they might have been at protecting me, were more upsetting than any complaint she could have uttered.

My mother's departure left a hole in me that summer. I wandered around the house feeling her absence. Sometimes I found myself sitting in my parents' bedroom on Mother's *escabeau*, her stool which seemed forgotten in front of her vanity mirror. Gone were all the lovely cosmetics, lipsticks, and creams, the brushes and combs that she liked to arrange in a long and narrow crystal tray. The drawers were empty. Her side of the armoir compartment looked at me with empty eyes, her Coeur Joie perfume and hopes of a joyful heart had dissolved in disappointment. A couple of wooden hangers were left behind, naked on the sad rod. The top of her vanity had collected a fine cover of dust. There was only my own image in the mirror, and a vacant space where my mother's used to be.

4 MOTHER'S ILLNESS
Mid 1980s

S o many years after I'd lost my mother the first time, I found my connection to her eroding for very different reasons. Nearly two decades after I left home, the business of life in America—raising my son and launching a career in social services—had swallowed up all my energy in my late thirties. There were days when I hardly thought of Greece and could no longer remember how it was to keep track of my mother in our faraway home. But in the winter of 1985, I did truly begin to worry about her sparse correspondence. Perhaps she had just become busy with one project or another, but the thought slipped into my mind, *Was there trouble? Could she be sick?*

The distance seemed vast, and her day-to-day life was obscure to me. But then she came to visit in the night without warning. I hadn't dreamed of my mother in years, but that night I woke up frightened. The woman in my dream had spoken with a thick and desperate voice, distant and otherworldly. It was a faceless voice calling me, first with a sigh, and then by name. And I knew it was my mother.

"Sophoula *mou!*" she called, two or three times. Awake, I shivered with a sense of dread and troubled premonitions. But then, nothing. There was no message, no revelation. For days, I couldn't shake that sense of dread. Was it a sign? The urge to know what it was about stayed with me.

On the days I lived with my father at my Kouidis home, I would sometimes carry worries about my mother's household because, during my teens in Greece, immediate communication with her was limited to weekend visitation. During these visits with her, plans for the day usually came about in the morning after my arrival. We would make it up spontaneously, whimsically, depending on mood, resources, and weather. "A movie sounds good on this rainy day," Mother would say. Then we would scan the newspaper, getting it away from my grandfather, who had it by his side most of the time. Occasionally, some planning ahead was required: "The circus is in town. Shall we get tickets for next time?" That was the extent of our planning. You see, word of mouth, neighborhood news, and the radio influenced our daily whims and added freshness and surprise to each visit, something we were used to.

Long distance changed our ways out of necessity; letters became the primary carrier between Mother and me except for the infrequent tape-recorded messages that Mother would send by mail, an expensive but newsy method as my mother, her mother (Yiayia Athena), and her sister, Aunt Marika, took turns speaking their news and asking questions about my friends, the classes I took, and the like. But years later, when my husband, my son, and I vacationed in Thessaloniki, we would revert to our old ways of showing up and making plans on the spot.

My father installed the first dial telephone in our house when I was in high school, and it took time for us to get used to it. I put it to good use rotating the dial when I needed to work on tough school assignments with classmates or to arrange get-togethers with friends. If I hung on the line too long, I was often scolded and asked to "Keep it short; someone might be trying to reach us."

My mother never could afford a home phone, and mail was ever so slow. In truth, I had never investigated a way to communicate with her in case of emergency. *Aren't parents here forever?* But that night, when I dreamed of her with disturbing force, my mother's broken voice had pierced my sleep, reaching me wispy and ferocious—and I realized how little I had understood the weight of our transcontinental separation.

I'd sat up wondering if there was something wrong—or was it just a nightmare? Should I be open to telepathic communication, if it were truly intended for me, or was it a stray dream? The bedroom loomed large that night, filled with shadows, and the night-light by the doorway pierced the darkness, spreading a sickly yellow glow on the wall, flickering. The *tick-tock* of the alarm clock by my bedside sounded too loud and intrusive, and although I reached and shut it in the drawer of my nightstand, I could still hear it. I tried folding my pillow in two to rest my head a bit higher, but everything was annoying. After turning and tossing for a while, I finally cuddled with my husband for comfort and eventually fell asleep.

My mother had known this house, had occupied the spare bedroom across from ours with its large window facing the backyard and its built-in closet. In the early 1970s, she'd come to the US and lived with my husband and me for a short while—returning eventually to Thessaloniki, back to the place she had moved to after her divorce, the D. Gounary apartment. At the time, we lived in Portland, Oregon; our son had not been born yet, and we worked full-time jobs in social services. Since then, the whirlwind of time had brought about several changes. We'd moved to Seattle, bought a home, worked for state social services, and welcomed our son, a handsome, busy, bright boy who was growing up fast.

It is June of 1986. Our lanky boy has turned twelve, and once schools have closed for the year, I book a flight for me, my husband, and our son to Greece. I sent a quick postcard to let my mother know of our arrival, all along wondering if she is all right. But by the time my note reaches her, we are already in Greece. With jetlag behind us, the day just breaking, my spouse and I take our son on the bus to her apartment on Navarinou Square. On the way, busy looking out the window and pointing out familiar city landmarks—the burial site of Zeytinlik with its impressive brick fence and grand gate, the modern structure of the railway station—and chitchatting with my family, I am hard at work waving dark thoughts and lurking fears away. When we arrive, we find that Aunt Marika is in the hospital again, and my mother is just waking up from an afternoon nap. Beyond the cheery "Welcome home," her surprise waxes once she has opened the door. "Why didn't you let me know you were coming?" But my pleasure at watching her smile and her tucking each of us into her lap is too great to explain. Already, she is worrying that she doesn't have any treats in the house to welcome us with.

"Don't worry about it, Mother," I say as I gesture her to sit beside me so we can at last settle down to a mutual sharing of updates. That is when I notice my mother's poor coloring and wait for her to tell me what is wrong. But she is holding it inside, whatever it is. Slowly working up the courage, I ask her awkwardly, "Mother, did you call me recently?" Puzzled, she looks at me. I continue, "Was something going on in May this year? Were you distressed? Did you try to reach me?"

I can't be sure what I am asking. Maybe it had just been a nightmare, and I am being superstitious. But when my mother finally tunes in to my question, she speaks of troubled times. Kidney problems, she says—and, at about the time of my dream, she'd been hospitalized with kidney disease, falling into a near coma.

"Why didn't you tell me?" I gasp.

"Why worry you?"

"Oh, Mother! I should know how you are doing, no matter what it is. Are you okay now? In my dream, I thought you were calling me last month. Did you?"

"It was as if I was in a fog," she says, laying sad, intense brown eyes on me. "I did call for you, I know. Did you hear me?" I shiver, my pulse quickening. So it was true. It was she who had come to me in my dream with her unmistakable, disembodied voice, and I had heard her call.

I scold her and ask her to keep me posted but worry that she will not.

"I'm fine, now," she reassures me, never referring to her kidney problems. Still, she welcomes my arm supporting her and is having a hard time moving around.

After that, our visits to her remained confined to her apartment; we gave up the small pleasures of short outings or trips to city restaurants.

"Take care of your health, Mother," I would beg her each time, and she would nod a shallow confirmation but not linger over my advice or her own decline. Mostly, she wanted to enjoy our visits, especially getting to know her grandson. So, I fooled myself and decided that she would be strong, and, in time, she would recover. After all, she'd always been my own sweet mother, the one I could rely on, no matter what hardship befell us. I held my wish tightly, and I remained clueless about her ailment, denying a stark reality.

5 MOTHER
Before and After World War II

There may have been plenty of mystery about the past, but what I knew was that I loved her and called her *Mamá*, the accent on the last syllable. Before she was married, my hapless mamá had lived with her parents in a downtown apartment with a formal reception room where guests were received (not to be confused with the sitting room used by family members) and a turret. Everyone called my mamá "Nitsa," a familiar diminutive for Elenitsa or Helen. It was her childhood nickname, a name used by those who loved her, scolded her, shared intimacies and secrets with her; and it was an endearment that I sometimes used in my adult years, just as she called me Sophoula, all my life.

After she left my childhood home, she rarely came to the Kouidis warehouse on Egypt Street, and only occasionally stopping by at her father's dairy products warehouse on Katouni Street, one street from my own father's warehouse in Ladadika, the wholesale district. Were she still alive today, we would saunter down the cobblestone streets and settle on the small square with the fountain at the foot of Egypt Street, choosing the busiest restaurant for a meal ("The sign of a good chef," she would have said). Today, this neighborhood has evolved into a noisy entertainment center for Thessaloniki. Afterward, we would head to the waterfront for a walk along the bay to inhale the salty, misty air and the sight of the White Tower. We would talk about life in America ("Whatever happened to your ex-husband, Billy, after your divorce?" Or, "Are prices for groceries in America higher?" And,

"Do you like American or European fashions better?") and share a bar of chocolate to top off the day. I would walk her to her apartment, following the promenade, leaving behind Egypt Street where Gypsy children cluster to sell small trinkets and play the accordion for small change, and I would end the day by bidding her goodnight with a hug and a kiss. But my mother had passed away in her late sixties—and after all this time, I was still trying to locate her grave.

Nitsa was a modern woman for her time, a dreamer. My relatives tell me she was delicate, pretty, an eligible young woman who followed her mother's advice closely. She passed Yiayia Athena's wisdom to me in her letters to America when I was attending college: "Remember what Yiayia used to say, 'Don't worry, don't trouble yourself; study but laugh and sing whenever you get a chance. Work hard today to enjoy the fruit of your labors and to get what you want in the future.'"

But my mother was a positive soul, too, expecting life to be easy. "I used to bounce you on my knee," she'd remind me, before reciting Mother Goose verses.

My relatives used to say, "You have your mother's lips and your father's eyes." Mother would smile, and I knew I was special, her only child. In 1946, the year I was born, she was twenty-eight, and Father was thirty-nine. She was her parents' oldest daughter, and occasionally she liked to reminisce about her youth.

When she slipped into past recollections, she spoke of days with her sister and brother, days of pleasure that she treasured in the Hadjimichael family that had raised her well. My mother had a dowry. Her sister, Marika, had a dowry and a boyfriend. According to custom, my mother, as the oldest child, would have to get married first.

Born in 1918, Nitsa had lived on the first floor of a spacious, neo-classic apartment in the noisy center of town with her parents and, eventually, two siblings. Her father, Constantinos, was a wealthy merchant of dairy products, and her mother, Athena, a homemaker.

Mother was born a year after the horrendous fire that had destroyed so much of Thessaloniki, the capital city of northern Greece, burning most of its wooden houses like tinderboxes. It had been a fire too huge to be contained by the inadequate firefighting equipment of the day.

Young Nitsa and Marika, a year younger, had enjoyed luxuries not known to the more homogeneous people living in southern Greece. (Many of the million Greek refugees who relocated from Turkey in 1922 settled in or near Thessaloniki and influenced local customs and everyday life.) Because the bathroom of the Hadjimichael family, like most apartments of the day, had an indoor toilet but no bathtub, the two young girls fell into a routine of going to the crowded Bey Hammam once a week. Carrying a bundle of fresh clothes, the sisters would walk the couple of blocks to spend the day at the traditional Turkish bathing facility known as Paradise. Located on the corner of busy Egnatia and Mitropolitou Genadiou Streets, today it is being restored and occasionally used for exhibits. Paradise operated continuously from 1444 until 1965. It was built by the Ottomans right after they first captured the city they occupied until 1912. When they finally surrendered it back to the Greeks, it was the first and largest two-story hammam of Thessaloniki, serving both women and men in separate quarters.

The steamy bath was a sanctuary where modesty had no place. Women of all ages came, beautiful young girls and plump middle-aged ladies along with old and wrinkled grandmothers. Bellies, breasts, and all parts were simply displayed and checked out by all in the room. The sisters rendezvoused with their girlfriends and took the opportunity to show off fancy underwear. Mother was sociable and enjoyed friendships with classmates long after they had graduated from high school. They shared food and kept each other informed about boyfriends, engagements, weddings, and any other juicy gossip—especially about eligible grooms.

When she was young, my mother and her family kept watch for a man of good social standing for her to marry. Her mother advised her to marry an up-and-coming young man. In a letter to me during my college days, she would pass on Yiayia Athena's advice, even after her own failed marriage: "My little bird, at your age do not neglect your future family. Do not take it as a joke. I see your friends who are engaged, and I am jealous (of their family's joy and good fortune). And then there are other times I think that you are now preoccupied with your studies, and there will be time in the future to consider that. But I want to show you off, a beautiful bride with a handsome young man, as you deserve. Is that too much to dream about? What do you say? Is that going to be a distant dream?"

My parents found each other in the typical fashion of the day; theirs was an arranged marriage. It was the way most young people were wed in mid-twentieth-century Greece, and they were, like so many young couples, introduced by a matchmaking business acquaintance. At the time, the end of World War II was in sight, and people's hopes for a peaceful life were being revived. In 1943, as the German occupation of Thessaloniki was winding down, my parents were married at the orthodox cathedral of Gregory Palamas, filled with the hopes of a new dawn approaching.

Only three years later, I was born during another challenging time. Between 1946 and 1949, the Greek resistance that had countered the Italian and German occupiers became politicized and broke out into civil war. The Democratic Army of Greece, supported by England and the US, fought against the Greek Communists, who were backed by the Soviet Union and our Balkan neighbors, Yugoslavia, Albania, and Bulgaria.

In our safe neighborhood universe, all that was unfolding did not touch our daily routines. Carrying me in her arms, my mother visited daily Mrs. Katina, a heavyset, wide-hipped woman with long black hair. Our neighbor lived two houses over and was my wet nurse. She had delivered her daughter, Soula, about the same time that I was born. My mother would take me to Mrs. Katina's ample breasts, perhaps because her milk had not come in or perhaps because it was fashionable . . . not that it really mattered why. The two women would chat while I was feeding, and they enjoyed those conversations. Later on, Soula and I became friends. Everyone called us "sisters of the same milk." During all the years that my family lived on 25th of March Street, my childhood home, the two of us spent endless hours in play. It was a friendly neighborhood where my father's two sisters, Aunt Eleni and Aunt Ioulia, lived with their families. People met in backyards and left their front doors unlocked. Women carried on quick conversations during the day across fences and occasionally took breaks to share a cup of Turkish coffee and a cold glass of water with Yiayia Sophia and my mother.

Our house faced the main street. A couple of climbing roses tangled their branches in a tight embrace around the wrought iron fence surrounding the front of our house and took my breath away every spring when they flowered. Mother loved the yard and often brought flowers inside the house. Those small, sweet-smelling red roses were glorious in the spring and summer and contributed to the scratches and scabs on my arms and knees. An oleander bush on one corner of the yard flowered with pink-and-mauve blossoms all summer long, and the lilac bush hugged a corner of the house. An iron gate opened to the busy street. It creaked, and it was hard to unlatch and open. From inside the house, I'd hear it and loved running to see who might be visiting us. I always recognized my father from the sound of the car engine, even before he had unlatched the gate.

My parents had been married during the depressing days of the Second World War and managed to survive it in spite of many hardships. Nitsa and her sister occasionally talked about the German occupation. It was my aunt who revealed its dark history, one of the city's bloodiest secrets: the death and destruction of its Jewish community. Before the war, half the population of Thessaloniki was Jewish (about 70,000 Jews). Adolph Eichmann ordered his deputy, Rolf Gunter, to organize the SS and develop an extermination plan throughout Europe. Initially, the Germans forced all Jews to wear the yellow Star of David badge and confined them to living in ghettos. Later, they were rounded up en masse and transported to death camps. In 1943, in Thessaloniki alone, 50,000 Jews were rounded up in Victory Square and sent in packed trains to Birkenau and Auschwitz. The carnage accounted for the extermination of nearly 98 percent of the Jewish population of our city. Only the Polish Jews experienced a greater level of devastation.

"But my friend Anna, Aunt Marika, she is Jewish, and she is alive," I had challenged her, as I tried to make sense out of this time of terror. "We were together yesterday."

"If your friend was alive when the Germans were here, the odds would be against her survival. When was she born?" she asked.

"Born in 1948." Fortunately, it was after they had left.

Years later, I met Anna, also an expat, for a cup of coffee in Thessaloniki's Aristotle Square. We were only blocks from Victory Square. I had not seen her in a few years. Her parents had both passed away. Reminiscing about them, I saw deep creases form over my friend's eyes. With enormous sadness in her voice, Anna said of her mother, "Her death was a redemption for her."

I remembered our teen years, the arguments and the irritability we both had shared in dealing with our parents. They were such demanding people about "good manners." We scoffed at them because we considered ourselves to be on the right side of decent behavior. They were so intent on tracking our whereabouts whenever we chanced short side trips to talk or meet with friends that we felt justified in being annoyed at them.

Anna's mother was one of the eight hundred Jews who fled to the Macedonian mountainside to join the Greek resistance, mounting a fierce opposition against the occupiers. When I used to visit my friend's home as a teen, I had noticed her mother's unusual mannerisms, frequent deep sighs, and gestures as if she were chasing visions that blocked her sight and interfered with her breathing. I realize now she was chasing ghosts: lost parents, relatives, and friends who had been exterminated during the war. But she had her Anna, her only child, her solace and relief from the losses life had handed her.

My friend had grown up in a guilty city filled with prejudices. That guilty city lost not only almost half of its citizens during the war, but also the rich traditions of a once-thriving Jewish community. In recent years, Thessaloniki has been documenting and reclaiming its tragic past, but during my childhood, I could not fathom the destruction of life, nor the impact on the city, because it was not discussed openly.

On occasion, when my mother and I visited my maternal grandparents, she would bring along her knitting, and I would get to hear more talk about the war years. We liked to settle in the sitting room, heated and cozy, with its comfy couch and two armchairs resting on a kilim rug. Out would come her needles, gray wool, and a sweater in progress. One day she picked up a skein and asked me to help. Six years old with no experience knitting, I gladly agreed, pleased to be asked. She draped the yarn over my arms and began winding it into a ball. Aunt Marika had settled down on the couch and was making small repairs, like sewing loose buttons on a dress.

At the sound of sirens going by my aunt said, "Nitsa, that siren reminds me of World War II."

"A miserable time," my mother replied.

"What happened?" I asked.

Aunt Marika pulled an embroidered handkerchief out of her pocket and lightly brushed her forehead. "The radio told us to run to the nearest shelter at the sound of the sirens," she answered, tucking the hankie in her sleeve.

"I hate the sound of ambulances," I said with alarm, picturing blood, nightmarish screams in the night, and panic.

Mother's hands busily moved loops from one clicking needle to the next. She said, "Remember? In the confusion, that fist time, the five of us grabbed two coats and ran down a flight of stairs. We barely made it to the shelter. We huddled with our neighbors, wondering if our home would still be there when the bombing was over." My mother's face grew even darker. "Buildings shook all around us when the Italian bombs hit the ground. They later struck St. Sophia's Orthodox Church. It took several months to restore it."

In the cozy Hadjimichael living room, the women were knitting the sights and sounds of war-torn Greece. It was as though invisible gears were in charge of people's lives, and they reacted to the threat by clinging harder to life—living to restore the ruins of war. My mother had witnessed destroyed buildings and people starving, desperately looking for their families, salvaging their belongings, and burying their dead. At night, the city was quiet, like a graveyard. In the morning, the city carts collected the dead from the streets and parks. "Gone were all the old merry gatherings we loved to attend," she said, then fell silent.

Aunt Marika was more willing to talk about the German occupation, usually in my grandfather's absence. She spoke about the German invasion and their hold on the population following the Italian bombings. The occupiers stationed their Balkan headquarters in Thessaloniki because of the city's strategic importance. They requisitioned buildings and set up offices in the center of town all around where my mother's parents lived. I learned that their army base and the Nazi torture cells were near our 25th of March home, in an area we called the Karagatsia and downtown on Tsimiski Street.

"Neighborhoods were not safe. No matter where I went during the day, I ran into Germans," Aunt Marika recalled. "Impossible to avoid them. Both Nitsa and I took to walking fast past them, making no eye contact." She sounded scared and vulnerable, so unlike herself. "They swore at us as if we were disgusting: '*Schweinerei!*'"

My mother's ball of yarn ran out. She laid her needles down, settled a new skein of yarn around my arms, and began to wind a new ball in even strokes. "We drew dark curtains over the windows to keep our lights from showing to the night sky," she said. "The Italians aimed their bombs at Thessaloniki's downtown, the port, and the western suburbs. We were right downtown."

"I remember when they bombed us during the day, Nitsa," Aunt Marika interjected. "Father was still in his Ladadika warehouse near the port," she said, looking at my grandfather, Papous, who had just walked in the living room. He sat in his armchair, took the paper, and started reading, half listening to his daughters.

My mother looked at her father directly. "It was a relief to see you back home, safe, Father." Her voice was tender, and Papous nodded. My grandfather had his own stories, but he never shared them. He was not a talkative fellow and did not care to be reminded of war times. Mother had another ball of yarn to lay in her knitting bag as I quizzed my grandfather about bombs and air raids. But he would rather listen to our trips to the movies or summertime adventures than be reminded of those times.

My mother's ways were gentle in raising me. At age six, I finally learned how to float on my back in Poseidon's realm, a summer imperative for all of us preschoolers. Back then, there were no swimming pools or lessons available, so we learned by watching adults and other kids. The salty sea was calling with its calm, then windy, and everchanging shorelines that hugged, flirted, and tempted us year-round. As we ventured into the shallow waters, we shivered, dove in, tasted her, splashed each other, and eventually learned to float.

My mother held me as she walked into the sea, speaking softly as she drizzled the salty water over me. "Here is some on your head; it will protect you from the sun." Slowly, we moved into deeper waters, sinking my feet, waist, and shoulders in. Then for a while she let me rest on her arms and relax, floating.

"Stretch your arms out and angle your legs," she instructed. "Stay still." Soon, all it took was one finger touching my spine for me to float. And then, realizing her hand was gone, I almost sank to the bottom. Quickly reassured by her presence, I was willing to stretch my limbs again and float, trusting my body to the lifting arms of the sea and the warmth of the sun. I could not wait to tell my father and Papous.

6 MOTHER'S PASSING
October 1987

The beauty of learning buoyancy and feeling invincible in child-hood, of course, is that we think it will never run out. But some-how, decades had passed; I was a full-grown woman, and my moth-er's ailments had been troubling her for years now. So, it was to be the trip in August of 1987 that marked the last time I would see my mother alive. Hugging and kissing her on that final day of my visit was more about my need to hold on to her. Afraid to leave her, I didn't want to believe that this could be our last time together.

It took great effort for her to see us off. She held her back and leaned on my arm, shuffling away from her bed, as we all moved toward her Hadjimichael apartment doorway to take our leave. Fearing that her death might come before my next trip back to Thessaloniki, I took a deep breath and wrestled with the thought, struck again by the dark circles around her eyes and the taxing effort it took for her to walk. At the door, we kissed again and lingered, looking at each other for a long moment. My eyes teared up after my husband and my young son shut the elevator door, but once we arrived at the apartment building lobby I collapsed, letting out a primal, uncontrollable sob that I could no longer hold back.

All along, I had not wanted to burden her with my worries. Just like her, I saved the flood of grief and worry for the moment after her door was shut. Was she crying too? My husband watched me for a minute, silently handed me his handkerchief, and took our son for a stroll. When my eyes were dry and I could compose myself, I found them at a café across the street, facing my mother's apartment building. I joined them briefly for a cup of Turkish coffee, and we were soon walking down the sidewalk toward the ever-present bay, following my mother's favorite walk along the promenade, for some fresh air.

Two months later, on the 27th of October, an overseas phone call came in the middle of the night. Damn these distant continents. I don't know who I talked with, my father or my stepmother.

"Your mother . . . gone . . . the burial is tomorrow."

Everything around me turned murky and wild. I could not take it in. "Do you want us to do anything? A wreath of funereal flowers?" They were thinking for me. My mind had stopped.

"Yes!" I replied.

"What shall we say on it? Something like, 'To my dear mother?'"

Numb, I finished the message, "From your loving daughter, Sophia." As I hung up the phone, overwhelming guilt overtook me. A salty stream of tears burned down my cheeks. All I could think of was, *How could she leave me?* The day felt empty. In truth it was more, *How could I leave her back there in Greece so close to death?* I could not deny her passing any longer.

The next day, I drove at midmorning to the empty Greek Orthodox Church of the Assumption in Seattle. The door was unlocked, and no one seemed to be there. In gilded frames, saints and angels stared down at me from that otherworldly place. Reaching for the candles, I lit one and set it in the sand tray in front of the Virgin Mary, crossed myself—a practice I had gotten away from—and took a seat in a pew for a minute. In the silence, I recited a whispered "Our Father, who art in heaven . . ." staring at a mosaic of the Virgin over the nave.

The priest in his black robe surprised me when he entered through the back, asking what he might do for me. Before I knew it, I'd told him of my mother's passing. In response, he walked me to the front of the church and started to recite prayers for her soul to rest. It was a jumble of words that I could not follow, and yet a ceremony I welcomed. It felt like balm as I listened to the soothing singsong of the priest's voice.

Sometimes I wrestle with my demons, and other times I snuggle with them in silent, unsolved debates. That is how it is with the church and me. I was still numb, feeling hollowed out in the vastness of distance and my helplessness, and still debating the finality of her demise. In spite of the priest's invocation of everlasting life, all I knew was that she would not be home to answer the door next time I would visit Thessaloniki, and that seemed inconceivable.

7 FEVER
June 1953

A dusting of snow spread a white veil over peoples' worries and sins the early spring that my mother left my childhood home, but it did not sooth my heart or body. By the summer I turned seven, I had fallen ill—grief made visible for all to see—and was diagnosed with measles.

Divorce was not a word that I had in my vocabulary. It was a rare occurrence in the Greek society of the early fifties, and Father seemed so remote, almost always returning home late, tired, and frequently speaking to Yiayia in Turkish.

That year, I needed Yiayia and depended on her love and care. And my steady grandma was there for me. "Wake up, *yiavri mou*— my little bird," she would call every morning in Turkish. Then, at the end of the day, she'd settle me down to homework, dinner, and bed. When I called for Yiayia, I was calling for my mother.

The blue camphor pouch with the sliver of wood from the Holy Cross always pinned on my jersey did not protect me that year. I was a thin child, but other than colds and an occasional bloody nose, I had been healthy. But this time a high fever sapped my energy. I could not tolerate light. My father fashioned a hood made of newspaper and fastened it over the light fixture to keep the light away from my eyes. Lonely, I stayed in bed in my half-dark bedroom, missing out on summer play with my friends and cousins.

"Time to take your temperature," Yiayia announced when she saw me curled up and sweaty on the couch. The cold mercury thermometer on my underarm pinched me, but my protests were limp, and Yiayia would have none of it.

Next came her cold compresses on my forehead, and then I heard her tell Father that he should call the pediatrician.

In those days, doctors still made home visits, and the pediatrician who arrived with his black leather bag prescribed daily injections of antibiotics. An eternity seemed to pass while I lay on a shiny stainless-steel bed with its side rails raised, the shutters closed and curtains pulled, sleeping a lot. Because I was contagious, my friends did not come around. In truth, I was not up for playing with them anyway.

"Here she is," Yiayia warned me each time she ushered in the nurse with her small bottles of antibiotics and syringes from Tousa's pharmacy. Each time, the gray-haired old nurse, dressed in black, set up the blowtorch on a low table next to my bed and sterilized the syringe and needle in boiling water. It was an ominous sight, a forewarning of the dreaded injection.

"Turn around and stay still," she would order, and I obeyed, biting my lips and waiting for the sting with my eyes shut. Then she would collect her equipment in her black bag and leave.

Occasionally, Aunt Eleni would come to check on us and bring some food. Yiayia Sophia was now in her late seventies and needed some relief from mothering—but nothing was the same as my own mother. When Nitsa would come into my room on days I was sick, her eyes would search my face, and she would sit by me and feel my forehead. Speaking in soothing tones, she would give me medicine along with a treat—rice pudding sprinkled with cinnamon—a taste I still love. Then she would leave me with a soft kiss on my forehead, turning off the light and whispering tenderly, "Sweet dreams, my rosebud, my sweet child." I wanted her always by my bedside.

But that season, my fever was high, and I took long naps alone. Sometimes, I woke up disoriented, thinking that Mother and I had been visiting my maternal grandparents' apartment. I guessed that Mother had to be with them in Thessaloniki. Where else would she have gone?

Waking again, I imagined her soft eyes, wrinkles plowing her forehead with worry. Thinking of her comforted me, and it was not only I who thought my mother beautiful. Before she married, she had been a sociable young woman with many friends and admirers, and close to her sister and brother. Her skin was smooth and clear, and she cut a trim figure. Aware of fashions, she tended to her coiffure, slightly shifting the look to keep it fresh and trendy. She used lipstick whenever she stepped out of the house and dressed in becoming modern apparel. She liked crisp dresses hemmed below the knee, with modest décolletés and full skirts in the fashionable length. Sometimes, she shopped for fabrics in the downtown shops and took them to her seamstress to sew designs she selected in fashion magazines. In her closet hung scarves and belts next to her blue winter coat and gray raincoat. She preferred matching purses and shoes and liked to wear belts that matched the fabric of her clothes. Nitsa was an elegant dresser, and she liked showing me how to be well groomed.

I used to sit next to my mother, who would turn to comb and part my hair. Sometimes, she tied a ribbon or placed a barrette to keep my hair out of my eyes. I loved to watch her carefully apply her lipstick before going out. When she was in a hurry, she leaned into the mirror, eyes focused on her lips, her hand steady, drawing lipstick lines. At night, she would apply cold cream to her face before going to bed. I loved the fragrance and its creamy feel, so she would invite me to "just try a little," and I would dip my index finger in the oval container and spread it on my cheek.

When she abandoned our home, she had taken all the pictures of the two of us. I wondered if she ever looked at the album, or if she missed me. Did she feel sad, like I did sometimes? Who brought her hairpins or her purse when she asked? Who was helping her set the table? Did she remember the rabbit foot she had given me? I kept it on a chain in my pocket. My mother had bought it for me from a street peddler. I rubbed my thumb into the softness and luxury of its white fur, seeking comfort. I kept it under my pillow at night and carried it with me during the day.

Sometimes, I hoped the doorbell would ring, and she would be there, like the apparition I'd seen. But as the days rolled on, my hopes faded, turned into sadness—and eventually anger—at her sudden disappearance. What had I done to make her leave? Was it because I had wet the bed a couple of times? Or because I had told a lie?

In time, the fever broke, and the old lady with her syringe went away. I was up lounging in the sitting room with my handful of toys, following Yiayia around the house, bored. Father brought me stamps in large manila envelopes. They were from the foreign countries where he imported coffee, with flags, exotic animals, and different alphabets. Yiayia and I would soak them in water, peel them off envelopes, and press them flat in books and magazines. Still there was no sign of or talk about my mother. This must have been the time they were negotiating their divorce, but I did not know about such things then.

It was the summer before first grade, when I suddenly sprang up an inch or two, a tall girl who looked forward to starting school. A tall, thin, motherless child, busy filling voids with dreams, acting them out in play. Simply sighing, I tried to make sense of the changes in my family.

Feeling caged in the house, I pressed my yiayia to release me to the outside. Finally, she conceded. Deprived of the outdoors and all my neighborhood friends, I ran and knocked on Soula's door. It was time to start another round of hopscotch as we waited for the summer heat to subside and school to start.

8 LOCAL HELP
November 1, 2015

I was up against it, the unbreakable barrier of stone wall after stone wall. All the bits and pieces of family history that I had patiently gathered up over the past six years only hinted at the answer to my burning question: How had my father gotten custody when courts routinely awarded it to the mother? In the patriarchal Greek society, our family was burdened by conflicting cultural expectations about the place of a woman in her home. Secrets told in Turkish between Father and his mother thwarted my own mother's understanding of what was truly going on in the house, and my understanding as well.

It has made me question myself about what clues to family troubles I might have missed. Was I totally unaware of the ongoing conflicts? And what kept me from asking more questions of my parents when this was all unfolding? An adult offering an explanation would have been so welcome. So many years later, throughout my work life, I learned how important it is to offer explanations and anticipate questions during times of trouble, even when children do not ask. The hardest moments of my child welfare career, for instance, were those when I needed to remove a child from the parental home because of child abuse and/or neglect. While transporting them to foster care, I made it a point to take time to talk to them. "You know your parents are having some problems. This is not your fault."

At first, children might return a blank look; other times they looked sad, puzzled, or they might look away as if trying to avoid the conversation. Eventually, some engaged by asking questions and advocating for what contacts they wanted to maintain, especially when they were supported by their adult allies. Some wanted to know when they could see a sibling, a friend, a parent. It was not always possible to arrange the contact, mostly for practical workload reasons such as distance and available time to transport and arrange supervision. Some of the toughest situations involved splitting siblings, largely because homes that could house them all were not available when needed.

For me it was about assuring their safety and giving them the message that parents sometimes need to be left to themselves to sort things out and work on improving their behaviors and environments for their kids, often with the help of some type of counseling. It was very important to let the children know that they would have visits with their parents soon. I knew that in court hearings right after a child's removal, the judge would issue orders that would specify the frequency and location of parent visitation and whether they needed to be supervised. During those early, critical moments, the younger children especially rarely asked questions. They were all eyes, and those eyes spoke volumes, dripping sadness when parents failed to show up for court-ordered visits. My heart broke for them whenever we waited for parents that no-showed and then returned to the foster home empty-handed; their disappointment and sense of loss was palpable.

By the fall of 2015, my own adult eyes had opened again as my awareness of the legal system led me to try to track information about my parents' divorce. I had located Thessaloniki's family court, hoping to find some documentation pertaining to the proceeding. I'd learned that it was within manageable walking distance from my home when I asked a waiter who worked in the neighborhood restaurant.

"It's huge like a fortress," he'd told me. "You can't miss it." Then he added, "Just keep walking straight on from Tsimiski." The imposing, modern structure of the Court House complex took over a city block and proved to be a labyrinth to navigate. People in suits, carrying cell phones and briefcases, were rushing in and out of the main entrance under the gaze of the blindfolded female—a mural, holding the scales of justice.

"Where is the family court?"

A hurrying man slowed down and pointed toward a heavy oak door. Careful not to make any noise, I approached, pulled the door open, and took a seat on the very back bench. It was a small but impressive room, and empty at the time. The bench and all the furnishings were made of richly varnished oak, adding a sense of official weight to all proceedings. Shutting my eyes, I could picture a man in robes sitting on the bench and opposing attorneys dressed in smart business suits shuffling papers across from him at the two tables to the right and left of the bench. The room was suddenly filled with onlookers and witnesses. *Who might they be?*

The Greek family court proved to be hard to navigate, although I had experienced the American courtrooms as a child welfare advocate and as a divorcée. I also refused to acknowledge the emotional cost of the effort. Yet, that took its toll as each failure to unravel the past felt like defeat. Occasional sleepless nights and an obsession with figuring out how to infiltrate the bureaucracy, enlist help, and ask questions consumed the days of my recent vacations in Greece.

My frustration was compounded by a system that was naturally hard to penetrate, a bureaucracy that was infuriating, especially early on in my attempts. How was I to know how to do things when there was no place to read instructions about what processes were in place to obtain information, what documents were needed, or where one was to go for them? And then I discovered that it was not so bad as I had originally thought; it was partly my unfamiliarity, my impatience, and my inability to decipher the Greek court system. For many answers I discovered the KEP, Citizen Information Centers, a free public service for citizens with everyday needs relating to government institutions. There was hope! But the court system seemed insurmountable, and I was getting tired.

Stepping out in the wide hallway, I looked for the right window or counter to get request forms and apply for copies of records. I needed identification, fees, reasons, paperwork. It turned out to be impossible to sort out where the archived petitions and orders were, and where the right clerk was stationed. Attorneys seemed to move around with ease, greeting clerks and going about their business systematically. I recognized that local professionals would have a much easier time getting access. After an hour, I gave up for the day. In the Greek setting, it turned out that I was an amateur.

But my stay in Thessaloniki was nearly over, and, as in past years, I was drawn to the new city cemetery where my father and other relatives and friends were buried. Talking to them, I sought to exorcise the resistance that I'd felt from the bureaucracy and from some friends and relatives. It was as I had observed when I was on the other side of the bureaucratic desk, when I worked in the public agency for child welfare. Young adults who had grown up in the child welfare system, had been in foster care, and were eventually adopted by families that raised them to adulthood, were asking for information. The agency kept files, sealed to them, that contained all that history in the system, including the identity of their birth parents. The cries of the children, who had grown to young adults—their yearning to know and understand the past, their hope to meet their birth parents and find out what had happened, why they had been placed in an adoptive family—came loud and clear through phone calls, letters, and personal inquiries to see their files.

I was happy to experience a shift in the system that was trying to respond to this demand, this instinctive, powerful call for roots, for identity, for knowing. Information inaccessible to them in the past—the cruel seal of the law—was loosening. What mattered now was that both child and parents of origin wanted to find out about each other. Early on the calls that reached me at the agency head-quarters came from the most courageous young adults, willing to test the system and demand what was perfectly reasonable. Community agencies began to search for natural families and register mostly mothers' interest to communicate with their birth children. When both parties were reaching out for each other, we could go forth and release contact information, at first with a lot of fear and uncertainty as to the outcome, but with more confidence as time went on, since most of the time these reunions would sort themselves out. Redacted records were made available to children, some of whom needed the information for medical reasons.

The calls were awkward, uncertain at first, "My name is . . . I was in foster care and then adopted . . . I want to find my natural parents!" Some were hesitant. Then as the system began responding, they became demanding. That was a good day, a courageous move for young adults to read and discover, to understand, to cry, to accept, to reject, after knowing.

I had missed my chance to meet, to ask more directly from my parents what had happened in the past that split our family. My youth, the distance, and the course our lives had taken had cheated us from this vital and direct kind of sharing and knowing. That is why my urge to find them, even in a cemetery, was so strong. It was not just a plea or a request, but a demand.

These dead, I thought, they had to release to me, to respect my right to know my own story, a right that I was not willing to forfeit in America's self-exile. I was not alone in leaving my birth home for another continent. So many others—call us immigrants, refugees, émigrés, and asylum seekers—decided to relocate and acted out of compulsion for self-preservation, a powerful force, a driving need for us ever since we inhabited this earth. History records so many groups that have moved en masse because of wars, conquests, political and religious atrocities, injustice, and discrimination, in order to seek a better future. Over the centuries, my homeland, Greece, mothered a lot of these groups that moved to it from all points of the globe in search of hope. My own father's family escaped genocide, resettled in Thessaloniki, and built their own family empire for the next generation. Today, fifty thousand refugees are fleeing violence in Syria and the Middle East and are pouring into my country. It is no different in my second home, the United States, where its southern border is becoming a survival battlefield for Mexican, Guatemalan, and other Latin refugees who are fleeing to escape poverty and possible extinction, people who take high risks in the hope of getting a second chance.

Many are the reasons that motivate radical decisions like this, and individuals and families become economic, religious, and psychological refugees with the will to act, move, and change the conditions of their everyday lives. For me, it was fundamentally a case of looking for release to a productive, constructive future, unburdened by a challenging family life. An optimistic youth, I sought to try my wings, fly away, see a new world free of an environment harboring whispers, leaving my childhood behind. In my mature years, I hoped that the family secrets about my parents' divorce might still live in memories, scattered documents, and papers in the city's nooks and crannies. Some of my best plans to ask my relatives and old friends direct questions, the search for documents and study about the backdrop of time and history in libraries, were brewed in the cemetery my father was resting in, but just now I was hitting a dead end and felt enormous frustration.

The following day, in desperation, I blurted to Efi, my trusted high school girlfriend, when we met over lunch, "I need someone impartial to my story who has the time to track documents in family court."

I confessed how my own efforts had met with limited success. "Can you help me find someone?" Her daughter-in-law, I knew, ran a law office and, to my relief, Efi agreed.

Later that week, the phone rang with a call from the law office. Even though the time to conduct a search was short, they were willing to take on the task. I spoke up: "Please, give this to someone young and not shy about pushing against dead ends." *A last effort, I owe it to Mother, Father, and myself,* I thought, feeling hopeful.

The next day, I called my cousin to firm up our plan for our annual visit to the new cemetery where the Kouidis family grave was and where his parents were buried too. Away from the noise of the city, the Kouidis family grave held four people's remains: Yiayia Sophia, my father, my stepmother, and her father, the general. Their bones huddled under the marble top of the grave, and white pebbles covered its surface, hidden from view under the shadow of a white cross and the pair of vases I would fill with white chrysanthemums. Their presence made it into a peaceful, companionable stop, softening the distance and the years apart. Clearing weeds that cropped up between the white pebbles gave my hands a purpose, and the ritual of lighting candles in the marble box at the bottom of the family grave was a greeting, and a sign of repose and thanks, a moment of honoring them.

My father had said "time is money." He saw it as an investment in living. Yiayia Sophia, my quiet, steady grandmother, called me *arsiziko,* a teasing word of her own I took to mean rascal, and her support and care gave me courage to explore the world. My stepmother, steadfast and industrious, had helped convince Father to let me go to America. Her father, the general, had bought me my first pair of nylon stockings. There was synchronicity of their spirits that orchestrated my days, and on this day, I experienced a strong sense of companionship, their presence, the essence of bones.

My mother and father must have had good times before and even after my birth. In recent years, my sister of the same milk told me a story that I will always treasure. Her parents, who lived in the same block with us, had witnessed Father and Yiayia's preparations for my parents' wedding. The day before the ceremony, they noticed that Father was placing paving stones on the uneven dirt yard, inside the fence, from the gate to the front door of the house. He had a plan he carried out right after the church ceremony. When a special car decorated with flowers brought the bride and groom home, my father stepped out of the vehicle, opened the door for his bride, and carried my mother into the house through the front door. He was a romantic man. Oh, how I wish I had asked them about their courtship and sweet early days! But I had been too young to ask, and now I would never know.

My mother was the greater mystery to me, mainly because my time with her had been limited to weekend visitations for most of my teens. She was prone to staying positive, avoiding gossip and negative news. But despite what I did not know about what she was made of, her experience and reasons for compromising on who would get custody of me, I still had a strong desire to track, touch, see, and hear her with adult eyes. A grave does not bury a precious person we remember; it is the physical space of connection. And no matter what the past was, I wanted to honor her for her love, her way of being, and what I learned from watching her; but most of all, because she is my one and only mother. This had to be the year I found her grave, seeking out her grace and loving spirit. Persistence.

9 EGYPT STREET
In the 1950s

If my mother remained an enigma, the circumstances and routines of my father's life had always been physically clear and evident to me. Most of his life, he spent endless hours at the store on Egypt Street, a narrow cobblestone street lined with warehouses a few blocks from Thessaloniki's seaport. After the financial crash of Greece in 1932 and the civil war that followed World War II, business owners in the 1950s had to work hard to start and grow their enterprises. Fortunately for my father, the Greeks from Turkey had brought their love of coffee to Thessaloniki, and more quickly than anyone would have guessed, his business was booming—which was good for him and for me as well.

In the central wholesale market of Thessaloniki, hamals loaded and unloaded sacks and boxes of goods every workday of the year in a thrum of energy that was fascinating to a young girl. Business owners answered phones, took orders, and arranged for the transportation of goods. Here, perennial congestion and noise reigned. It was the world of Hermes, god of commerce, a world of hard labor and sweat. I loved the adrenaline of the wholesale market and the constant activity of the street: donkeys and horses pulling long beds and carts, hauling in merchandise. Motorcycles, their sidecars loaded to overflowing, crowded in too, and our "jalopy," the company truck, was often parked next to the warehouse, waiting for a load. It barely fit in the narrow street. There was no sidewalk left for pedestrians to pass, as all types of vehicles occupied the curb to get as close to the storefronts as possible.

From the time I was five years old, my father, then in his mid-forties, brought me occasionally to "the store" as he called it. A Lilliputian in a world of giants, I was caught up in the centrifuge of activity and the adrenaline of rushing men, even though I tried to stay on the sidelines, hovering near my father's office after school. He worked in a small wooden modular space that stood next to the steel coffee roasting machine, right off the entrance. The crowded space housed a metal desk covered with receipts, ledgers, notes, and a constantly ringing black rotary phone. Perched on the visitor's chair jammed in the office, I sometimes watched the activity, but I much preferred to wander around the warehouse.

Besides the attention I got, there was a lot to love about being there. My senses were filled with the aroma of freshly roasting Kouidis coffee. Dozens of hemp sacks full of coffee beans lined the floor and flooded the Greek marketplace, ultimately making a fortune for the family. Carried in from the port, these sacks of coffee beans were imported from Latin America, Africa, and the Arabian Peninsula and stacked floor to ceiling all along the left side of the warehouse. Brazilian, Colombian, Madagascan, Ethiopian, and Ecuadorian coffee beans and spices filled every square inch of space.

All around me wafted the comforting aroma of roasting coffee, ground into rich, smooth, and sensuous combinations of imported varieties. The high art of creating the desirable flavor, the bouquet, with these handpicked beans depended on climate and soil conditions that varied from year to year, similar to the alchemy of winemaking. My father and his brother presided there. Father selected which beans to blend, the length of roasting, and the fineness of the grind for the Greek market. He considered taste, aroma, and the body of the drink, aiming to successfully release the essence, the tannins, and the caffeine. I had often watched my father sample raw and roasted beans, as well as the ground powder. He made adjustments every step of the way. He was a gourmet when it came to coffee. I loved watching him reign, competent and friendly with his clients and knowledgeable about the coffee and all the machinery he maintained. There was plenty to admire about my father, and I was proud to be his daughter.

Moreover, had he been born in Thessaloniki, perhaps his marriage to my mother might have lasted; but my father had come from a place with different customs. His birthplace was the village of Dinar, in Cappadocia, Turkey, though he had soon moved with his family to Istanbul. The culture of Greeks living in Turkey was more closed and conservative when it came to women, who were chaperoned and devoted to household chores and raising children. My mother was not one to be confined to the house, and cooking was not her strong suit, unlike her mother-in-law. Yiayia, especially fond of her young son, would have naturally expected his wife to spoil him, too, according to the traditions she held.

My father was Yiayia Sophia's last son, a boy with deep brown eyes and an easygoing disposition. In his boyhood, he was the little prince on whom his two sisters and mother doted. They fetched and ironed his nice clothes, saving the best bites of fruit to feed him while his older three brothers were attending boarding schools in Smyrna. Only his father got more care and attention.

When he was fifteen, he came to Thessaloniki with his parents and five siblings. They had left hearth and home behind in Istanbul when they relocated to avoid the genocide of Greeks by the Turks in 1922. It was a time when orthodoxy was targeted in the old Ottoman Empire, and many Christians who continued living in Turkey subsequently lost their lives. My father spoke Turkish fluently with some customers, as well as with his business partner and brother, and with Yiayia Sophia at home. As for me, I spoke only Greek and never learned more than the half a dozen Turkish phrases from my yiayia.

But even if I didn't speak that language with him, I liked to help him whenever I was at the store. On one particular day in 1950, we had arrived at the warehouse around noon, and I'd followed him out of the office toward the long wooden counter in the back of the store. A steel grinding machine as tall as me was bolted down on the counter. Maria, a trim and tall clerk, was packing the ground coffee into Kouidis brand bags for retail.

My father took a pinch of coffee powder from the box she was using, tasted it, and adjusted some levers on the grinding machine. "Nice flavor," he said to Maria, who smiled and continued scooping coffee into the bags. I could see why my mother always complained about the odor of coffee, hopelessly trapped in the fiber of his clothes. A fresh change of clothes became the first order of business whenever he returned home.

Near the counter, two hamals loaded a couple of hemp sacks of coffee beans on the imposing weighing scale. Once my father noted the weight, each hoisted a bag on his shoulder and carried it out to the customer's motorcycle sidecar. Then he turned to the back of the warehouse. "Maria, keep an eye on her. I need to make a couple of calls," he called out.

Just what I wanted. "Can I help?" I asked her.

"Sure," she answered.

Maria motioned me to climb on a stool that she sometimes used to rest from standing all day. She wore a coat like the kind that doctors wear, with buttons down the front, only it was brown, and she wore flat shoes. "Is this high enough?" she asked. I settled on the stool and nodded. She handed me a scoop.

"Watch me." She half-filled the scoop with ground coffee and poured it in a half-kilo bag, weighed, sealed, and stacked it in a row on a tray, all ready for the marketplace.

"What grade are you in?" she asked.

"Kindergarten," I answered, pleased.

Copying her motions, I scooped the freshly ground, aromatic powder into the branded Kouidis bag she handed me. Clumsy at first,

I spilled a little. Maria patiently placed my partially filled bag on the weighing scale, topped it off, sealed it, and set it on the tray. She smiled and handed me another empty bag and let me work on filling it. I never got as good and fast as she was, but I always liked working next to her. I lasted a while but soon jumped off the stool and started to wander.

Somewhere on top of the hemp piles, in between the stacks, two oversized cats patrolled. They had no names. One was a calico and the other was gray, and both were busy tracking warehouse mice and other pests. They were not the petting kind. I called them, "Psss . . . psss . . . psss." They ignored me.

Maria had watched the calico chase a rat the other night. "The cat won."

That gave me the shivers as I imagined a bloody fight. "Can I give the cats some water?"

But my father, who had returned to pick up a couple of bags for a customer, answered, "They drink rainwater, out on the street."

"Can I take one home?"

He laughed. "They belong to Egypt Street, Sophoula. Cats survive hunting mice and drinking water on the street."

But that seemed like such a cruel reality.

"Come on. I will weigh you," he said, gesturing toward the large coffee scales.

"She follows you like a tail," Maria joked. Did I see my father wink back at her? That seemed odd.

The scale, where the 150-pound hemp sacks of coffee were usually weighed, sat next to my father's office. I climbed on it and looked up at him expectantly. Had I gained some weight?

"Light as a feather," he announced, adjusting the weights. At about fifty pounds, I was considered a thin child and had to swallow my mother's awful-tasting spoonful of cod liver oil each morning to "stay healthy."

We returned to the office just as a boy, with his loaded coffee tray, poked his head inside the front door searching for my father.

"What would you like? A lemonade? An orange soda?" my father asked me, and when I answered he shouted out to the boy, "A *metrios* (with a level teaspoon of sugar) for me, and an orange soda for my daughter." He would have ordered another coffee for his customer, but the man had just left.

I watched the young waiter, who never stopped moving on the cobblestones of Egypt Street. Soon he returned with the coffee in a white demitasse cup and saucer along with a cold glass of water and my orange soda.

At the end of a full day, I rode home with my father in the jalopy, tired but content. He was "Mr. Periclis," a respectable, energetic, and successful man in the marketplace, but at home, I now realize, a man in the middle of a battlefield between his mother and his wife. Recently, he seemed noticeably preoccupied. He spent less time at our house, often returning home near midnight, a routine I did not think twice about at my young age.

There was the time I heard Yiayia Sophia say, "Nitsa burned the food yesterday. My son came home late, and there was nothing ready for him." Then she shifted to Turkish. The exclusive domain of the Turkish language that all the Kouidides were fluent in kept me and my mother out of such conversations. We were not on equal footing with those "insiders."

The unfortunate "burned food" incident sounded like an accident at first, so people did not think much of it. But it happened again, and Yiayia whispered it to her girls. And then it happened again. I imagine that the conversations changed to things like, "Again? How could she be so careless? Didn't she learn how to cook?" But as long as there was food on the table, I didn't pay much attention to this criticism of Mother. Yiayia Sophia, on the other hand, had rarely been criticized, having done a lot of the daily cooking throughout her life, serving

the delightful Constantinople cuisine for her family, and, therefore, she had certain expectations of her daughter-in-law. A woman
like my yiayia valued pleasing her family's culinary palate, and the
family was always looking for the treats that she had prepared and
placed proudly on the table for us to enjoy. She steamed fish skillfully, serving it on platters with parsley and lemon sauces. Her soups
were filled with celery, carrots, and seasonal vegetables, together with
chunks of fish that the family had loved when they lived in Turkey.
They were netted in the Bosporus and Black Sea, and, even after their
move to Greece, my father still sought them out in the fish markets
of Thessaloniki.

My mother's upbringing had been different from that of the family
culture into which she married. Her mother, for instance, had never
taught her culinary skills; and even from my earliest days, I remember how my mother's hackles went up at the slightest mention of a
cooking failure. She was simply not that kind of woman; she'd had,
from her own earlier years, different ideas of what a woman might be.
My mother lived in a conservative, patriarchal society, a merchant's
daughter who did not join the labor force that in her day was essen-
tially an extension of domestic responsibilities for women—house
cleaning, sewing, clerical or secretarial positions—although her
sister, my aunt Marika, had worked as a secretary for a pharmaceutical company for several years. To my knowledge, my mother had
not joined any women's advocacy organizations but held that women
were valuable, deserving of respect and dignity. People of that time
generally believed that a man's honor depended on the modesty and
purity of their wives, sisters, and daughters. It was still a time when
women wore corsets every day of their lives and pulled the strings
tight!

Yiayia Sophia's family clearly held more conservative views about
the role of women in the house. No surprise that there were tensions.

How could there not be? The women in my early life were of two different worlds. And all the same, together, they were my world. So even if sometimes Yiayia kept her comments to herself, we all felt the strain, the chasm and clash between differing histories and expectations. At times, the tense silence around us spoke volumes. And at others, my grandmother lashed out.

"Take the frying pan off the stove!" she might warn. "The fish is burning to a crisp. What will we have for dinner?"

"Didn't you tell me to leave it alone for four to six minutes?" my mother liked to counter, unwilling to accept criticism unless she recognized it to be well intentioned.

"And you fry it in lower heat, woman!" The put-down was always nasty, unflinching. "You will never learn." Not satisfied, she could carve her words sharper yet. "Such a waste. That was an expensive fish that your husband brought you."

It was not that Yiayia Sophia was uneducated. I understood that she spoke French, and of course Greek and Turkish, and had studied piano in her youth, but life's unforgiving turns had pushed her away from that way of being into survival mode, when she had to leave hearth and home to escape genocide. It was a miserable circumstance for Mother, who had to endure cohabitating with a very critical mother-in-law.

Taking care of and preparing meals for the man of the house was a universal expectation. My maternal grandmother certainly demonstrated those skills, maintaining a spotless home and preparing her family's meals herself. I understood that Mother had been a high academic achiever in her school days and perhaps had not been expected to help in her mother's kitchen. Was she spoiled? Had her mother expected her to marry into money and have household help? Or was housework something that my mother herself had resisted, an area of conflict between her and her own mother? That I do not know. Although a gentle woman and not a cook, she was much more than what Yiayia Sophia's slanted view gave her credit for. A smart woman with wide interests, kind and well bred, my mother had an active life beyond the home. She loved to engage in social and intellectual activities.

Thessaloniki was and continues to be a city that offers many cultural events, lectures, and art exhibits, and my mother's circle of friends would rendezvous at these venues to witness the creative life in those hubs. What we loved to do together later on was go to movies and shop for books. Our frequent stops at the Recos and Zaharopoulos bookstores were not only to purchase paper supplies, children's magazines, and the shadow puppet figures that I adored, but also to replenish her own selection of books and magazines. She loved to slow down, underline, and write brief remarks in book margins, reading mostly Greek literature but also harder to get original English and French titles. When I would visit her from the States in the 1970s and 1980s, I would often purchase a couple of magazines or books for her from the London and Paris airports to bring as small gifts. My aunt Marika also liked to curl up with a book and later deeded me her favorite poetry anthology, which I still have. They would ask me, "What are you reading?" and leaf through pages with me. The sisters also maintained correspondence with a Parisian teacher who later visited them, and an American librarian from Atlanta, reaching out to the wider world of educated women.

Unfortunately, my mother's skill in handicrafts, knitting various fancy stitches, home decorating, and her thirst for books, theater, and movies—which were valued in her parents' home—did not carry much weight with the Kouidises, nor did her good manners, wide circle of friends, and delightful social graces. She was a compassionate woman too. I remember hearing that she and her mother knitted socks for soldiers during the years of the German occupation, and she trained to give injections in the Red Cross, serving relatives and her own aging parents' needs—but none of those things mattered, once she was married.

In the early 1950s, my father often returned home after midnight, and by the time I was in my teens, I understood what was going on. In his time, it was not unusual for Greek men to have affairs, especially when they lived in failed marriages. So, he relaxed with his girlfriends, handsome as Adonis and vain as Narcissus. He was a successful businessman, after all, and able to indulge all his desires. In younger years, his photos show him to be a sharp dresser, carrying an especially fine cane for show in a picture that stayed in the photography studio window for a long time. Another sign of wealth was the way men upstaged each other to impress ladies when they contested among themselves who would pay the bill for a meal; my father was a champion at that and often got a good table at the restaurant for his group.

When my suspicions and shame about Father's weakness and betrayal grew, I would list Maria, the Kouidis warehouse clerk on Egypt Street, as a potential paramour of my father's in the journal that I kept in high school, wondering if she might have coaxed my father to send my mother away. I was totally wrong about that hunch, and my knowing cousin scoffed at the notion. "No way; she is too homely for his taste!"

There was that certain appreciative look that I came to recognize in my father's gaze when he came across a woman he liked. His eyes softened, and he stared a bit too long. Of course, I was guessing, but each time, I felt distress and resentment. Heroes, I was learning, do indeed have clay feet.

At the end of the day of my visit to the warehouse, we headed to a home that must have seemed increasingly inhospitable to him as the strife between his mother and his wife grew. I loved to watch him drive the jalopy. He started the ignition, his hand on the manual gear, and once he shifted, the jalopy lurched forward, bouncing away onto busy Tsimiski Street. Riding with him in the front passenger seat, I saw how he watched the dials, held the wheel firmly, and made the car do his bidding. Then he took that familiar road home.

"Did you memorize any new poems?" he would ask absentmindedly. Glad to fill the silence, I would recite one eagerly, flawlessly.

"My bright moon,
Shine the way along my walk. . . ."

Nights cover a lot that a pale moon cannot penetrate. I would deliver these lines at a holiday school performance. "Good," he'd said when I'd finished, but I didn't think he was listening. I imagine instead that my father must have been ruminating over dark thoughts, now that I realize the antagonism between Yiayia and my mother, living under the same roof all day long, created much strife. *How did I end up in this situation?* he must have asked himself. *I come home exhausted, and there is a story about how the floor is not swept right or the food got burned, and "I had to prepare something quick for you, Son!" My wife and my mother bicker. What a mess!* He did not see his part in it, although he caused his own problems; he perceived the situation as too burdensome, resenting life in a household with two women embroiled in conflict.

The gearshift ground on the cogwheels, protesting alongside him. We fell silent. I was almost asleep when we arrived home. My father headed to the kitchen to wash his hands and sit on that same kitchen chair with the wicker seat that my mother liked to use. He swallowed hungry bites of the food that Yiayia served him, finished, and went to bed quickly, turning me over to the women for the evening.

When my mother walked with me to my room after dinner she asked, "What did you do all day long at the store?" She reached for my nightgown under my pillow and started helping me put it on. "I helped Maria fill her bags with coffee," I told her. "I got weighed and got a soda." I was still standing there excitedly as she motioned for me to take my dress off, had me stretch my arms up, and carefully slipped the flannel nightie over me.

"Didn't you get bored?" Her eyes were questioning.

"I like it at the store. I told Father my school poem, too, and he liked it," I lied, covering up my hurt from Father's inattentiveness.

"Which one?"

"*My bright moon,*

Shine the way along my walk. . . ."

I recited the whole poem for her again. My mother glowed. "Good job! I used to know that poem, too, when I was a little girl!"

She kissed me, covered me with a light linen blanket, and turned the light off.

10 MEETING CHRISTINA
November 6, 2015

A few days after seeking assistance from the law office in searching for legal documents, my doorbell rang in the midmorning, and I heard a young woman's voice on the intercom calling my name. Rushing down the steps from the loft, I met the attorney waiting on the cobblestones of Egypt Street. The morning rain had evaporated from the heat of the midday sun, leaving the streets clean. We shook hands, and she introduced herself in a soft voice, "Christina." I liked her firm handshake.

Young, tall, soft-spoken, and professional, Christina was dressed in a dark blue suit with low-heeled leather shoes and was holding a bundle of paperwork in her left hand as we moved up the street. She needed my signature, certified by the police, giving her limited power of attorney to conduct the document search, she explained. I smiled to myself, noticing that I was dressed casually in an orange short-sleeve top and jeans that morning. How very American she must have thought me.

Moseying along toward the nearby police station, we crossed busy Politehniou Street and ducked into Todaylicious, the crowded, fast-service coffee shop facing Egypt Street, for a quick cup of coffee. "Different," I said, nodding toward the remodeled two-story, glassed-in segment of the city's Byzantine wall where the coffee shop was housed. "And the same." Christine nodded as we took a seat at the counter by the window that faced the street. If she asked herself what conflicts in my father's home might have led to the divorce, she didn't say. Christina was only in her early thirties, and I wondered if she had seen situations where parental struggles were eclipsing the needs of a child. For her part, she probably wondered what had taken me so long to start exploring the past; but if she did, she made no comment.

In fact, I had gone to some lengths to learn about the past after my retirement from social services. A few years before I set about my mission to find Mother's grave, I had already started to ask questions about my roots and reconnect to ghosts of the past. To begin with, when I was in my sixties, I had studied maps and traveled to places where my father had grown up; the actual experiences of these journeys were much richer, immediate, and touching. Walking on the soil, looking at the landscapes, finding places where he had lived were adventures that often started with a map, a suitcase, an airline ticket, and a bus ride; they unfolded in feasting my eyes on neighborhoods and experiencing customs, food, people, and cultures that rang familiar and brought to life stories Father had shared with us. Though this was my first encounter with these places, they felt like old friends I recognized.

Chios, Constantinople, and distant Dinar were my primary destinations, places located East of Thessaloniki. The walled medieval town of Mesta charmed me when I roamed the Greek island of Chios, and I stopped breathless at the sight of Homer's Rock, where he is said to have taught his students the craft of epic storytelling. This was the Greek island where the Kouidis family was said to have ancestral roots, a place so far east that I could see the Turkish coast. Not far and north of Chios, cosmopolitan Constantinople with its rich sultans' palaces straddles Europe and Asia, bridging the continents divided by the waters of the Bosporus Strait. I visited marketplaces, seaside cafés, and minarets; woke up to the lilt of daily calls to prayer; and marveled at Hagia Sophia, the architectural wonder of Orthodox emperors. This was the city where my grandfather had met and married Yiayia Sophia and where his children had thrived until they'd had to flee to Greece.

Then, visiting deep in Turkey's Cappadocia during Ramadan, I traveled by bus to the small town of Dinar, the ancient Greek town of Arc (Κιβωτός) where the Euphrates River springs. There, just as Father had told me, I walked the street along the riverside to the main railway station on the line to Baghdad that my grandfather had managed, searching for my father's birth home without success. I knew little about the world as a child, and now I relished seeing, hearing, exploring on foot these exotic places, for I did not want to let time erase the past. Kouidis footsteps had marked this land, and I imagined the siblings growing up here, playing in the countryside and meeting friends at school, their voices ringing in the yard and in their home, their footsteps muffled by rich hand-loomed carpets and their palates satisfied by Yiayia Sophia's rich cuisine.

As Christina and I were finishing our coffees and getting ready to walk away from the Ladadika district to the police station, I noticed two- and three-story brick buildings across the street, a few still in ruins from the 1978 earthquake that had devastated the city, and others now restored, turned into nightclubs and covered with posters advertising musical groups performing till the wee hours of the night. "Everything changes over time," I commented, and began to share with her a bit about myself and my work experience in my late twenties. "I started to work for child protective services in 1980." Christina's curiosity was piqued, and she asked what this job entailed. An early experience came sharply to mind of my visit to see a baby boy and his parents who lived in public housing in West Seattle. "The young couple answered the door and let me into their living room, naturally worried and alarmed when I explained I was there to investigate a complaint about the care of their son."

"I can imagine," Christina replied, her eyebrows furrowing. "An unwelcomed visitor!"

"It was the woman who asked to see some identification, and I handed her my business card. The man pretended to ignore me and barked at his wife, 'Where is my breakfast, woman? Did you leave any clean dishes or are they all rotting in the sink?' And I remember how she'd looked up at him, her expression going watery with anger. 'Wash your own dishes,' she shouted, already leaving. 'I'm going to my mother's, so you'd better look after your baby. You don't have a job to go to anyway!'"

I could still flash on the picture of the neglected, lonely toddler who was holding onto the side of a crib filled with soiled diapers, rice, a knife, and a spoon, and was beginning to cry. Neither parent paid him any attention. In the midst of their power struggle, they didn't think to pick him up to comfort him, to clean the crib, or even to make excuses about this being an unusual circumstance—that their lives were not always like that, and that I shouldn't take their child away. In a stony way, they displayed their family dysfunction.

Christina blanched. "That poor baby!"

"Parental blindness magnified." Then I went on, "My family didn't have such extreme difficulties, but parents in the midst of divorce often lose their compass about their children's needs." By then, though, I sensed that Christina was getting restless; she must have appointments to attend to, I thought. We paid the bill, bused our cups, and stepped out into the noisy street. Her time was valuable. Walking along the pavement, we turned instead to the business at hand. I thanked her for being available on short notice and asked, "Which documents might you be able to track down today about my parents' divorce?"

"We will not get the entire case file," she warned.

"What then?" I asked anxiously.

She assured me that family court should have the divorce decree.

That was better than nothing, but I had been hoping for more. We resumed our walk to the police station. The streets were already jammed with busy traffic in this unfamiliar part of town, lined with storefronts and seven-story buildings that mainly housed offices, and I kept pressing Christina for information as we jaywalked across Dodekanisou, another busy street. Her demeanor was serious, and her explanations clear. "At the time that your father filed for divorce, family court was only accepting petitions after spouses had been married for ten years. They had to complete pastoral counseling and attempt reconciliation," she explained, gesturing all along for emphasis.

"Ten years? Astonishing!" Moreover, I wanted to know, "Was this counseling mandatory?"

"It certainly was. The church would issue a document certifying completion. Only then could the petitioners proceed to file for divorce." Such an irony, I thought, that the church was involved in the divorce proceedings for a couple of agnostics like my parents! *One power of attorney for the church that is always meddling,* I thought.

The wide Dodekanisou Street was flanked by tall buildings with storefronts that offered all sorts of products to the marketplace—hardware supplies, industrial equipment, a small nursery, a couple of banks, and the like—interrupted by large building lobbies dressed in fancy marble floors and walls. These were high-rises mostly used for office space, built to impress the pedestrians and create an ambiance of affluence and professional expertise. Still, occasional cafés had tables spread out on the wide sidewalk, and restaurants were getting ready for the lunch crowd, lighting their charcoal and setting spits of chickens, gyros, and *kokoretsi* (entrails wrapped in intestines) on their barbecue equipment. In a while, the street would be filled with customers sitting around the tables, unable to resist the waft of appetizing odors inviting them to a nice meal.

"I will check with the Orthodox Cathedral first," she went on.

"Today's laws have changed. They allow people to file for divorce after six months of an unhappy marriage." There was a tiny smile on her lips.

"More sensible," I agreed, glad to know that she already had a plan for the search that I had asked her to conduct. Watching her eyes, I saw her willingness to answer more questions without prodding for my reasons. "When did it come about?" I asked, tracing shifts in the Greek laws. Christina told me that the change had come in the late 1970s, after a battle with the church, which opposed the new legislation.

"Church control and hypocrisy," I exclaimed. "I heard that couples sometimes went on hunger strikes to advocate for these changes back then. Is that true?"

"It is," she replied, and I wondered if she had run across these situations herself, but I didn't want to sidetrack the conversation.

"The church is so self-serving," I murmured, not realizing that this was an easy target on which to place blame, instead of my parents—but Christina did not seem to mind.

"Some marriages just don't work. So many children of lovers who coupled with a married partner had to grow up with the stigma of 'bastard' back then because their parents couldn't remarry, not before the ten-year requirement for divorce of the post-war era was met. The usual grounds for divorce were proof of adultery, a difficult finding for a new family to live with," she added.

I liked this young woman. She understood the issues of irreconcilable differences, family interference, and financial considerations creating obstacles. I felt supported to have her on my side, ready to penetrate Greek bureaucracies for answers.

Ahead of us, a couple of old, tottering retirees, one with a cigarette hanging out of the edge of his lips, had stopped to greet each other by a kiosk, blocking pedestrian traffic. A younger man accompanying the taller of the two smiled, enjoying the scene while the second, holding a set of worry beads around his wrist, greeted his friend enthusiastically: "I spotted you from a distance. It has been so long! Did you see me?"

"Sure did. How are you, old man!" answered his pal.

There was something heartwarming about watching these old codgers on this street, thrilled to happen upon each other in the marketplace. We circled around them, careful not to disturb. Christina chuckled when we made eye contact and continued her explanation. "We now operate under laws that allow for a 'no fault' divorce. I will also search family court and vital records." Those were the second and third releases she needed me to sign.

"You are well organized, Christina. I just hope you can find a trail," I told her, wishing with all my heart that she turned up a lot of documentation.

The Greek flag over the entrance marked the police station which was in a high-rise on a side street, and a policeman sat as a guard in a small wooden cubicle by the door. He looked up from his newspaper with a questioning expression. We explained what we were there for, and he dryly answered, "Third floor," and returned to his paper.

We silently began climbing the poorly lit stairwell. Suddenly my mind turned to the other puzzle that my mother had left for me to solve, the location of her grave. Although not relevant to the business at hand and not knowing if she would know the answer because of her profession, I decided to see if Christina might have any suggestions to offer. Besides, time was of the essence with my return trip to the States looming soon. I stopped climbing momentarily, turned and asked, "Christina, I don't know where my mother is buried. I'd like to visit her grave before this trip is over. Any ideas?"

At first surprised, she thought for a minute and suggested that I check with relatives who might have attended her funeral, which made sense. I thought I would approach my mother's side of the family. Although I could have asked my Kouidis family who had notified me of her passing, I assumed they would not have attended nor even noted Mother's funeral. Besides, it had been an old childhood habit to live in two separate family worlds, so it did not occur to me to ask one side for information about the other. To be honest, in the past, the thought of locating her grave had not even occurred to me, but I found it haunting when I realized that I had visited my father's grave but did not even know where Mother's was. I was trying to resurrect anything and everything I could touch that spoke of her, of us. My broken family could never be restored, but Mother and our story could.

For the rest of my time in Greece, I persisted, turning to friends for information and suggestions, since my cousin seemed to be out of reach. Soon, learning that there were a number of cemeteries in and outside the city, I trusted that I would eventually find Mother's grave and visit her tomb, in a peaceful, quiet location outside the city walls; a place where I would join grieving relatives, priests, and fresh graves. In fact, I had purchased extra candles to carry with me to her grave once I found it.

However, my search turned out to be a bittersweet quest that led me to my mother's bones. After the fruitless church visit, I had called Stella back to ask about the cemetery, but she had only attended Nitsa's funeral service. Still, what she'd heard about it was astonishing. Without much warning, she'd blurted, "Your father came to the service." I just about jumped. Was there love, guilt, perhaps some fondness for his first wife, after all the years? Had this marriage held promise in its beginnings? What was I to make of all this? There were several arranged marriages that I knew of that had worked. Although the past felt slippery, and I was prone to look for days of happiness, I visualized Father standing near her casket, a tear in his eye, as the priest recited «αιωνία η μνήμη», evoking her memory in everyone's minds. Imagining them all there, my own tears burned my cheeks as I set the phone down in its cradle.

In moments of frustration, when my "realist" self would raise her voice, I would ask myself, *What would finding her grave answer?* It would not tell me more about who she was or help me understand her decision-making about the divorce at a deeper level. Who was she, really? How well did I know her? Was she a strong, decisive woman who dealt with crises well or a stoic, indecisive young woman of that era? How was I like her?

The next day, I resorted to calling the cemeteries in and near the city. When one man finally acknowledged that my mother was listed in the computer records of the cemetery of Stavroupolis, my heart skipped a beat. Hopeful, I asked, "Where is her grave?"

"No grave. Her bones were placed in the common grave."

"Common?"

"With everyone else."

Someone else was asking the clerk a question, and without delay he hung up, heartless and rushed. Had I understood this right? Common? A dugout filled with people's bones? This was an indignity I had not expected—and it was another moment when I felt my mother slipping away from me, this time in the harsh anonymity of bones. Her silence was not of her own choosing—because I came to understand that after a period of six years, her body had been exhumed and the bones had been deposited in a common grave, for families who cannot afford the fees to store their dead in the ossuary.

No one had told me anything about the rituals of burials, and I had left the land of my birth too young to know about Greek funerals and customs. Still, I wish that someone had called me in time to take some action, to make some arrangements for my mother. *Why hadn't they?* I thought, feeling a blind rage welling up within me; but all I could really do was feel my own heaped up guilt for not being there. Had I lived in Greece all my years, I would have known that cemeteries in large cities in Greece and elsewhere in Europe were overcrowded with bodies. That is why today it is required by Greek law that, after some years, the space had to be recycled for the new tenants. Only for exorbitant sums of money could families like my father's rent plots and renew the lease every five years to keep them for family members.

At the time that I was focused on finding Mother's grave, I was not entirely clear about what propelled me to search for it; I would still be left with my aching questions about the past. I had experienced motherhood, had watched my then husband relish our son as he grew to be a young man. How was our childrearing experience different than theirs? Was this simple curiosity that motivated my search, or was there a deeper need to understand myself and my own family? Was it another way to fathom what my son thought about my divorce? Most likely all of that, but what I knew was that whenever I visited my father's grave, I found myself thinking of the man, our times together, his loving ways, and our bond. I had a sense of caring for him as I brought flowers, lit a candle, and cleared the site of weeds. And when all that was done, a deep sense of peace and contentment would linger in my heart. I was looking for the same moments by my mother's resting place and resented the thief of time and distance that had stolen the precious conversations we might have shared about what she held important in life, what she could tell me about her divorce and relinquishing my custody, and what she wished to leave with me as her legacy.

But for me, Nitsa's daughter, there is no plot on earth to tend, no visible place that would mark her existence and passage. I contemplate all that on my own. Left without bones or dust to mourn, I find myself returning to the rituals of my ancestors, and, having made my peace, I light a candle in her memory at a church every October, wherever I am.

11 JOUR FIXE AND TURKISH COFFEE
April 1951

My mother was an elegant and genial hostess, worth every gold coin of her customary Greek dowry. With her three languages and good education, she was an accomplished woman; but being a well-polished hostess was all that really mattered to the social circles in her day.

It had been a year and a half since the last gathering at our house. For a couple of days now, my mother had been preparing for her *jour fixe,* the day when she would hold an open house for friends and relatives.

"Bring fresh ground Turkish coffee and tea," she told my father as he was leaving for his coffee warehouse on Egypt Street. Aunt Marika was to buy a box of *fruits glacés* from the downtown patisserie, Terkenlis in Aristotle Square. The morning of the gathering, my mother placed a vase of musky, sweet lilacs from our yard on the golden-fringed Persian rug design that she had cross-stitched to decorate the living room table. She dusted the furniture and set out polished trays and a teapot. Silver-framed pictures of her parents and a recent studio photograph of six-year-old me were placed on the table. A pair of her embroidered pillows with geometric designs of baskets full of flowers rested on the ends of the couch. I liked watching the preparations and anticipating the gathering. A spick-and-span home, treats in the kitchen, and a living room filled with Mother's lively friends gave me a rush and made me feel like a grown-up!

When the first guests arrived, Aunt Marika handed me a couple of napkins in the kitchen. My job was to give one to each guest as soon as my mother offered treats. Trim and poised, Mother wore her golden cross on a chain, and a simple navy blue short-sleeved dress with shiny gold star buttons that ran down the front. She moved easily in and out of the room, tending to our company.

"Give one to Marianthe and the other to Maria," my aunt instructed me. Early hostess lessons, under the tutelage of my mother and aunt, were meant to train me in the hospitality arts and care of our guests. My mother's classmates were sitting comfortably on the couch. It was their monthly routine to gather, and my mother's turn to host them.

In the kitchen, small crystal dishes with *kourabiedes,* cookies dusted with powdered sugar, were lined up on the counter next to assorted cups and saucers for Turkish coffee and tea, and water glasses. On the red stove, next to the sink, was a pot of water ready to boil for tea. The blue enameled Turkish coffeepot, the *brique,* waited ready to brew Turkish coffee, which my mother would serve in delicate demitasse porcelain cups.

"Where is your mother-in-law?" asked pudgy Marianthe, a woman lucky enough to have a sizeable dowry and no mother-in-law. "Will we see Yiayia today?"

"She is helping her daughter, Eleni, next door. They are preparing breads and sweets for Easter. You know how that goes. She may pop in later."

"There is no rush," Marika winked, smiling.

"Here, sit by me," my mother urged me. I was expected to stay with the grown-ups until they all showed up before joining my friends in the backyard. I climbed on the chair next to hers, and she put her arm around me as I smoothed my dress around my knees.

Aunt Marika, in her gray suit and a matching set of pearl necklace and earrings, returned to her seat next to mine. We were expecting a couple more "girls," as they called each other. Aunt Marika seemed to know all of Mother's former classmates, even though she had attended the French lycée while they had gone to the second gymnasium, a public girls' high school in Thessaloniki. She was a regular at these gatherings, almost always accompanying my mother.

The ladies finished their *fruits glacés* and raised their water glasses to Mother and Aunt Marika, toasting, "Happy Easter," "Good health," and "May we meet in 1951 and be well." In Greek homes, exchanges like these filled the season in April.

"Did you see the editorial in the paper last week?" Maria, a tall, lean woman asked. "It was about dowries."

Marianthe leaned forward, her deep brown eyes staring at Maria, and spoke in confidential tones. "My niece's engagement was broken up because her parents couldn't provide the dowry that the groom demanded. He insists on an apartment as part of the dowry. Her parents can't afford that."

"It may be the end of the girl's chance to get married. She is getting older. I am afraid she will be an old maid," Maria commented.

"What are women whose parents just make enough to feed the family supposed to do?" asked Aunt Marika. "Are they supposed to run away with their beau if they have one? Go to waste and become old maids? Have children out of wedlock?"

"Men look for dowries to preserve the lifestyle that our parents have provided for us," answered Eli, walking in with Anna, a tall woman with striking features. They handed their coats to my mother, who had answered the door.

"It's a terrible custom that invites grooms to negotiate a price for taking a bride," continued Eli, who had received a paltry dowry because her parents had first had to find grooms for her two sisters. The word was, though, that my mother's own dowry had been considerable. Father was an up-and-coming young merchant marrying a wealthy merchant's daughter, and it is reasonable to assume that he invested my mother's dowry in our new home and his growing business.

"Nothing wrong with dowries. They work when young couples get along well," added my mother, "but I have seen some disasters." She looked at her sister, who nodded in agreement.

"And then some boyfriends play the field, and as soon as they have stolen your heart, they take off with another," added Aunt Marika, taking a careful bite of her *kourabiedes* that dusted her red lipstick with powdered sugar until she wiped it daintily away with her napkin. Even back then, I'd heard that Aunt Marika had a boyfriend.

"But the port and train station fill with abandoned girls who are forced to become prostitutes, and syphilis spreads rampantly in the city. I just hope our men don't find their way to those quarters," chimed in wiry Anna, the provocative member of the group.

"Let's get rid of dowries! They are only trouble," she continued, twisting her wedding ring on her finger. "I would love to live in a world where women choose their partners because of love rather than money. Parents have too much say because they control the size of dowries." I loved the lively dialogue, as I listened to my mother's friends, seated in the chair next to her.

Yiayia Sophia had entered the room, hunched over with scoliosis, her graying hair pulled back in a bun and wearing her usual black widow's dress. She took a chair by Eli, the only blonde in the room. Yiayia Sophia had been widowed since the mid-1930s. In her youth, she had been a popular beauty who lived in Istanbul and was raised by her aunts. Back then, young men swarmed around her. Likely home-schooled, she was brought up with piano lessons and all the graces demanded by the wealthy Greeks of her time, and was, undoubtedly, a desirable bride. She'd married her handsome French tutor, Leonidas, a man educated in mathematics in Liege, Belgium who had lived abroad for over ten years. The couple had raised six children.

Anna's challenge, though, annoyed Yiayia, and she countered, "What makes you think that parents want anything more than what is best for their children? Do you have any complaints about yours arranging your marriage?" She looked questioningly at my mother.

"You didn't do too badly, Anna," agreed Marianthe. "Your husband turned out to be good to you. He adores you. But look at Persa. They say her husband beats her!" She spoke in confidential tones.

"That is exactly what I am talking about." Anna made a fist. "She would never have chosen him. She gave up her relationship with her boyfriend, obeyed her parents, and now she's miserable." Anna was a close friend of Persa's and knew the situation firsthand.

"It makes me angry. Parents don't always know what is best. All they think about is their social status and good name. Her mother could have saved her from that marriage," Anna continued, her cheeks reddening. Later, my own mother would tell me that Anna was a lucky woman, in charge of her household, with a husband who listened to and trusted her. She was my favorite of my mother's friends, and I guessed that, if she had this perspective to speak from, one should listen.

"So sad. If her parents had only known," Aunt Marika said, reaching for her glass of water.

"I wonder how Persa treats him, to make him that angry," Yiayia Sophia interrupted, sitting menacingly erect in her chair, her voice stern. "I know how women can get carried away and argue with their husbands. And what do you expect from men, then, but a strong reaction?" She spoke with the authority of a crone who presumed to correct the frivolous girls.

Much later, I learned that Yiayia had made compromises in her life. She had married a jealous husband who worked for the railways. Before their marriage in cosmopolitan Istanbul, he had watched her admirers flirting and vying for her attention. When Sophia dressed in her finery to accompany him to social gatherings, he threw fits, criticizing her for "showing off." I am told it got so bad that she refused to leave their house, worried about his displays of jealousy. He even moved the family to faraway Dinar, in Cappadocia, a village of 2,600, to remove his wife from big city life and her troublesome friends, accepting a job as the director of the freight distribution system for the French railroads that connected Bagdhad to Smyrna. Yiayia had to go along, then, and make her peace with being trapped in the small town; and that is where my father was born in 1907, followed by his sister, Ioulia, in 1913. Eventually, the family had returned to Pendick, a suburb of Istanbul, when Yiayia was in her forties, only to have to abandon their home in 1922, when the tide turned against the Greeks who lived in Turkey.

"Mrs. Sophia, the world is changing, and, if you ask me, not fast enough," Anna spoke up, disregarding "good manners" and respect toward elders. "Persa is a very intelligent and sensitive woman. She had a great relationship before this disastrous marriage. No woman deserves a husband like hers."

Even on a cool April day, I could feel the air in the room getting heated.

"You are young and don't know the world. Men need to be pampered. Women need to obey them and look after them, as they deserve," Yiayia proclaimed, pulling rank on her. Then she rose to leave in a huff. "I just wanted to stop in and say hello to you all. We can visit longer next time. For now, have a good time."

With that, she turned her back and walked out of the room hastily, straightening her back to loosen her joints. People intrigued me, and I hated to see Yiayia Sophia so irritated that she walked away.

"I had to bite my tongue," said Aunt Marika, looking toward my mother. "I didn't say anything more because I don't want to create problems for you. But she is so Old World. We no longer live in harems eternally pampering the sultans of the household." Her voice was sharp, and I watched her carefully. There was something in my aunt's angry tone that I did not care for. I did not like conflict in the family.

But I didn't have much time to think about it because the door-bell rang just then, and the last two guests walked in. Mother hung their coats, offered them chairs, and soon presented them with the box of *fruits glacés*. Watching the exchange like a hawk, I got off my chair and moved to the kitchen to bring in a couple of napkins, the last set I had to deliver. Finally, after changing into everyday clothes, I was free to join the kids outside. I ran out into the yard, leaving behind me a room full of tension and women in their finery, some in two-piece suits, others in dresses and high heels, wearing necklaces, rings, and earrings. I valued my playtime, but I was also intrigued by adults and how each viewed the same story so differently from the others.

In later years, I realized that, on days like that one, my aunt Marika had seen how my mother was willing to conform to her parents' wishes, accommodating the customs of my father's home. My aunt herself, though, was more independent, even though she, too, expected to receive a dowry and settle down with a husband. In the old days, once a woman was married, she had no rights to her own dowry. In today's Greece, parents who have the means still provide dowries for their daughters. However, when couples are divorced, the assets are returned to the women. Stories of ex-hus-bands enriched by keeping women's dowries are now history. Even though I lived in America, when I married the man of my choice in my early twenties, Father felt duty-bound to provide me with a dowry, which neither I nor my American husband had sought but were grateful to receive.

It had been a successful gathering, and Aunt Marika was getting ready to return to her home after helping Mother get the dishes washed, dried, and put away. The fancy pillows and embroidery were tucked into my mother's trunk, and she had changed to her everyday clothes and was resting under the plane tree in our backyard. As dusk settled in, the two sisters shared a cup of Turkish coffee and *kourabie-des* with Yiayia and Aunt Eleni while I sat on the kitchen stoop with a glass of milk. My father would soon be home.

"For women your age, your friends sure were noisy and silly," Yiayia said, half seriously. "Especially Anna. Did they like my *koura-biedes*?" Was Anna gaining a reputation for her radical point of view with Yiayia? I could not see what was objectionable.

"They loved them. You are the best," my mother told her, acknowledging that Yiayia Athena was right when she'd advised her that a successful marriage demanded that she get along with her mother-in-law.

Yiayia Sophia smiled. She far exceeded my mother in the culinary arts and took pleasure in drawing attention to that, a note that was an unspoken put-down of my mother, who collected the cups and saucers in a tray and took them to the kitchen. When she came back, she settled in her chair, and the women chatted more about Easter.

My ears perked up when I heard a car engine outside. Father had arrived back home. I could recognize the distinctive sputtering of the engine anywhere. The pistons sighed as they slowed to stillness, and I rushed through the kitchen to open the door for him. He walked in and saw my mother's smiling face.

"Was it your day with the girls?"

"They have come and gone, and it went very well," she told him, pleased. Then she noticed my muddy hands. "Why don't you go with your father to wash in the bathroom?" And she followed us, bringing in a fresh towel.

My father was pleased to see his wife entertaining her friends. It must have reminded him of the old glory days of the Kouidis family when he was growing up in Constantinople among affluent friends and family. In those days, my father's hard work was slowly improving the family's finances, so things were looking up. Father and his older brother, Uncle Antonis, were partners by then, and their joint efforts at the warehouse had expanded their business. The family name was winning a good reputation in the marketplace as the brothers imported "colonial products," mainly coffee and spices, and distributed them in the city and countryside.

"Eli said she loved your coffee. She will ask her grocery man to buy from you from here on out. They all wanted coffee." Back then, my mother knew just how to please my father, and she moved next to him to help him take his coat off. "You should change clothes before you settle down. You smell like roasted coffee beans!" Indeed, my father was a hard worker. He wouldn't even hesitate to pick up those heavy hemp sacks of coffee beans himself and move them around when needed. That distinctive odor permeated his clothes when he returned from the warehouse.

The next day during our afternoon visit with my maternal grandmother, Yiayia Athena, my mother and Aunt Marika related much of the previous day's events to their mother. "It was a great gathering, Nitsa," Aunt Marika exclaimed. "Next month is at Eli's. Hopefully Persa can join us." And then she added, "I must say, I was not surprised by your mother-in-law's opinions."

My mother nodded.

"What did she say?" asked Yiayia Athena, her interest piqued.

"It was all about how wives must treat their husbands 'right' or they deserve to be abused like Persa," Mother reported, testily. "Thank God Periclis (my father) has no such inclinations."

That gave me an opening to ask, "What happened to Mrs. Persa?"

But Yiayia Athena preempted with a short answer. "Some men are mean to their women. But never you mind. That is rare." Then she turned to her daughters with, "You need to watch what is discussed in front of the child."

It sounded like she was scolding them. *Adult talk,* I thought. I liked to listen to adults, even when I didn't understand them. It made me feel grown up. Besides, often I would be able to figure things out later.

Aunt Marika and Mother recounted Yiayia Sophia's exchange with Anna.

"She is so old-fashioned," Mother exclaimed, looking over at Aunt Marika.

"You can tell a happy home," Yiayia Athena spoke, her eyes on my mother. "There is harmony between the husband and his wife."

Aunt Marika was silent, but I knew that Yiayia Sophia had annoyed all three Hadjimichael women. I did not really like their disapproval, steeped in the traditional Greek culture as I was. Once more, I thought, *adult talk,* trying to ignore these disagreements that I would someday set out to understand.

12 WHAT WILL TURN UP?
November 6, 2015

When Christina and I climbed the steps of the police station to the third floor, we found the office door locked and a few other people waiting. They said the officer was expected to return anytime. The day was still young, and my attorney had time to wait with me, so we stood outside the office, leaning on the whitewashed wall of the poorly lit corridor, and Christina set out to deal with my high hopes.

"Court testimony and supporting documents would have been destroyed. The law requires keeping these documents for only ten years. Don't expect any of the proceedings," she warned me.

Yes, I nodded. I had already heard this from friends, but I kept hoping. "Why not? Don't they store anything? Not even on micro-fiche? Not even for estate matters?" I quizzed her, amused and disdainful of the disorganized Greek bureaucracy I had experienced firsthand in the past.

"We don't have such systems here," she answered, matter-of-factly. "Our best hope is to locate the divorce decree. That is what is reasonable to expect." Then she added, "Remember, you're reaching back to days when women had just earned the right to vote." That change had come about in 1952; not surprisingly, it was so late in coming to the patriarchal Greek society.

"What about women's dowries, Christina? How has that tradition evolved?"

Christina had tracked these changes. "Brides were required to have a dowry by law, and dowries belonged to men, even after a divorce. But no more. Since 1983, dowries now stay with women."

Traditions do die hard. I knew that parents still tried to furnish dowries to their daughters if they could afford to. I did not know whether my father had ever returned my mother's dowry after they'd divorced, but I hoped to find out.

"Well, I guess we've made some progress since 1940." We both laughed and exchanged a knowing look. I checked her hand. She was wearing a ring. Then we chatted about where I lived now and how long I had been away from Greece. "But I never really left Thessaloniki," I confessed.

When the police officer arrived, he was a balding man, and his desk was organized with several sizes of stamps and embossing seals sorted in a variety of trays. When our turn came, Christina handed me the power-of-attorney forms for signature. The letters of my name flew off the tip of the pen onto the paper with a secret plea, *Please.*

In his official, practiced way, the officer certified my signature once I had produced my identification, stamping each document, dating and signing it. He returned all copies to Christina.

"Good luck," I told her, restraining my hopes to just two words, and we climbed back down to the street.

Before going our separate ways, we agreed that Christina would scan and email me documents as she located them. We shook hands as we parted, and Christina headed for the court complex, just blocks from the police station, to begin the search. Filled with hope and doubt about this effort, I was aware that I was slowly exhausting all means available to me to uncover more of the story. I tried to forget about her mission, how soon and how much she would uncover, because I could not stand the wait. Fortunately, the wait was short. It took efficient Christina less than a week to unearth what information was available. Even before I'd left the country, I was staring down astonished at my inbox.

"She did it," I whispered, feeling a strange kind of reverence on the day of my departure for the United States, just as my cousin Leonidas was coming to Egypt Street to give me a ride to the airport. I would be leaving my loft behind, locked and silent to wait for me until my next trip back to town. Before finally shutting down my laptop, I had noticed a gripping email from Christina. She had written to say that she was attaching two documents from family court and one from vital records. She'd added that my parents were married in 1943, and my father had filed for divorce in February of 1953 and remarried in 1955.

How had she done it? I breathed, both relieved and nervous as I downloaded the attachments to my hard drive. She was already forwarding documents. How had she found things so quickly? Before I could so much as open the first one, though, the doorbell to the loft rang. My cousin Leonidas had arrived to take me to the airport, so my heart would have to thud with anxiety for a while longer. I sighed, snapping the laptop shut after one more moment of dizzied anticipation and hurried downstairs with my luggage. *What could she have found?*

I'd have to wait to find out, though, because the drive to the airport was long, and the wait there even longer. On the way to Thessaloniki's airport, my cousin chatted about our time together and what lay ahead for each of us that fall. It was an effort for me not to bring up hiring the attorney and the looming computer download. As much as I guarded that activity, hoping it would yield answers to questions hibernating inside me for years, I also feared that little might come of it. And although I trusted my cousin and sharing something like that would have been my normal response, I wanted these hard-earned and as yet unseen documents all to myself. So not a word about the precious attachments. My cousin would have to wait until I knew what I had. They were for my eyes only.

Clutching the padded black bag with my laptop inside it and

dragging my carry-on, I boarded the plane. It was not until we lifted off for Munich that I opened the computer and located Christina's email. Even though I felt crowded in my aisle seat and wished for private space, I could wait no longer.

PART II

13 THESSALONIKI TO MUNICH
November 19, 2015 (9:10 a.m.)

Sometimes a single day is not enough to absorb what it brings. Early that morning, my flight left Thessaloniki on schedule for Munich, Germany, beginning a twenty-some-hour saga of a journey back to the Pacific Northwest. In the past couple of years, I had wrestled with which actions to take and how far to go, and I could not help twirling the same questions in my mind over and over again. Would this effort lead to a nightmare in which all my fears of abusive and hurtful interactions between my parents would turn out to be true? How close to the truth did I want to get, and how painful could it be to find out? Would the record get me much closer to the true story or remain an exaggeration? Some might think I was prying where I had no business going. Let sleeping dogs lie, they say, but this is my childhood, my story, my right to know. At times it felt like a leap into the unknown; and as much as I know that every story has many sides, I had made up my mind to delve into it, no matter what the cost, and this day, Christina's email might hold some answers.

On the wing of the Airbus, I had taken an aisle seat and set the airline blanket, my purse, and a computer case under the seat in front. A young couple arrived and slipped into the two adjoining seats, an athletic, blond man and his lanky, freckled companion. Once they were settled, I asked, "Where to?"

"Munich. It's where we live. We were in Greece on a business trip," the man who had settled next to me answered in Greek with a thick

German accent. "How about you?" He seemed friendly enough and was about my son's age.

"I'm returning to the States in time to celebrate Thanksgiving with my son's family." He nodded, and I smiled, content that I had timed my return trip just right for this celebration. I missed my family. The couple indulged me a bit longer when I reached for my cell phone and shared school pictures of my grandchildren, bragging about their soccer teams and their latest victories.

Ahead of us, the flight attendant walked down the corridor rushing to check seat belts and overhead compartments a bit late, as we were already off the ground. Leaning slightly, I peered out the window, sad to leave behind the incredible expanse of Thessaloniki's bay mirroring the blinding glow of the morning sun on its waters. There were only a few clouds below us, surely a good sign. The view lasted a few seconds, and then the airplane rose upwards into a thin, hazy gray sky. Soon, we were above a thicker layer of clouds, straddling the Balkans and heading north.

I kept shifting and tossing in my seat, feeling crowded in the narrow space, wishing I could turn on my laptop when we were allowed to lower trays. "How long is our flight?" I asked a passing flight attendant.

"Just over two hours. A short flight," he smiled.

The German couple carried on a conversation and shared a spanakopita. They wore wedding bands and spoke in their native language. A ping of envy struck me as I watched them, young and warm and friendly, chatting with each other, seated next to me who was just an observer, a fellow traveler, returning home alone.

Warm and lovely touch wanes away when relationships fall apart, I thought. In 1993, forty years after my parents' divorce, my own twenty-five-year marriage had dissolved. Ours, though, was a relatively civilized split. There was no need to hurl accusations at each other. We had agreed to seek a divorce, and since there was no custody to settle, we had elected to follow mediation. Our only son, eighteen by then, had graduated from high school. Even though he was a young adult, he had become a child of divorce as well, and I worried about how he'd felt receiving the news when his father and I had delivered it to him. Neither my husband nor I were at our best, going through that process.

So yes, we'd needed help, too, and I still remembered how, in a corner conference room on the fourteenth floor of a downtown sky-scraper, the mediator, a lawyer, had coached us on how to proceed. "You need to make a list of assets. Washington is a community prop-erty state. Your husband shares . . . you share."

"You're kidding!" I exclaimed. "You mean, everything has to be divided equally between us?" That meant that the dowry my father had given me would not be considered all mine anymore. What would my dying father think about his gift to his daughter who was failing her own marriage, had he known all that was transpiring? All I had known up to that point was that the Greek laws had evolved since my parents' divorce, and dowries now were returned to the woman when a couple divorced—but not so in the United States.

However, when my husband learned that his substantial retire-ment funds would be treated the same way, he had a similar reaction. "Split evenly between us?" his temper flared. "That can't be true."

In the small family courtroom where we sat, the judge assured us that it was. "According to Washington administrative law and bar-ring a prenuptial agreement, all assets have to be listed and divided evenly and fairly," he emphasized. Truly, though, fairness is a concept influenced by one's culture, as it turns out, and is reflected in the law. It's not surprising how people from different traditions make differ-ent assumptions.

So, things were as amicable as possible, yet still painful, with spi-raling bouts of anger, loss of trust, and sadness. I was giving up what I had hungered for and labored to create for myself in America: a family. A sense of failure was stirring a feeling of being lost at sea, about what life would look like tomorrow, yet I was thirsty for this to end and yearned to regain a sense of direction and set new routines. *Alone again!* But I also knew that *this too shall pass*, as I repeated to myself what had been Mother's favorite expression. But my son's puzzled looks spoke volumes that day, weighing me down with guilt, even though he was about to start attending university. Is there ever a better time to tell such news to our children?

Friends we both knew had gone through divorce, which, at least, offered us some measure of feeling "normal" about it all—a luxury my parents had not had. Still, my world was tumbling. I was no longer living in the pastoral scene, a contented family, but rather in a gray landscape, shrouded with ashes. Keenly missing my family in Greece and their soothing presence, I rushed back to Thessaloniki for a brief vacation break—but eventually, it was time to return to the States, fall into a daily rhythm of work, deal with my empty nest, and try to regain my sense of vitality and purpose. And just as my mother had before me, I did eventually regain my footing. A single woman with a grown son and plenty of time to devote to my work, I rose ever more quickly upward. Promotions came about, and I soon moved into supervisory and managerial positions. That, at least, was one small solace—one that my mother hadn't had.

Twenty minutes after takeoff, the flight attendants allowed us to adjust our seats and lower our trays. I reached for my laptop, hungry to view what might be looming in the research files that Christina had attached to her email and fished out of my purse my trusty notebook and my Staedtler Tradition 110 pencil. On a blank page, I would be jotting down more questions, my fears, anger, or delight at the news. Would I be able to find words to describe the torrent of emotions that was threatening to flood my heart? Would I be overwhelmed, shocked, mad, or even possibly indifferent? No matter what I might feel, I wanted to preserve it.

A click later, I opened the first file to find my mother's birth and baptismal certificate, a one-page printed form, its blanks filled in by hand in legible ink. Baptized as Helen, the document said, she'd been born at noon on August 6, 1918, when Yiayia Athena was thirty-eight years old. They were small details, perhaps, but it felt satisfying to have a solid grip on my mother's birthday. Scrolling forward, I saw that the second document had new information about the divorce—the surprise of a joint petition.

In my early adulthood, I'd viewed my father's philandering and my mother's unwillingness to accept Yiayia Sophia's expectations as the cause of the divorce. My cousin, though, had warned me that any Greek divorce in the 1950s had certainly been a vitriolic process. After all this time, my surprise was not that both of them had wanted out of this marriage, it was that my mother had been actively seeking a way out. Delighted and relieved, I found myself spontaneously springing up and prancing to the rear of the plane, basking in the news that my mother, who lived in an era when women stayed in and suffered unhappy marriages, dared to leave hers.

In 1953, divorce petitions were beginning to crowd Greek family court calendars. With World War II over, couples were no longer preoccupied with basic survival. It was time to put an end to relationships that had failed and remained unresolved because of the cruel ten-year marriage requirement. Quickly, my mind flickered back to the couple sitting beside me, and I wondered how long they had been married and what laws guided divorce proceedings in Germany.

On the flight, I found that I had to suspend my own experience, to imagine what it had been like for my parents in their time. Shutting my eyes, I let my mind drift back to a black-and-white photo of them enjoying ice cream cones seated under the shady reed cover of a seaside café, Mother with sunglasses and a colorful scarf tied under her chin, and my father with his tan fedora with a black ribbon around the rim. They looked happy and elegant.

Although my mother had always managed her money just fine during regular life events, I was almost sure that the financial negotiations for the divorce would have been handled through their attorneys, with input from my father and maternal grandfather; that part would not have been my mother's strong suit. All the same, according to the documents, their attorneys had filed the petition on February 16, 1953, four months ahead of the ten-year mark. It was their response to their earnest desire to dissolve a marriage that was already dead. They must have obtained the required church certificate since pastoral counseling to reconcile them had failed. The purpose of the open court hearing, then, was to find out if their petition met legal sufficiency, what the cost would be for the proceedings, and to determine the blame for each plaintiff with the help of witnesses (sworn testimony), along with finally deciding who would have my custody.

In my mind's eye, I could imagine my mother's distressed voice telling her sister, "I am so embarrassed. What will these attorneys say in court for all to hear?" My father would likely have thrown himself into a hard day at work, just as I had done, anticipating the freedom to enjoy his dalliances and get relief, an end to getting caught between two warring women, my mother and my paternal grandmother. All the while, silent adults had turned into protective shields around my six-year-old self, keeping away from my ears whispers of a stormy time. My memories and curiosity mixed with anxiety were overflowing and found me sometimes eager and other times reluctant to harvest the fruit of my labors.

14 MY FIRST VISIT
Fall 1953

The turbulent spring that had upset me started on the day of my mother's departure in 1953 and continued beyond my sick days in summer with the measles. It lasted for months; I truly no longer could remember how long. The fickle adult world had spun my life around. It was after my seventh birthday that I started to protest in my childish ways by staying away from the house, playing with neighborhood friends or alone as long as I could, often ignoring Yiayia's calls to return home. My life turned around again when she told me suddenly one fall morning, "You can visit your mother at your grandparents' this Saturday."

"Really?" I cried. "She's still in the city?" Not a day had gone by that I hadn't been craving time with my mother. When Saturday came, I ran in the kitchen to finish drinking my milk and dressed in a hurry, choosing to wear my pleated skirt, the one my mother loved. Then I ran to board an empty public bus that took me along the familiar route into downtown. The scruffy man who issued passenger tickets from a small counter by the rear bus door and I were the only ones on this bus besides the driver. He handed me my ticket, and I took it, returning a wide smile, grateful that I was so close to seeing Mother. "Thank you," I added with exaggerated politeness, and he looked at me, surprised. Such niceties had no place in the bus-riding etiquette, but I was not into etiquette alone that day, and good manners had always pleased my mother. I placed the ticket carefully in my wallet and gingerly took a seat on the rear bench of the bus, keeping the keychain with my house and locker keys out to fiddle with. How in the heck could she leave me like that and be gone so long? Could I ever forgive her for her sudden disappearance? Why hadn't she explained anything to me at all?

Still more excited, though, than anxious to see her, I moved and sat next to the back door of the bus, eager to get off. Traveling along the wide breadth of Queen Olga Avenue, I marked off Salamina and the fish market, the School for the Blind, and eventually the Pate Movie Theater. *So many other passengers!* I glared. *Couldn't they board any faster?* But no—an old man with a cane delayed us quite a bit as he struggled to climb aboard and find a seat; tapping my foot on the floor, I resorted to looking out the window to avoid being obviously disrespectful and bothered, but watched him secretly out of the corner of my eye until the bus started up again. As the bus neared my stop, I wound up my toy wristwatch. It was almost ten thirty, and I had to be back to my Kouidis home by nine at night.

When I arrived, my grandfather would be reading the Saturday paper Mother had bought from the nearby kiosk that morning. She would be back home. I couldn't wait to see my family, of course, the people I had lost for an entire summer. What would I find when I knocked on their door? And it was not just about seeing the tall pendulum clock with the Westminster Abbey bells that rang every fifteen minutes, nor did I wonder much about where Mother had displayed the fine embroidery that she had taken away from the Kouidis home. Much more than that, I wanted to learn about their summer, their health, and most of all, why they hadn't come to see me when I was sick. But the bus could not be hurried; it took the same sweet time that it always did along this long and winding road to my grandparents' house, a route my mother and I had taken together so many times before. Outside, sheets of rain were pouring. Inside, anticipation burned until finally the sopping, steamy bus stopped at the avenue near my grandparents' apartment.

Then, speeding through uptown with an open umbrella from the bustling Tsimiski to the wide Egnatia Street, I turned, just past the Paradise Hammam, onto my grandparents' street. The uphill walk was short, and my stride lengthened when I saw the heavy double doors to my mother's building, left wide open as usual. And sure enough, my mother was watching for me from the turret window, the curtain drawn to the side, her eyes soft and a smile blossoming on her lips as she waved when she spotted me. I waved back and then ran up the stoop into the building, flying up the marble staircase, holding onto its wooden banister for balance. Then I heard their apartment door creaking open, and there was Mother, standing on the landing. I reached for her, out of breath.

"My sweet child! Let me look at you! Oh, my!" she exclaimed, and took me in her arms, hugging and kissing me. "You *have* grown taller." How could she be so warm and loving when just a while ago she had left our household?

I hesitated for a moment but, searching her eyes eagerly, I stepped back and turned on my heels to give her a full view, and my vision blurred. "It has been so long, Mamá!" She dabbed her eyes dry with a wrinkled handkerchief and squeezed me tightly. My mind was soothed and my heart full.

In my imprinted memory of that day, I locked my arms around her waist in a possessive way, feeling the comfort of her familiar body, the soft silk of her blouse against my cheek, my every fiber now content. Breathing in the aroma of her favorite perfume, Coeur Joie (Joyful Heart), I watched her eyes glisten and her cheeks brighten with a healthy, rosy glow. She wore her hair in a French roll, a new style. That was different.

My tall aunt Marika stood right behind her, leaning down to collect her hug and kiss from me. I half climbed up her frame to give her a quick peck on her cheek. "*To tzoutzouki mou,*" she said, calling me her sweet child. Then she laughed, teetered to gain her balance, and squeezed me before releasing me to the floor. Yiayia Athena joined us from the kitchen.

"You've grown! My goodness!" Her voice was hoarse.

Soaking in their attention, I felt reassured, pampered by their love. Would I see them a lot, could I stay with them for a while, or would this be just a fleeting moment, never to return? A quick wish crossed my mind: Maybe my mother would come back to our home with me at the end of the day. But really, I did not wish to face another disappointment. *Wait and see*, I told myself. I was an observant child, sensitive to the adults around me, and as my eyes relished the sight of their familiar shapes and faces, I was looking for any clues. My mother looked tan. She must have gone swimming. Was she happy here, away from me? I held her suntanned arm and admired her. "I like your hairdo, Mother, and your tan. How many swims this season?"

"Just fifteen, my sweet," she replied. "I bet you have gone swimming a lot more than I have."

"Not this summer. Only ten. You know, I had the measles," I answered, checking her face carefully. She seemed surprised.

"You had the measles?!" Mother hesitated, her eyes strained, filled with shock. "Why was I not told?" She looked up at Aunt Marika, who was biting her lips. "They will hear about this," she mumbled, and looked out the window, squashing her anger, pain, and bitterness. Then she turned to me. "Did you go to the pediatrician?" her voice pitched anxiously. "Did you get antibiotics?"

What? She didn't know? No wonder she hadn't come. My mother had been kept in the dark! Why had Yiayia or Father not called her to tell her I was ill? All the neighbors of my 25th of March Street knew. Even the milkman. Suddenly, I felt a weight lift off my heart. "So, you would have come to see me," I asked, "if you'd known?"

"Sophoula *mou*, of course!"

I waited for a moment, wanting to tell her how angry I'd been about her unexplained absences, but now my head was spinning.

That is why she hadn't come! But why hadn't she been told? Instead, the relief of seeing her chased all these questions away. "I had to have injections," I told her, nestling against the warmth of her hip. "You know I hate needles."

Still shaken, she asked me, "Who gave you the injections?" She patted my arm gently. "The old woman from the pharmacy on 25th of March Street?"

"Yes," I told her. "The same one that came for Yiayia. I missed you!" Wrinkles plowed Mother's forehead. She knew and disliked the nurse who had come and gone from our house before, without a friendly word, just doing "the job" and getting paid. But it was not just the nurse.

"I should have been there to look after you." She ran her hand through my hair. Then she stood up to straighten her embroidery that had been askew on the table.

Yiayia Athena, who always pressed us to action, interrupted us, "Go to your Papous. He has been waiting for you." Had she noticed Mother's pain and discomfort, her effort to contain it? Was my wise yiayia giving Nitsa some space?

As usual, my grandfather sat in his spot in the living room arm-chair, dressed in his suit and vest. My sweet Papous, with his deep wrinkles and sparse white hair, turned and smiled. He was a tradi-tional Greek man, old-fashioned and gentle, and I kissed his right hand to show my respect. With his calm exterior, he was burying who-knows-what worries for my sake. I had missed him.

"Come," he motioned me closer. "Let me give you a hug." Lifting myself up to sit in his lap, I wrapped my arms around his neck, like old times. Then I asked Aunt Marika where the radio was, and if I could turn it on.

"Sure. Go ahead. It's on the cast iron table in the corner," she pointed. It was sitting on the gilded, clawfoot antique table that had always made an impression on me. The dial was set to a station that played popular songs. Next to the radio was a framed studio portrait of Mother and me. I glanced at Aunt Marika, pleased. Our picture had found a new home. She smiled back.

Years later, on an audio tape she mailed to me in the States, Yiayia Athena would confide in me how hard that summer had been on my mother. After leaving our March 25th home, she'd shed bitter tears, but not about that alone. Back then, my mother would have battled with the bundle of mixed emotions every divorced woman has felt: relief, pain, fear, anger, and even regret at times, emotions she kept from me, sharing only the joy of reuniting. Often enough during those early days of our separation, Yiayia disclosed, she would take our picture from the brass table, hold it on her chest, and pace. She'd hold it like that, seeking comfort, but instead, it just broke her stoic, lonesome, and proud heart. Across town, in my dreams and awake, keeping her image alive, I would linger in the space between love, loss, anger, and pleas for her return, wrestling with the stone walls of unanswered questions. I can see her awake, pacing in the early hours before dawn and after dusk, holding her picture album, turning its pages, kissing some and tearing up others, wrestling with the riddles of life in endless monologues.

But back then, during my first visit, the morning had passed with me and Mother leafing through magazines, reading comics, and working on crosswords and puzzles. We were settling down to a new routine after the first excitement of seeing each other. At noon, Yiayia Athena called us to lunch, and I sat down next to Mother to devour my food. I rarely took naps, but Yiayia suggested one after lunch, and Mother started preparing her bed with fresh sheets and a new pillowcase. At first, I helped her, but then, feeling restless, I jumped up on her bed, grabbed the pillow from her hands, and shouted at Aunt Marika, who was standing by the door, "Look up!" Quickly, I tossed it, but she was on to me, seizing the pillow with one hand and tossing it right back.

"You will break something—an arm, a leg, or a porcelain statue! Get off that bed!" Yiayia Athena commanded, waving her hands madly.

But my mother ignored her. "Go to the hallway. The coast is clear there," she said, pointing in that direction. For a moment, I paused, not expecting that kind of permission from my mother, who usually demanded good behavior, but then I raced past my aunt, exchanging volleys.

After a while, when my aunt called, "Truce!" I was ready to quit. Giggling together, we walked back to the living room.

The next time I held a pillow up above my head to Mother or my aunt, they knew. It became our signal to provoke future pillow fights and giggles, even though Yiayia Athena never approved. It was a simple outburst after a summer of fear and loss, a way to celebrate our reunion.

"Time for your nap, Sophoula," Yiayia instructed me as we walked into the living room, glad to see us settled down.

"Would you tell me one of your stories?" I bargained with her. My yiayia wove funny and exotic yarns, and that day I knew I could ask for anything I wanted. She loved storytelling time, unlike my yiayia Sophia, who was always too busy. Yiayia Athena's stories always ended well. She wisely called on Blue Bird, a touchstone in her plots, to explain and help me understand the temporary loss of my mother. Blue Bird, the little bird who knows all, heard a distressed call coming from a soft, gray hatchling in a nest that hung under the window of a village stone house. The baby's mother was nowhere to be seen.

My yiayia continued softly, "Where is your mom?" Blue Bird, now perched on the sill, asked. Dry from thirst, the baby clicked and clacked its dry tongue.

"You must be thirsty. Time to look for food and water," she said, and she flew away.

"Chirp, chirp," the baby cheered when Blue Bird carried back water from a puddle on the ground and brought food.

"Did the baby get well fed, Yiayia?" I asked, shifting around to get a better look at her.

"Yes, Blue Bird took good care of the baby and stayed with it until its mother returned," she crooned.

"Where was she?" I frowned.

"A falcon hunted her down when she was looking for food."

"Did she come home, Yiayia?" I interrupted, worried.

"She had a young one to care for, sweetie." My yiayia Athena looked into my eyes. "That made Mama strong and clever, and she hid well from the predator. Once the falcon gave up the search, Mama Bird jumped on the wind's wings and came back to the home nest."

"Go on, Yiayia," I urged, hoping for more, though my eyelids were heavy. But she bent over and covered me lightly with a sheet, her last touch that afternoon, and started for the door. Not old enough to form them clearly, I did not ask her the questions I would raise years later about my mother and her sudden parting: Why do mothers— dedicated to loving and protecting their children, parents who long to see them launch into a happy life—abandon them suddenly?

"Time to get some sleep now, Sophoula," my grandmother said, as she stood up gently to leave the room.

I stirred once, then twice, and drifted into sleep. The house fell quiet until I woke up from a short nap. Listening to the silence around me, my grandmother's story came to me again. My loving Hadjimichael Blue Birds, it seemed, were nurturing me now with a new narrative—balm on a day when I was struggling to reconcile a paradox of life, where love breathes in the same space as the fear of loss and betrayal.

15 SOUTHERN EUROPE TO MUNICH
November 19, 2015 (9:40 a.m.)

There would have been the usual bustle in the crowded court that March morning of 1953. Three men sat on the family court bench, one substituting for the regular judge. Clearly, it was going to be a long day of disputing parties. With some reluctance and curiosity about how my parents would argue their case, openly pitted against each other, I followed them in my imagination.

"Case 928," noted the secretary, and the judge called out, "In the matter of Periclis, son of Leonidas Kouidis, petitioning for the dissolution of his marriage to Eleni, daughter of Costantinos Hadjimichael, and her countersuit against him. Ready to proceed?" The family court judge and his secretary shuffled the new set of documents on the bench.

And apparently, they were, whether or not they could yet imagine just how nasty it would all get. Flash forward sixty-some years later, on a flight over the continent, and I was about to come face to face with the harsh and unforgiving language of litigation. As I leafed through the files that my attorney had tracked down, my parents' Pandora's Box was springing open, explosive and revealing. I was about to discover just what kinds of anger and betrayal my mother had been trying to shield me from during that first summer of our new lives. But maybe she shouldn't have—maybe knowing how complex that story was would have helped me in some way. Would learning more bring me peace or keep me unsettled and wondering? Certainly now, all these years later, that story was not at all what I had expected. And what does it mean to revise my whole understanding of my history and family during my retirement years? Is it simply a matter of fact-finding? Is it an act of self-help? Is it healing? I was about to find out; my mind leapt, overwhelmed but too far enmeshed now to turn back, to an imaginary courtroom to watch the proceedings I had been too young to witness.

I returned a smile to the German man sitting next to me, careful to avoid the trap of another conversation; and, anxious to unlock a stronghold safe that had resisted me for years, I scanned the pages where Mother's and Father's lawyers had summarized their grievances. Strapped in my seat, traveling between Greece and the United States, the five-page document that Christina had forwarded burned my eyes. It contained a summary of the hearing that took place in open court on Saturday, March 7, 1953, when my parents' two attorneys had filed their respective petitions. It had been typed on a manual typewriter, with each page initialed in the margins in someone's curvy, self-important, and unreadable strokes. The last page, dated and signed by the presiding judge and the court secretary, ended by ordering another hearing for witnesses to appear in court and testify. It was clear that the family court was attempting to weigh responsibilities and attribute fault to the parties. I flipped to the beginning, sighed, and dove into the allegations the judge and his secretary were reviewing.

> *The wife remained attached to her paternal household, ignoring the petitioner and his family. Easily angered, jealous, and selfish, she created scenes against her husband on a daily basis without cause.*

My mother must have sensed that my father, like many men, was philandering. She would certainly have discussed it with her sister, my aunt Marika, likely venting over what could have been the smallest of details. Had it been, for instance, a pair of tickets to a movie that had tipped her off—or perhaps receipts from a dance hall cover charge, forgotten in my father's coat pocket? Surely, she had called him out, and he must have known that his clever explanations were suspiciously clumsy. Although he never openly acknowledged a girlfriend, his siblings had known, which I gathered from talking to my first cousins, even though it had taken plenty of prodding. Although they had been aware of all that history for decades, they had not volunteered anything until I started pressing them. Why was it so hard? Why hadn't they been more forthcoming, even after my father's death? Was it all just because the "face"of the family mattered that much? Did we really still care about all that? Or was it just that my years in America had shifted my way of seeing such things?

My imagination took off, piercing the moment with guesswork. "Marika, I don't know what to do! He is not faithful to me. I found evidence, but be careful, it's not to be trumpeted around." No matter what her evidence was, my aunt would have answered, "You better have it out with him, Nitsa. It's stupid to sit on this. Talk with him, but don't bother with his mother. You know her. She will defend him to the end."

No matter the suspicions, no matter the evidence, I expect that my father would not have admitted to anything. "What? Are you serious? It's your suspicious mind. I didn't know you were the jealous kind. Hush! Don't make me angry, now!"

All over again as I read this passage, I, too, felt deceived imagining this scene of denial, this smoke and mirrors act, and I looked around the airplane, my eyes blurry and sore from concentrating and pained by my cheating father—and now his attorney, too, who painted my mother as an insufferable, jealous woman. Even though I had seen lawyers in action and understood their role, a flood of anger filled my lungs reading that man's poisonous words, witnessing what, I believe, were Father's put-downs and unjustified accusations. I felt the distance between him and myself widening. He was, after all, distorting concepts expressed in Paul's letter to the Ephesians, always recited by the priest in Orthodox wedding ceremonies: "A man leaves his father and mother and is joined to his wife, and the two are united into one." I smiled at the irony, for the original text pointed out my father's failing, his strong attachment to his mother.

In my mind's eye, my mother's pensive face came to visit me when I shut my eyes. I could imagine her regarding these words with horror. All the effort she had made to join the Kouidis family had been dismissed in just two sentences in a petition! Turning to her sister, who sat next to her on a couch, she would have whispered fiercely, "Marika, he's blind. Totally blind. And I had to get along with his mother who lived with us. Who would have put up with that?!"

"Sis, not just blind. Really he turned to a scumbag." Marika had been a frequent visitor at her sister's home and had a good sense of the situation.

"I thought he was a sensitive man when I first met him."

"I'd thought you would have a good life with him, Nitsa," Marika spoke, wringing her hands, her voice dropping.

I see her sitting there, my mother rubbing her forehead in a gesture of despair. "It's like I stopped existing in that house," she sighs. "I can't tell you how glad I am to be with my family again. His and his mother's household is pathetic, and he is a creep."

In their days of courtship, though, I know that my mother had come to enjoy the Kouidis family gatherings, especially conversations with her husband's sisters. They had lived in a city that offered plenty of entertainment: dances, movies, lovely outdoor cafés, and beaches. They'd had such a good time when they were newlyweds frequenting these places in the evening, often finishing their outings humming songs. Father had played the mandolin back then, and their love of music had rubbed off on me. For years, I turned out to be the family crooner who led everyone in song on family outings when Father drove us in the jalopy, a WWII British military truck he had purchased to use in his business. Those were my moments of glory, when the family joined me in song to celebrate the good, carefree days of weekend fun.

Back on the plane, though, with the German couple nodding off sleepily beside me, I returned my attention to the screen and read on:

> *Since 1952, Nitsa took to abandoning the home of her husband, and together with her daughter, she would stay at her father's house from morning to night.*

True sophistry. I found it strange to see the attorney describe my mother's and my visits to my grandparents as acts of abandonment. I loved being in the presence of my attentive and loving Papous and Yiayia Athena. Nothing seemed more natural. We would walk into the house, toss our coats onto the wicker couch, and head down the hall to the sunny sitting room to greet the family. I can still see my Papous sitting in his favorite armchair and Mother chatting away with my aunt Marika. Often, I would leave my mother's side to go look for Yiayia Athena in the kitchen and check out what she was preparing, watching her awhile and occasionally giving her a hand by carrying a glass of water to my grandfather, or asking for a treat. She always obliged. It was a peaceful and orderly home, and I felt special and treasured among them. It was an oasis, a place that had offered Mother safety, a family nest of love and support that both my mother and I thrived in.

16 MY NEW BLENDED FAMILY
April 1954–April 1955

It was a springtime afternoon in 1954, and my family had handed me another riddle. Yiayia Sophia was taking me somewhere downtown. It was one of her rare outings, "A visit," she said. My cousins would be there. That was good news. They had been my steady childhood companions, more like my siblings. When I dressed up in my pink velvet dress, the one with ruffles on the skirt, and black patent leather shoes, I could not imagine that I was about to join in the celebration of my father's engagement to my future stepmother. Walking alongside Yiayia Sophia past an oak doorway into an apartment building in the Diagonios neighborhood, though, that was just where I was headed. Slowly, we climbed up four stories of a dark circular staircase; as we approached our destination, Yiayia told me carefully, "Mind your Ps and Qs, today. There are people who do not know us here." It always mattered to make a good impression.

Then we stopped briefly on the fourth-floor landing for Yiayia to catch her breath. When she was ready, she let me ring the doorbell. The door swung wide open, and a hostess welcomed us to a well-lit reception room of a large crowded apartment. "Good afternoon," she greeted my yiayia, and fixed her eyes on me. "Come in, come in."

I was curious about this new place and, although about to be blindsided, I looked forward to meeting my cousins and noticed that the hostess seemed to recognize us. I had seen her before and needed to figure out what she was doing here. Her name was Evdokia. She was a woman in her early thirties with black hair, brown eyes, a small forehead, and a broad smile.

"Thank you," I replied politely, with my best eight-year-old deportment, unsure if I liked her exaggerated manners. The entry hall was spacious and warm, a relief from the humid April evening outside. Even before we left the house, I knew that this would be a special affair. Really, you don't dress up like that for just any visit.

"Here, I will find an armchair for you." Our hostess moved ahead of us into the beige walls of a richly furnished room, and we followed her. Yiayia Sophia, now in her late seventies, was seated comfortably next to her youngest daughter, Ioulia. The two began a polite conversation with a heavyset lady, and I began exploring the room.

It was crowded with people, many unfamiliar faces, mostly adults, some sitting, some standing, holding drinks and small plates with *kourabiedes*. Men wore suits with bowties or long neckties, and ladies were all dressed up wearing necklaces, earrings, bracelets, and perfumes that clashed with each other. The room was filled with a pleasant hum of chatter. Quickly, I glanced around, and once I spotted him, I ran directly to my father, who made room for me on his lap. As I always did, I looked to him, checking in to size up his mood; finding it relaxed, I let myself feel comforted by his presence.

From across the room, one of my aunts noticed me, exclaiming, "What a pretty dress, Sophoula!"

I smiled, smoothing the ruffles self-consciously among so many new faces.

The hostess, a bit stocky in a brown velvet dress embroidered with ribbon around a V-shaped neckline, served drinks and *kourabiedes*, first to Yiayia and then to me. She held herself erect, moving about the room pleasant and chatty, tirelessly offering treats to her guests. She seemed middle-aged. Then I noticed that my father was smiling at her, and I wondered why. But I couldn't figure it out, until I remembered that I'd seen her, on a couple of occasions, drift into our Sunday Kouidis family gatherings. It might have been obvious to anyone else that the point was for Evdokia to get acquainted with our relatives, but that awareness still eluded me.

Scanning the room for familiar faces, I spotted one of my older cousins who came bouncing up to me. "Look what I got!" He pointed to his chest. He was wearing a bright red tie.

"Is it new? Where did you get it?" My voice wavered with obvious envy.

"This man gave it to me," he said, pointing to a well-groomed man in his thirties. The man, who stood talking with the hostess, had thick Brylcreem slicked into his hair.

"What did you get?" my cousin asked.

"Nothing yet." My voice sank low.

I followed him to his mother, Aunt Ioulia, to find out if there was a gift for me. Just about then, Yiayia Sophia called me and handed me a small pink package to unwrap.

"Isn't it pretty?" my yiayia asked as I took a plain golden cross out of a box lined in blue velvet. I lifted it to my chest, half smiling. "Let me keep it for you. We will get a chain so you can wear it with your red velvet dress. Miss Evdokia got it for you."

"Here," I answered, and returned it to her. I would have preferred a toy, but I knew that Yiayia valued religious trinkets. My mother would have chosen something better. She knew I loved to wear her rings and bracelets, and much to Yiayia's chagrin, I was indifferent to the icons and religious books that she kept around the house. Every time Father provoked her with his favorite blasphemous pronouncement, "I light a candle to God and one to the devil," I took delight watching her smile fade away.

"Go, find and thank her," Yiayia Sophia told me, but Evdokia was not in the room when I looked for her, and I gave up. As I roamed around the house, I realized that Evdokia's family had gifts for every member of my family, a tradition that my father reciprocated with ties, scarves, pins, and cufflinks.

My cousins, the sons of my aunt Ioulia, and I explored the house. We tasted more treats spread in large and small silver trays in the kitchen and the reception room and found heaps of coats in a bedroom and a forgotten set of dentures in a glass of water that made us laugh.

Time went by, and strangers, several of them with friendly smiles, began to leave. Yiayia got up from her chair to say goodbye to the hostess, and Evdokia helped her into her black coat. That's when I thanked the hostess for the cross, getting an approving nod from Yiayia. I reexamined her closely. She had dimples when she smiled and wore a golden pin of flowers, studded with tiny, precious stones over her heart.

"Let's go, Father," I called before starting for the door. People were coming up to him, chatting away, holding him up, and he did not yet have his coat on.

"Go ahead without me," he replied. "I'll be home later." Disappointed, I moved closer to Yiayia, who held my hand. Out of the corner of my eye, I saw Evdokia smile at my father. Instinctively, I knew that this was a connection to track and perhaps interfere with if I could. Then someone walked with me and Yiayia down the staircase and hailed a cab.

In the back seat, I turned to her and asked, "The lady that gave us presents, what is her name?" I wanted to be sure I knew.

"Evdokia, and she is your father's fiancée," Yiayia answered, explaining that the wedding would be soon.

"Really?" It took me a minute to swallow the news. Surprised, I felt stricken, idiotic, but it all added up now: the party, my dress, the treats. Later, I even learned that a Greek Orthodox priest had been at the apartment earlier in the afternoon for a religious ceremony. Yiayia and I had arrived only in time for the reception that followed. But that event—it had been my father's engagement to Evdokia.

Who was this lady? Would we get along? "We were just fine before—" I muttered.

"But we need to get some sleep now. Remember, you are visiting your mother tomorrow," Yiayia interrupted me. But my heart shrank. *What would I tell my mother? Did she know?*

When we arrived home, I headed for bed, although I was not sleepy. There were more riddles to solve and Gordian knots to untie. *The grown-ups should tell Mother,* I thought, resenting the thought of having to face that moment. *Besides, how could Father get engaged? I should have known something was up.*

Thankfully, though, I learned that my mother already knew about the engagement. In a curious, detached way, she asked me what I thought of the gathering, who was there, and what my present was. "Many people there," I told her. "I got a cross. My cousin got his first tie. The woman, she is okay." My answers were brief and stingy, but there was still so much that I was sorting out. My mother, in response, wore an inscrutable, blank expression, a face I would copy decades later in my work with troubled families in child welfare.

Years later, my stepmother and I would laugh, remembering the engagement party. "You had such a pretty dress on," she told me, explaining how she'd noticed my entrance immediately, and my orientation toward my father. "And you seemed so serious."

I remembered it too. Where else would I go but to my father's lap, to the person I recognized and trusted in a room full of strangers? At that early age, of course, I was totally claiming my father. That was my first glimpse of the space that Evdokia would occupy in our household, the room she would take up, leaving less for me. I felt her presence when she filled my time with chores and errands, crowding me in an uncomfortable way. No wonder I turned watchful and serious; I had not been around my own mother in that way when our family was intact.

The wedding day was approaching with a rush of activities, several of them invisible to me. The weight of preparations was born mostly by the bride, who had to choose and have her dress made and ready, select the best man and put the guest list together with her future husband, and get her personal belongings packed and moved into her new home. The groom's share, I believe, was lighter with purchases of a black suit and a suitable tie, rings, and bouquets, chores mostly taken care of away from our house. In that whirlwind of preparations there were two unmistakable signs of the upcoming, major change I could not deny: my brand new and very special dress for my father's wedding and the move of Evdokia's personal belongings to our house.

My dress came from an exclusive children's clothing store in downtown Thessaloniki. I still remember the store, Ariston, gone now but elegant at the time, with its year-round fine window displays. It was where I had to make a couple of trips to get measured for my flower girl dress with furbelows around the skirt, that was hemmed just right. Later my yiayia brought a barrette with delicate flower decorations for me to wear in my hair. When all that arrived at home, I had to try the combination on and look in the vanity mirror that my mother had left behind. I looked so fine, so delicate! "So pretty!" my yiayia agreed, spying on me.

One afternoon before the wedding, my father came home early driving an overloaded, lumbering jalopy, bringing what were Evdokia's personal belongings. What I remember most of all was her upright piano, black and heavy, that a couple of hamals carried up the circular staircase moaning and groaning. With it came the special bench and a box of musical scores. I had been taking piano lessons for a year or two, and I loved the thought of having a piano right in the house. However, that also meant that my new stepmother would soon be living with us, and I was not thrilled about that.

No matter what my feelings were then—or what I learned years later—there was no stopping what had already begun. My father and

Evdokia were married in the Basilica of Resurrection, the Orthodox Church in Thessaloniki, on April 18, 1955. At the time, my father was forty-two, my stepmother was thirty-one, and I was nearly nine years old. This was the second arranged marriage for Father and a first marriage for my stepmother, who was a bit older than most brides. It was a wedding with all the trimmings, fancy dresses, a decorated car, many guests, flowers, and bonbonnières.

On a festive morning filled with good will and hope, I stood by quietly, feeling sidelined and skeptical. The bride's father, a proud man and a lieutenant general, with his daughter, the bride, rode to the church in a white Studebaker decorated with ribbons and flowers. It was not unusual to hire oversized American cars for important occasions like a wedding. Dominating the roads next to the smaller European cars, their presence always gave passersby the signal that some special occasion was at hand. I watched the bride in the pretty, floor-length gown and decorated car arrive outside the church, impressive to look at but with reluctance, because this was a strange day for me, a day when my father was replacing my mother. I was not in the mood to celebrate.

Outside in the churchyard, the jolly guests kept arriving, but my world as I knew it was shifting, and I felt tense and uneasy greeting them in my white chiffon flower girl dress. They came in crossing themselves, some lighting a candle to the icons by the narthex and standing in groups making small talk in the nave. Glancing around, uncertain about what I was supposed to do, I leaned in the shadows of tall wooden pews next to the entrance. A flower girl in my own father's wedding. How odd!

Up to that point, I knew nothing about divorce, nor could I fathom that a few decades later, half of the marriages would end in divorce. All I knew was that my mother was gone, and another woman was trying to take her place. What was certain was that I was the only one among all my cousins and friends who had lost her mother. I alone understood that when marriage ends, the child loses a bit of herself. My own family would now bear the stamp, the shame of being broken even though we carried the proud Kouidis name. I was becoming the product of a lost mother, a wayward father, and a new stepmother, and would alone struggle to understand what it meant to be the loneliest child in the crowd. And, of course, I wanted the impossible; I wanted my mother back.

But for the moment, we just stood waiting for the bride to arrive. Byzantine icons and frescoes of saints looked out from the iconostasis that separated the nave from the sanctuary in a splendid chorus of color. We were surrounded by elongated, vivid images of sainted, angelic, and demonic creatures painted with pure, vivid red, blue, purple, green, and silver paints on mostly gilded backgrounds.

"Come and meet your new cousin, Peter," Aunt Ioulia said, coming in from the outside. A four-year-old boy in his black velvet suit reached for my hand and looked at me with large, overwhelmed eyes.

"Hi," I replied, following my aunt, who was ushering us to the center of the floor.

In a long white gown, the bride linked arms with her father in his dark gray suit and walked through the crowd toward my father, who was waiting in the center of the church. My new cousin and I took our places across from Father, and I stared at Evdokia. She left her father's arm and walked slowly to my father's side. Their eyes met with a smile, and he handed her an artfully arranged bouquet with white roses, lilies, and baby's breath.

I had seen photographs of my young mother, but none of her wedding to my father. I wondered who had torn them up, lamenting those lost years. A sharp dresser, she would have been much prettier than Evdokia, and I imagined her wearing one of those floor-length gowns with a wide décolletage and a tiny waistline, fashionable in the 1940s. She would have been youthful, slim, and graceful as she came down the aisle with my grandfather, Constantinos. He would have walked with her to the center of the cathedral in his pinstriped suit and vest, all smiles and dreams for his daughter. But back there, in the moment, it was getting hot in the church because of all the burning chandeliers and the guests who had begun to crowd around us, trying to get the best view of the couple.

"Blessed is the kingdom of the Father, and of the Son, and of the Holy Spirit." In a practiced voice, loudly, to get everyone's attention, the priest started the service, swinging the thurible, its silver bells gently ringing. Everyone, still standing, quieted down and came closer in. My father, I noticed, did not seem to know that I was there. He had found a new preoccupation with keeping track of his new wife and relatives. Was it time for me to move on? But I was still too young to attempt it.

Another pair of cousins joined us just as the service started, hurriedly pushed forward by their mother, and we formed a circle opposite the bride and groom, holding the space open for the priest and the couple during the ceremony. The priest wore his silky liturgical vestments in Byzantine gold and blue with a red stole over black robes, and presided over the ceremony.

It was a long service, too long for us flower children to stand still the entire time. Along the sidelines, I shifted from one foot to the other, poking my cousin a couple of times, and we snickered. Bored and anxious, I stood as still as a young child can, weighed down by the gravity of the occasion. Who was this woman about to take over my home? This was undoubtedly her moment, but up until then she had been a single unknown woman who, no doubt, had a dowry and some mysterious connection to my father. Everyone in the church and in my family circle seemed to make room for her: my father, of course, but also my yiayia Sophia. And what about me? *How would she be with me? Would we get along?*

The priest took a pair of plain golden bands, blessed them, and placed them on the Bible resting on a table in the middle of our circle. Then came the Dance of Isaiah, the moment that the guests had been waiting for gleefully, when Father and Evdokia circled three times around the table with the Bible, led by the priest. The couple stopped every so often to receive more blessings, while guests showered them with rice. In those moments, the bride is supposed to step on the groom's foot during the dance, according to custom. This is an opportunity for the new bride to dominate the moment, even if fleetingly, in our patriarchal society. The crowd laughed as it always does, and so did I. Finally, the priest placed the rings on the bride's and groom's fingers, and more blessings followed until the final amen.

Once the service was over, guests lined up to congratulate the couple, and each guest received a bonbonnière with white Jordan almonds wrapped in white tulle. The first one in line to kiss the bride and groom was my yiayia Sophia, overcome with a sweet smile on her lips. I watched her with surprise; for a woman who did not normally show her feelings, she was glowing. She wrapped her arms around each of them, kissing them on their foreheads, and then she peeled away, making room for the next well-wisher, as a broad smile lingered on her face that softened her eyes. I had never seen her act as sweetly as that. What a complicated world this was turning out to be!

But as for me, I did not line up to wish them well. I had a job to do. Leaving my vantage point, the loneliest child in the crowd, I moved to the sidelines to hand out bonbonnières to each guest, greeting them with my pretend smile, wondering what tomorrow would be like. That day was one of a kind in my Greek world, a divorced man marrying again. Was I the only one feeling awkward about it all? Did my mother know? She must have, and she must have been miserable that day. In the Greek society of the day she would have been used goods, suspect, someone who must have done something wrong, someone who abandoned her child, and, of course, a woman unlikely to remarry. What did she have to look forward to for herself? Affairs, going it alone, or leaving the area? But I did not know about all that then. I watched all our merry guests who seemed to be enjoying the occasion as they lined up to congratulate the couple.

After the service, I hardly saw my father and stepmother. They had packed their suitcases and "flown off to the island of Rhodes for their honeymoon," Yiayia told me the next day.

"Why a honeymoon?" I quizzed her when she returned to the living room, already knowing her answer. They had not taken me with them, and I meant to complain.

"Will Father come back?" I worried.

"They *both* will," she replied. "Your mother will live here with us." I arched my back and walked away. That was my first clue that I would be expected to call this new woman, Evdokia, my "mother." Silently, I tried the feeling of it out on my tongue, but, feeling disloyal to my own mother, I squashed it.

The last two years had been a blizzard of shifts: living with Yiayia Sophia and Father, visiting my mother only on weekends, and now facing a stepmother. Certainly, I realized that there was no good time to bring a stranger into our home. Still, the sun is tireless. It rises in the morning, sets at night, and embroiders our minds with perplexing thoughts that ferment and allow for the birth of a new, unconventional family. I would have to improvise even when I looked for words to describe it. No one else I knew had a family like mine.

17 OVER SOUTHERN EUROPE TO MUNICH
November 19, 2015 (10:05 a.m.)

I have little recollection of my parents' arguments. Nor do I remember long stays at my maternal grandparents' home because that would have meant missing school—and I rarely missed school. Those accusations, then, that I found among the detailed archives of my parents' divorce proceedings must have been lies—manufactured ones, likely aimed at justifying divorce in the eyes of the court—which made me wonder how much more of that document before me was accurate and how much made up, as my cousin had warned me.

We were halfway to our destination in Munich when a middle-aged woman seated in front of me was calling for steward assistance by pressing an overhead button over and over again. When no one showed up she got loud, complaining about the service on this flight. I wished she could wait her turn, as her high-pitched, cacophonous voice was taking me away from the page. "Is there no steward available? Where is everybody?" she shrieked. Luckily, the commotion settled down once a steward showed up. But by then, irritated because all she needed was a newspaper, I stopped looking at the screen for a while.

However, she was not the only one with unreasonable demands. When I turned back to my computer screen, I reread that lie again, and went on:

> . . . *As a result, she did not prepare meals or take care of household chores. Whenever her husband scolded her for her*

frequent absences, she would swear at him, adding, "This is
what is, and if you don't like it, I will leave you forever."

Was it realistic to expect any woman who was challenged, criticized, and ignored to act like a "happy housewife?" With Yiayia's
dominance in the kitchen, there was little room left even for an
experienced cook. All the years of caring for her family had made
Yiayia not only an excellent cook, but also one who could not recognize that she was exceeding her role in her son's home, now that he
was married. No wonder Greeks talk about «κακιά πεθερά», or "evil"
mothers-in-law. What was worse, though, was that in my father's
eyes, my mother must have been a woman incapable of managing the
kitchen. Next to his mother, he thought my mother was a disaster.
She's become a burden; not a support for me, he must have thought.
Her mother did not raise her right.

Turning to his attorney all those years ago, I can imagine how he
had poured out his frustrations. "I have had a lot on my mind. With
your help, I have got to get this divorce over with. Work, customers,
managing equipment, business travel . . . and then this headache! I
leave at dawn and come home in the dark. I cannot be bothered with
her anymore . . . and don't be fooled, she is feisty and stubborn as a
mule." Oh, how his voice might have gone on, menacing. "I hope she
stays at her parents' while this is going on. Mother will be happier,
and I know that my mother looks after Sophoula well." Did he consider his part in the problem? I doubt it. But this marriage needed
to be over with, for both their sakes and, in the long run, mine. For
when things are that far gone, they only fester more.

Perhaps he'd shared his frustrations about the home situation over
a glass of beer and a souvlaki with his attorney at the busy Modiano
Market, buzzing with housewives who were shopping for the dinner
table. That particular fast-food stand was close to the attorney's
office, a place that Father frequented often for a quick meal. If they'd

sat there together over drinks, no doubt the two men had made a plan to return to the law office soon to finalize the petition.

"I have built a whole business, starting with nothing," I can imagine my father complaining. "She's still clueless about what it takes. After all that hard work, a man needs to relax too!"

No doubt that rotund attorney would have smiled then, taking another sip of his beer. He could have guessed that Father was not the type to bother and scold my mother—but used that statement to make his client look good. It wasn't true; it couldn't have been, as far as I remembered, because Father, distracted as he was and gone so much from our home, was not likely to notice the inner workings of the household; it had to be Yiayia Sophia who had raised the issue. As for Mother threatening to leave, I can certainly believe that she must have warned Father once she'd reached her limit.

Still, in that day, women were expected to serve their husbands, manage the children, and maintain the household. Unlike her sister, my mother had not developed job skills, which would have made her slow to come to the decision to move out. And, of course, there was the still standing legal requirement that couples must wait ten full years before earning the right to seek a divorce.

No women in the post-war Greek social sphere of the 1950s wanted to be a divorcée or an old maid. I often wondered what women who worked in attorney's offices who answered phones, used manual typewriters, and watched men's machinations at work thought about marriage. Still, even they had better finances, I suppose, than my mother did—who, leaving her marriage, would have had nothing to fall back on because she never planned to seek employment.

With a few keystrokes, I magnified the text on my screen. I could see that the divorce petition had been typed on letter-size paper, and m's, as in "mother," were worn out, rendering the bottom of the letter invisible, trimmed, κουτσουρεμένο, like Nitsa's endurance in the Kouidis household. Reading those lines, it was so easy to picture the typist at the attorney's office reading her clever boss's masterful twisting of the truth. I imagined her smiling sarcastically when she eavesdropped on the men's planning conversations, and pictured Nitsa's plight. She knew that the way Periclis's attorney was presenting Mother, in service to his client, was manipulative. Long ago, she had become a doubting Thomas about "facts." Even through the silence of distance and years, I could hear the *click-clicking* of her keys, and I shared her sinking feeling, watching the way that patriarchy imposed its version of the truth. How could the judges trust the veracity of these statements? At least, I supposed, they had sought witnesses to further investigate the case. But what had those witnesses said? Would they have offered a different kind of story?

18 SHIFTING LOYALTIES
1955–1957

Spring had arrived—the season to watch the seeds of a newfound family sprout among the weeds of the garden. Aunt Eleni's chickens noisily trotted around the fenced yard next door, and I was still in charge of collecting their eggs from the chicken coop. Running to the *alana* to find my friends after school, I did my best to hold onto what I knew of our lives. My father and his old jalopy continued to take us to family outings, and Yiayia presided in preparing family meals. But some things were shifting and, although I still hungered for my old life, change seemed inevitable.

In the days that followed the wedding, I watched Yiayia Sophia and my stepmother sit on the living room couch and sew, iron, and chat. It was instant compatibility. They talked about recipes ("less oil, more salt"), added fuel to the oil lamp, and lit the wick under the iconostasis. "Don't forget to get some wicks," Yiayia would warn. "We're running out." All the while, my father kept long hours at work. "Keep some food warm for Periclis," I'd hear one woman say to the other. That was all they spoke of it but, regardless of my father's habits, the two women got along; they had more in common with each other than my own mother had had with Yiayia. Quietly, I slithered around a house that felt more peaceful, watching them quietly and taking it all in.

So Evdokia, my new stepmother, had joined our Kouidis family, and she seemed to be adapting just fine. Refugees, the Kouidises had settled in Greece in 1922, leaving their two-story home in the

Sakiz-Agats district of Constantinople to settle in Thessaloniki. Back then, my father had only been fifteen years old, and everyone in Greece knew that another one and a half million Greeks had abandoned hearth and home in order to avoid extermination by the Turks. Many of them had settled in Thessaloniki—with its Greek Orthodox churches, synagogues, and minarets—to start life over again, finding their new home after sleeping under the stars for five days.

That history is still such a contrast to my own days, which, despite some hardships, have been so easy. Especially during my girlhood, they simply could not compare. In those days, my mornings had begun with, "*Yiavri mou*, I have some toast for you. Do you want butter and marmalade or just butter on it?" My toast always came with the tea that we shared in the kitchen. My yiayia Sophia was my steady breakfast companion. She would boil water in a small pot that we used for tea or Turkish coffee. Then, she'd add the black tea that came from my father's warehouse, teas imported from Ceylon in large trunks marked with a canary and the country's name. I looked for the containers stacked up in the back whenever I visited Father at the warehouse.

In those days, my grandmother took to calling me *zizanio*. A physical child, I loved climbing the tree in our backyard, which gave her palpitations. "You little troublemaker," she would call me in Greek, clearly worried. "Come down right now!" But I was not persuaded easily. I liked the view from above, watching the neighborhood activity.

"Come and get me!" I would challenge her.

"You will fall and hurt yourself," she would warn me, but I never did, and I enjoyed her pleas that followed. When I got noisy or argued with my girlfriends in the house ("Leave my book alone, you are tearing the page," or "I am not talking to you, you make me mad!"), she would alert me when my father was home, repeating the words in Turkish, over and over: "*Babacin geliyor! Babacin geliyor!*"

(Your father is coming) until she got my attention. My mischievous moments, though, usually amounted to little more than running inside the house, disputing ownership of toys, and physical pushing and shoving jovially with friends—or momentary enemies.

In those days, during our boisterous play, Yiayia Sophia was prone to lapse into Turkish from time to time—a language my stepmother did not know—especially when she carried on confidential conversations with my father. But even if she didn't understand their language, my stepmother was dutiful, seeing me off to school and preparing my after-school snacks. She expected me to comb my hair, urged me to "look in the mirror before you go out," and to avoid appearing like "a rushed, disheveled child." In return, I had acquired a new chore, dusting the furniture and setting the table for her. And no longer did I sit next to my father at that table. Instead, Evdokia occupied that seat herself, while I sat across from them, next to Yiayia.

Was that what a child of divorce was to expect? Who knows? But, at the time, I was still a little girl, and I resented having to move over from my usual place at the table. I'd sit there, sulking a bit and wondering if there were "rules" about how to live in a second family. But there was no one to ask. Certainly, I couldn't ask my mother, and there was no one else, adult or child, around me who had experienced such a major change. Father was the only man with a second marriage in my known universe.

Life went on—perhaps not with clarity, but with habit. "Bring back a loaf of white bread and a small loaf of black," Evdokia would say a couple of times each week and send me shopping, sometimes adding more items. "And don't forget to grab a couple of ripe tomatoes and an onion for the salad."

She was a woman who revered food, marking special occasions with special meals. For instance, a couple of months after the wedding, Father returned home for an early dinner. She called it their "sixty-day anniversary," and she had set the table using our good dishes and placing a pitcher of red wine next to the pitcher of water. The menu was luscious: a spicy roast seasoned with rosemary and thyme, steaming oven-baked potatoes, a green Constantinople-style cabbage salad with shredded carrots and walnuts chunked in, dressed with mayonnaise thinned with lemon and oil. A heaping bowl of bananas and apples sat next to the bread cutting board. We took our time at the table, enjoying her delicious meal. Evdokia moved clockwise around the table, serving us and fussing over Father as she sought his opinion about her dishes.

"Is it salted enough?" she'd ask. "How is the sauce?"

"Fine."

"Delicious."

He offered compliments, even when she had not asked. When he wasn't talking, he stuffed bites hungrily into his mouth, sipping his glass of wine slowly. He even poured a couple of sips for me. When the meal was over, Yiayia and I cleared the dishes.

Over the past few days, Evdokia had been practicing popular Attik songs. After dinner, she moved to her piano, now dominating our living room, set the score of "Few Hearts Love" on the music rack, and opened the fallboard. With her fingers poised on the keyboard, she looked at my father, smiled, and fixed her eyes on the sheet of music. The introduction was soft and lyrical, and I watched her fingers moving gracefully as she pumped the sustaining pedal, filling the room with the romantic tune. That night, she'd chosen a popular song that my father knew—we all did. And, by the time she'd reached the slow refrain, my father had left the table and was leaning on the piano. With his fine tenor, he sang away, his eyes half closed as my stepmother paced the accompaniment to his voice.

Few hearts love, like my heart,
Most of them forget as soon as the night is gone.

A crescendo followed Attik's refrain and had us exhilarated. We all hummed, following Father's pace, except for Yiayia, who just smiled.

Do not leave me dear, and look elsewhere,
Few hearts love like I love you.

Whatever else I might have been feeling in those days, I knew that this was a special evening. A sense of harmony and joy was palpable in our household, a lifting of spirits. And the truth is that, although I was undecided about what to make of father's good mood, I was too swept up by the song and the moment.

Finally, once our singing was over, my stepmother had one more surprise for my father. For days, she'd been laboring to perfect the finest baklava recipe—and she served each of us individually.

"Just the right amount of honey and cloves in the syrup," Yiayia commented approvingly.

"Bravo! Outstanding!" my father exclaimed.

Yes, I thought, all this is fine, but, all the same, I couldn't help feeling torn. Taking small bites of this dessert I found too sweet, I sensed that I was losing my place of privilege in this family. Everyone was busily enjoying their meal, emptying their dishes in no time while I lingered on discontent, with a sense of falling deep into the hole of being sidelined. Hestia, ruler of domestic life, had long ago abandoned our old household together with my mother. Still watchful and skeptical, I felt unsettled. Who was entering our home now? A wise Athena, the seductive Aphrodite, or Demeter the sweet mother of Persephone? Perhaps some of each. Fearful of accepting her, I yearned only for the wise Athena.

Time passed, and our home was calm, cheerful. So, I cannot explain it, but I was beginning to feel reassured that Evdokia was a well-intentioned stepmother—as I recognized the finality of my parents' divorce. Being an introvert, I carried the pain of losing my mother inside me, tucked in a corner of my heart, trusting my feelings only to my journal. It was a standard notebook—journals with locks were not available back then. I kept it by my nightstand, under the box with socks, or under the mattress, careful to keep it private and safe. In fountain-pen blue ink and thick lettering, I had placed a warning on the front page in case it fell into someone else's hands: PRIVATE JOURNAL/READ NO FURTHER. It was a place where I trusted my stories about my mother, stepmother, friends, and my father, a place of intermittent confessions, idle gossip, and words about hopes, victories, disappointments, and anger.

But there was a record of good moments, too, including evidence of my stepmother's intentions, which came soon on the day we visited my Aunt Ioulia's family, who had recently moved to a new apartment near the city center. As we prepared to leave, though, Yiayia announced that she was tired and would stay home.

"Take a jacket along for later," she told me. But not a leaf was moving that morning; the day promised to be hot. Still, I went along with her. She had always been leery of cold nights and "drafts" that bring illness.

But then, my father was sitting in his new acquisition for the business, a used truck, another jalopy, the engine on, waiting for me and my stepmother. He always got impatient, and I knew to rush outside when he honked the horn. I draped my light blue jacket over my arm and waited outside for my stepmother to lock the front door. She took the passenger seat next to Father, and I crowded next to her, leaning out of the open window once the car was in motion. There was little traffic on the rutted neighborhood roads, and seat belts were not required in cars back then. My parents were debating whether we had time to stop and get some patisserie treats for my aunt's home. It was a custom to "never go on a visit empty-handed," as Yiayia put it.

But before long, we were past the army base and the soldier with the bayonet on guard duty and had turned on a tree-lined side street, a shortcut that my father often took to downtown. Suddenly, he swerved into a dusty square. My father must have realized in a split second that he was about to miss the turn. As the passenger door unlatched and flung itself wide open, my own body swerved, doubling over. Gravity pulled me easily out of that cab, life unraveling like confetti into a thousand pieces as my head almost touched the dirt road. There was a dark fear, but quicker than anything, I felt a hand grab mine to pull me back in as I reassembled myself back into my body. Then the brakes screeched.

"Evdokia, my God!" my father gasped, as it had been my stepmother's quick reflexes at work that had saved me. My heart pumped in my ears like a kettle drum.

"My Virgin Mary!" My stepmother screamed, catching her breath.

I sat upright and disoriented. Shaken, my stepmother and I looked at each other, barely aware that the danger had passed. Then she turned to my father, asking pointedly, "What happened, Pericli?"

"Wrong turn," he said, getting out of the jalopy to check my door. He pulled hard on the handle to ensure the latch was securely shut, then returned to his seat and started the engine—and soon we were taking the elevator up to my aunt's home, arriving empty-handed.

So my savior was my stepmother, the woman who sat between me and my father. Now, I owed her my life. But, for those moments, I simply sat thigh to thigh with her and embraced her. I did not want to feel this way, but giving her a hug came easily, especially when she reciprocated.

In my aunt's living room, still plucking a chord of discontent, I took a deep breath and sank into conflicting emotions. I did not know where I belonged anymore, but other things were easier. Already, I had forgiven my father for the fright he had given me. What else could I do? It had been an accident, after all. So now I owed my life to my new stepmother, who had taken over six days of my week, leaving just one for me and my mother. This new guardian angel controlled my days—a right she had not earned by giving me birth—but it was all still too much to think about. Not surprisingly, that afternoon I did not feel like playing, choosing to retreat instead onto the couch with a magazine and look at cartoons. And even now, as I am recounting those moments years later, I'm still struck by the strong impact that one episode had on me. Maybe she was trustworthy, I had begun to realize—even as much as I had resisted it. Maybe she was more like Artemis, the mighty daughter of Zeus and protector of vulnerable children. Fearful of accepting her, I still yearned for the wise Athena.

19 OVER NORTHERN EUROPE TAKING OFF FOR CHICAGO
November 19, 2015, (1:00 p.m.)

When we landed in Munich's Franz Josef Strauss airport, I turned in the forms that the flight attendants had distributed to the customs official who stamped my passport with a practiced, decisive motion. Clearing the metal detector, I glanced upward at the departures schedule. There were still two and a half hours before my flight, and the gate was comfortably nearby. *Try to clear your mind,* I told myself, turning toward the nearest gift shop, a brightly lit duty-free shop filled with aisles of merchandise. There was a long lineup at the cash register, and I lingered to see what other shoppers were buying—mostly brightly packaged candy for kids, boxed liqueur bottles, and fancy perfumes. Then I quickly settled on Toblerone chocolates for each of my grandsons and a bottle of Amaretto for my son's family. At a nearby restaurant, I set down my bags with relief. Even though I had landed in Germany, I still hadn't left Greece—not yet. My homeland would stay with me all the way to the Pacific Northwest, halfway around the world.

The lunch menu was limited and had exorbitant prices. "Fish and chips, please," I told the waitress when she approached.

"Something to drink?"

"Water." My response was flat.

A few minutes later, she brought me a red plastic bowl with a plate of airport food, bland as cardboard, but it would have to do, even if it did leave me suddenly yearning for my grandmother Sophia's delicious cooking. During all those years together, Yiayia Sophia had prepared food that always met with Father's and everyone's approval. During the holiday season, Yiayia would lead the charge, assigning shopping to my father, kneading and chopping to my stepmother, and cracking walnuts or almonds to me. I also got to do "go fetch it" chores while Yiayia mixed, spiced, and tasted the ingredients, filling our kitchen with such smells of satisfaction that I could barely remember much about my mother's role there at all.

On those long days in the kitchen, my father would walk into the house with an exclamation of, "What smells so good?"

Our home on those days would be filled with delectable food and special desserts like baklava, kataifi, saragli and kourabiedes. These were the treats we all loved, the delicacies from my family's homeland, as Yiayia Sophia had retained much of the cuisine from her Anatolian background. Evdokia was no stranger to this culture, so her addition to our kitchen was seamless. "My mother grew up in Constantinople," she told us. "She was educated as a teacher there." And my yiayia seemed pleased, as was my father. Even I could tell that Evdokia was a good fit for him. One of my older cousins had told me that. But my mother, on the other hand, born in Thessaloniki, had never quite meshed with my yiayia and her customs—not her food, not her habits, and certainly not her expectations for her son's wife.

Shaking off these reveries, I shoved aside my tray of half-eaten fish and chips, paid the bill, and checked my watch. By the time I reached the gate, my flight had started boarding. Lining up with all the passengers, I stretched slightly and waited for my turn. The longest leg of my journey—one that would not be long enough for me to absorb all my computer screen was pummeling me with—was about to begin. We would travel over northern Europe, the Atlantic, and Canada, landing in Chicago ten hours later.

Ahead of me, a woman was laughing about someone she knew. "A sleazy man," I overheard her say.

"Don't be so critical. He is a poor bloke but not sleazy," her partner answered.

As I listened to their banter, I remembered our old 25th of March Street neighbor, Mrs. Katina, who lived next door and loved to gossip. She used to talk about our neighbors like this: "She's so stingy," she'd complain. "She won't even share a cup of coffee with us!" And, complaining about her husband, she'd equally gripe, "He can't even get a glass of water for himself."

As a girl hearing these things, I had always wondered what she might also be spreading about our own family—behind our backs. Oh, that woman did enjoy gossiping in colorful language! But did my mother have a reputation in the neighborhood because of that? Something about swearing at my father? If she did, I hadn't ever heard about it. Or, what about my father swearing at her? I couldn't believe that, either, but really, I would never know.

Slowly, we began to move forward, showing our boarding passes to the gate personnel and taking our seats. Then the crew started in with their routines: greetings, shutting overhead compartments, delivering safety demonstrations, and checking seat belts. Finally, we were on our way—but all I wanted to do was get back into those legal documents to resume studying them. After several long minutes of acceleration up into the skies, we could use our trays again. Quickly—but anxiously too—I turned on my laptop, anticipating more unwelcome news.

> *Her behavior toward her mother-in-law was crude. She treated her [Yiayia] like a maid. She did not heed the advice of relatives and friends, urging her to change her behavior toward her husband and his mother.*

All I could do was sink further into my airplane seat, seeking comfort, and feeling even more restless at the beginning of that long flight. How odd it was to be reading such a personal document there, surrounded by strangers. And how I wished I could talk to my family, my friends. The petition had started with "*. . . frequent absences . . . scolding . . . threats . . . perhaps behind closed bedroom doors.*" Again, none of that rang true. For one thing, my father was not the kind of person to make an effort to reform my mother's behavior. And had he tried, my mother would have reacted in anger. I would have too.

Still, it was easy to imagine the attorney writing up these allegations. Based on my own former work in child welfare court cases, as well as my Greek lawyer's descriptions, I could visualize the man moving through the courtroom. He would have turned toward the bench, adding to his list of arguments, laying out each one with conviction and force as he tried to influence the judges. He was standing up in the courtroom, a venting orator, gesturing to impress rather than speak the truth.

But anger welled up in me when I pictured my father's attorney painting Mother as a selfish, offensive, and unresponsive wife. Those harsh descriptions made me flinch. I needed to rest my eyes away from the page for a minute. Never had I seen my stoic mother turn harsh, but I could imagine her being persistent, defiant, and unwilling to cooperate with her mother-in-law. There was a time, for instance, when she'd refused to put down her book and prepare the dessert Yiayia wanted.

"Nitsa, do you have to read that book? Why can't you go to the kitchen to make some halvah or something, for our dinner?" Yiayia Sophia commanded as she stormed into the living room.

I had been six or seven then and had felt the chill in the air from the floor where I was playing with my doll. My mother never gave up her reading, even though it was disrespectful in our culture to ignore an elder. Likely, my father heard about it all from Yiayia Sophia. But had my mother really had outbreaks of rudeness?

"She is treating Mother like household help, Pericli," his sisters likely informed him.

The matriarch of the Kouidis family was not about to put up with her daughter-in-law's demeaning ways. Having endured the rush of a sudden relocation from Turkey to Thessaloniki, as well as the hardships of starting life from scratch in her forties, Sophia was a proud mother who wanted to see her children thrive. Hunched over now with scoliosis, she'd brought with her the culture of the old country where she had grown up, a conservative culture, and one that clashed with my mother's own upbringing. All her life, Yiayia Sophia had spent endless hours in the kitchen, bent over the stove, wearing an apron, peeling potatoes, and preparing meals to feed her six children before and after her husband's death. By the end, though, she had hoped to live with a son and a daughter-in-law who would respect her and appreciate her commitment to the family.

Most of the Kouidis wives, all of whom had their roots in Turkey, had tried to talk sense into Nitsa, advising her to soften the way she addressed Yiayia and take less space in her own household, but my mother had ignored their advice. What Yiayia Sophia must have hated most, though, was Mother's open resentment of her and neglect of her household responsibilities. She must have thought, *My son deserves better care and attention.*

That was not what I craved. In my childhood, what I yearned for was a loving, nurturing home, a place to feel safe and secure. I had loving parents, but the adults covered up their troubles. Perhaps my instinct to survive could have blinded me to recognizing all that strife. I was a teenager driven by my need for independence that propelled me to find my own path. But then, there on the plane, suspended in the long-distance flight between continents, a new awareness rose in me, one that I had never felt before. As I read the petition, a surge of resentment toward Yiayia and the insidious role that she had played in the decay of my parents' marriage suddenly raged within me. In my cramped airplane seat, I was regressing into a despairing child, in turmoil, as the typewriter letters whirled around me in a mad dance. The tension and confusion of those last years of my parents' marriage were choking me. I gulped down some water and noticed that people around me were settling down to watch movies and read. Needing to stretch, I took my empty cup to the rear cabin for a refill from a flight attendant.

Back at my seat, I glanced again through all the allegations. I had started translating them into English, thinking that this would help me keep hold of them in my head. "... *Her behavior toward her mother-in-law was crude. She considered his mother [Yiayia] to be her maid.*" And so, I looked for and finally determined that, somehow, there was no mention of Father's affairs. Why not? My mother's attorney certainly would have taken the opportunity to inform the court and establish "fault" against my father. There would have been financial benefit for Mother. For me, though, it was confirmation that my mother had not known of my father's betrayals until after the divorce. He'd been skilled, it seemed, in covering his tracks.

But eventually she had found out, and when I was twelve, I remember vividly the Sunday afternoon when I witnessed her wrath and contempt for my father. It was a scene for which I was unprepared.

20 AN EXPLOSIVE AFTERNOON
1957

I had never really understood who had started the divorce, my mother or my father. Once it was underway, though, I found myself talking mostly in hints and whispers; in 1950s Greece, almost no one got divorced. On weekends, I would get up early in the morning as if it were a school day and get dressed right away. Before anyone else got up, I'd sit in silence over my toast and breakfast tea, checking my pockets for bus fare and my student pass. But no one ever said a thing. Didn't they care? Did they notice how all that silence was turning a twelve-year-old girl's world on its head? Finally, just before leaving the house, I'd tell my father's family simply that I was going "over there," to the downtown apartment where my mother now lived with her parents. Still no answer. And so I'd leave.

But traversing two households meant more than getting on buses or arranging rides to and from one parent's house to the other. Leaving my father's house meant entering another world—and my mother invariably made plans for us there.

"What are we doing today?"

Silently, my mother would answer with comic books and magazines, crosswords, walks, movies, shopping, and swimming excursions in the summer—all activities that had to end by the evening hour. There were times that she waited for me with small surprises: chocolate treats, a barrette, or a rare visit to a restaurant.

"Mother, I love your surprises." I made sure she knew it, which her smile told me she did, but there was still something to her silence that I couldn't trace and didn't understand—not for decades.

Like my mother's transition from married life to seclusion in the home of her younger years, my own bus journey regularly took me from one hushed, holy place to the next. In Thessaloniki, my cosmopolitan hometown in northern Greece, where mostly Greek Orthodox churches dotted the horizon, I would ride the bus that I boarded by the Church of the Resurrection and, half an hour later, get off at the Church of the Savior. Back then, it was still safe for a twelve-year-old like me to ride the public diesel buses by myself. They puffed black, choking clouds of smoke, and the brakes screeched at each stop. The ticket collector would shout out the stops. I listened for "Diagonal," and would ring the bus bell to signal my stop. Minutes later, there would be my mother—both familiar and silenced, as any jilted woman back then must have been.

But that silence was easy. Our city was large enough for my biological parents to avoid seeing each other, though small enough to transport juicy news about everybody's business. Through the currents of all that silence, my parents had begun traveling in different social circles entirely. Still, when they ran into each other, they rarely exchanged greetings, other than a stiff nod and maybe a hello. The scale of their relationship had tilted in a way I could no longer understand. Although not attuned to the degree of disruption before my mother moved out, I'd noticed that she would put me to bed long before father returned home. He would often arrive when it was pitch dark, betrayed by the midnight strike of the clock and the dying jalopy engine outside the house. I paid little attention to his long hours. My grandmother had said that he often worked long hours in the business; that's why he was so successful. In those days, my mother had more frequent confidential conversations with her sister. Even though they held them at a careful distance away from me and Father's relatives, the two of them sometimes whispered my father's name in ways that let me know there were secrets far beyond what I knew. Their frowns and worried faces betrayed their distress, and I turned increasingly into a watchful child, tracking smoke signals that I could not decode.

On rare occasions, at the end of my weekend visit, my mother would walk me to Egypt Street to meet Father, who would give me a ride home in the jalopy. She and I would stroll from her apartment through the handful of blocks to the Church of the Assumption of Virgin Mary. Next to it stood a grand movie theater built in 1930, surrounded by two-story columns outside the lobby. A vertical three-dimensional sign raised above its entrance spelled I LY S I A. Outlined in bright neon lights and painted red, it was visible from some distance. In the early days of film in Thessaloniki, people formed long lines outside the Ilysia to watch new productions.

"Did you know that the Ilysia was controversial when it was first built?" my mother reminisced. Church officials, she explained, had strenuously objected to its existence. It was not just an offensive neighbor to a church, but it was also a wellspring of sin that would contribute to the deterioration of morality of the citizenry.

"But we love the shows, Mother. Come on, let's go see what's on right now." By the time I was born, all such controversies had died out, and I regularly dragged my mother to view the black-and-white photos and colorful posters on its bulletin boards to see what was playing.

"This one is R rated," she would read out loud. "Too old for you—but let's see what else is coming next." Whenever she could, my mother always tried to please me, which was easy enough because there were so many simple activities that we enjoyed together. One of her favorites was window shopping, so we'd walk along Tsimiski Street looking at window displays. Tsimiski has always been a beautiful downtown boulevard that stretches from the famous White Tower to the port of Thessaloniki and offers shopping opportunities for every budget. Small boutiques and large department stores, movie theaters, coffee shops, patisseries, and all manner of temptations lined both sides of the street. When we reached Aristotle Square with its open views of the bay, I knew that we were close to my father's warehouse. My mother, who would not leave her apartment without lipstick, her watch, and high heels, disliked walking on the unsteady cobblestones of Egypt Street, so she aimed to get Father's attention right away and then move off quickly. Once we turned the corner to the warehouse, she would announce our arrival loudly, making small talk with me.

"Here you are. I wonder where your father is." She looked around. "Are you ready for Monday, or do you still have schoolwork to finish?" On occasions like those, she would linger, sometimes repositioning her purse, resting it on her arm, hanging it on her shoulder, or making sure her buckle was exactly centered, and wait for my father's response. But my father was just as reluctant to meet her. Instead, he might simply peek out of the warehouse door or shout from somewhere inside, "I'm here."

Once we knew he was aware of us, I would hug and kiss my mother goodbye, and she would walk away toward the busy Tsimiski Street to enjoy checking the latest fashions in its boutiques and fancy window displays. Left on my own, I would walk down the short distance on the cobblestones, often oblivious to the activity around me, and reorient my thoughts toward Father and the rest of the day.

"I think I will walk you to Egypt Street today," my mother offered one Sunday when most businesses were closed. My father, who was very handy, often liked to spend the day at the warehouse to troubleshoot and repair the equipment that needed his attention. That was a spring day, pregnant with unexpected turns, enhanced by the warm sun, a pleasant breeze, and the lapis-colored sky. But my mother, my cultured and dignified companion, seemed less talkative than usual. She had forgotten her shopping list at home and fumed about her forgetfulness; then, she was dithering about which road to take to get to the warehouse, not that it mattered. We approached the corner of a deserted Egypt Street, a lifeless row of store roll dins padlocked to the cement floors except for the Kouidis warehouse. My father was bent under the hood of the jalopy, working on the engine. Unlike her usual habit, though, she didn't stop on the main street once my father was visible. Instead, she kept holding my hand and walked me practically next to the wreck that was parked in front of the warehouse and took off her sunglasses.

"Hi. Do you plan to work again next weekend? Shall I bring Sophoula to the warehouse again?"

"Hmm. Yup," he grunted without looking up.

"How late will you stay? We'd like to see a movie that ends at eight."

"That's too late," he cut her off.

"So accommodating!" she countered, annoyed. She was silent for a minute, then tried again. "Just this once, so Sophoula can see that new show. What difference could an hour make?"

"It's too late because I say it's too late."

My mother adjusted the bag on her shoulder, pulling it roughly to her side. "What would you possibly do with her at that hour if she were here. You're always working," she gestured around us. My father was almost invisible below the frame of the car.

"Sophoula needs to be in her home. She's more comfortable here."

"But I'm her mother! You can't tell me I can't take her out once in a while for something fun." She tugged again at her shoulder bag, the color in her skin rising in a way I almost never saw.

"She's a child. She needs to learn how to be accountable." My father glanced up briefly, then turned back to his work. "Life's not all about galivanting around town."

"Galivanting!" my mother's voice burst forth, a torrent of words leaping out of her chest like I'd never heard before. "Here you are under the hood. Hiding, no doubt, without shame," she spat toward my father. Her words sounded so unlike her that I looked up and noticed her eyes lit up with bolts of anger. In all my twelve years, I had never heard my mother sound so challenging.

My father looked up momentarily, then bent back down into the vehicle again, ignoring her.

"The secret is out, Pericli. I finally know what was going on behind my back all those years." Her voice was hoarse, barely controlled. I let her hand go and moved a couple of steps behind her, startled.

This time, my father surfaced from behind the car and looked at Mother steadily. "You have no right to talk to me. We are no longer husband and wife. Stop it," he answered. "Sophoula is here."

And my world shook.

"Oh, no," my mother pressed onward. "You get to hear it this time. You bastard!" She was getting louder now. "I put up with a lot, more than I knew! You and your addiction, you and your affairs. I detest you!"

"Why would I stay with a stranger? A man needs to have some pleasure in his life. You were not it," he answered stiffly.

"You stole my youth!" Her words were dripping blood from an old wound.

I froze in place, and mother turned swiftly toward me, giving me a quick hug and kiss that I could not respond to, and walked away, out of sight. I did not move and bit my lower lip.

"Fuck her!" he spat. He straightened up, momentarily stopping his work, but lingered under the hood. It was the death knell of their battle.

There was a hollow silence in my ears—and pain. I watched my father as he slowly started putting his tools away in a metal box, rolling down his sleeves, and wiping his hands on a towel, his face stony hard.

"Ready to go?" he asked. "Wait for me in the car."

I went directly to my seat, feeling the dark weight of trouble inside, refusing to let it sink in. For years, my parents' brief exchange that day continued to hiss and sputter like a discordant typhoon in my ears. Were those rumors I had scoffed at true? Was my father involved with a pretty store clerk? Had he been, even back when he was married to my mother? But there was no clear answer. My father's warehouse, long and narrow with its thick, ancient walls and cement floors stood by, a mute, stony witness.

Ours was a silent ride home that day. My face felt flushed, my eyes transfixed in the distance. Tethered by suspicion and shame, I did not want to look at my father. All I could do was shut down in Father's presence, while the quiet fires of adolescence were beginning to light up a new desire in me to be independent of my family. My parents had never fought in front of me before, and that day, they had been fierce. I never spoke to either of them about the incident. If I had to guess why Mother had confronted him that day, I would attribute it to his physical proximity and perhaps to what she might have recently heard about his affairs while they were married. She was laying years of suspicion and anger at his feet; and, in so doing, she revealed to me too that my parents' interior lives had been deeply troubled. They were, in their way, a philandering Zeus and a jealous, wronged Hera, displaying her rage long after it would do them any good.

The curtain of silence and pretense was drawn aside for good, and I could finally see the jagged edges of a marriage hidden from my view until then. Not long thereafter, I couldn't help but start to consider adults with suspicion and distrust, examining their actions and questioning their true intent. In my esteem, a long shadow had been cast over my father. My cheeks were painted with a constant flush of shame that the world might not see but that I wore for many years when I shouldered responsibility for the family name. Boys were marred and no longer trustworthy, casting a new complexity on my world that had caught me unprepared.

The shipwreck of this marriage unfolded in a part of the world that was very skilled in keeping untoward activities hidden. I did not know what to make of the father I loved, but all the shame of it certainly ran deep. I knew I could not share it out in the world. Our good family name mattered to my tribe. But just then, I was alone. Childhood demands simple heroes and villains, but they had deserted me, and I had to abandon living inside a child's cocoon.

21 LEAVING EUROPE, ON THE WAY TO CHICAGO
November 19, 2015

It was easy enough to imagine the attorney's courtroom manner during my parents' hearing, given all that I'd seen in my professional career. Before filing his pleadings, he would have scheduled an appointment to meet with Father in his office to learn about the situation and form grounds for the divorce petition. And yes, I could picture the man. Having accompanied my father to his office when I was a child, I'd seen glimpses of him. In a vest and pinstriped suit, he was tall, stout, and balding. His office was in the downtown Modiano marketplace, next to the old Turkish bath, Pazar Hammam, and behind the cheerful displays of flower shops that filled the corner sidewalk with colors, aromas, flowerpots, and seasonal bouquets. The lawyer was surrounded by dark wooden shelves filled with sets of impressive, hard-bound volumes. All those years ago, I remember thinking, *He must be important.*

On a recent trip to Thessaloniki, I found myself going to the entrance of the building to check out the list of occupants on the off chance that there was still some sign of his office or a successor. The building had not changed. The circular staircase was dark, and the steps near the banister were worn down from many years of people's worried footsteps going to the law offices that had handled their disputes. The landing on the second floor had the same tiled floor, edged with white marble. I imagined my father knocking on the door.

"Come in, Mr. Periclis, have a seat. He will be back in a minute," the secretary would have greeted him, hovering there for a minute. "He drafted the petition last week. Would you like me to order you a cup of coffee? Something else?"

Despite her calm demeanor and polite reception, I can imagine that what my father must have felt most that day was anger—and anguish, fueled by his mother's descriptions of Nitsa. Certainly, he must have hoped that he could conclude this unwelcome chapter of life as painlessly as possible. And likely he would. My father was a smart, well-connected man. He understood that most attorneys knew and ran into each other in hearings and courts. So his attorney, he would have reminded himself as he sat there waiting, would certainly have been the kind of man who knew how to get things coordinated and to get them done the way they needed to be . . . the kind of man who would know how to convince the judge that his client was in the right.

Although I had not understood this during my childhood, my father was a complex man. When he wanted to accomplish something, he went at it wholeheartedly. He did not hesitate to take things on by himself or with the help of competent people. At work, when no hamals were available, he would, all by himself, lift one of those 140-pound burlap sacks of coffee beans and carry it to a customer's vehicle, to accommodate him when he seemed to be in a hurry. Moreover, he had plenty of friends to call on when he needed assistance, and he readily reciprocated. There was certainly a hard side to him, that male energy and desire to succeed. He'd wanted that for me, too, and supported my getting a good education so that I could have good prospects for my future. But, all these years later, I ended up a single, divorced woman anyway, feeling angry at him for the treatment my mother received, disoriented, a bundle of splayed nerves, and upset with myself for all I had missed as a child—a normal, united family life.

Still, I knew that I loved my father. We were similar, strong and determined, he and I, and our connection, whatever else may have been going on around it, was a good thing. Perhaps it was during the years that I was learning how to swim that I experienced most his plotting and iron will—and the way that it might pass down, just a little bit, to me.

For instance, on a particular summer day when I was six, my father met his friend at the shoreline where he kept his rowboat; Mother and I also happened to be there practicing swimming. The rowboat had a heavy, broad wooden hull, painted dark green. Father had the oars, and his friend watched him. Without a rudder, he managed the boat skillfully, and I ran in their direction when he called out to me.

"Come with us for a ride," he told me. He rowed closer to the shore, made room for me to sit next to him, and handed me an oar.

With all my might, I copied his motions, but the boat was turning in circles. I could not match my father's powerful strokes and, watching me, he laughed, and matched his force to mine. For a while, we moved along smoothly while I continued rowing. Father was absorbed in conversation with his friend about work, and I enjoyed the mild lapping of the waves.

We stayed close to the coastline, gradually moving toward deeper waters. Then his friend signaled Father with a decisive, "Okay. Now!"

Now what? What I had not known at the time was that they had a mission for this outing—and, in that moment, they had deliberately turned the boat upside down to toss me into the sea. Horrified, I managed to keep my face turned upward and my body afloat by furiously treading water, my arms and feet flailing in panicky, irregular motions. I swallowed some saltwater, coughed, and felt my eyes stinging. At that age, I still did not know yet how to swim by myself.

Time was suspended; my mind froze, lost in that unpredictable moment. I was acting with an instinctive, primitive force. In the grip of the water's vastness, I felt lost, barely managing to stay afloat on my own for a minute, maybe two, hard to know. Then, I'd felt my father's hand holding my shoulder. "Here." I turned and grabbed his arm with both hands. "Rest up. You are officially a fish!" he'd announced. His friend was working on righting the rowboat. "You did it, kid!" They laughed.

Breathless and still overcoming my panic, I didn't know if I should be mad or proud. I broke out in nervous laughter, accepting the praise, my body feeling stressed and tight. It took a while before we climbed back in the rowboat. Seated in the bow, my back to the men and feeling safe, I shivered, collecting myself and realizing that I had survived what had seemed like a very close call. *I did it*, I thought as my father and his friend powerfully and efficiently rowed us back to shore. Yes, I thought, I had done it: succeeded for my father, managed it like a true Kouidou, and stayed afloat.

22 P. SINDIKA STREET
1955-1957

A few months after that visit to my aunt Ioulia's new apartment, after my near fall out of Father's jalopy, we, too, moved to a new house in a nearby neighborhood—though for a different reason. In our case, the change had everything to do with the war because my father had purchased our 25th of March Street home during WWII, in those trying days of German occupation. Families desperate for survival had sold homes and belongings for very little money, in an attempt to endure the bleak conditions of famine and deprivation that had loomed over them. Once the war was over, the Greek government had taken new measures, recognizing that homes sold during that period had been seriously undervalued. The new law required current owners to either pay the rightful price and back rents at fair value or vacate the homes and return the title to the original owners. So, in that climate, my father elected to return the 25th of March house to its prior owners and to find a new place for our new family.

Just as gusts of chilly autumn winds scattered the dry yellow-and-gold leaves of our plane tree on the ground, it was time to move. Perhaps it had been easy enough for Father and Yiayia Sophia to leave our home behind, marred as it was with our family's demise, but for me it was hard to leave the only house I had ever known. This was my childhood; it was my mother Nitsa's house and my own. My mother and I would not live under the same roof again until she was in her forties, when she moved to the United States to live in Oregon with me and my husband. That was years later, though, after I had left not

165

just a house but an entire country behind, moving to America as a teenager to pursue my studies in the hopes of a life free from the sadness of our past—a melancholy past in which I had let go first of my mother, and then of our home.

To me, abandoning our 25th of March house was leaving behind my childhood and family as I had known it, drawing a line in the sand between present and future. The rusty gate, the climbing roses on the fence, and the green doorway with the horseshoe above it for good luck that would not open again for me to run inside the house; at the time, I did not know the legal reason. Not that it would have mattered. What I missed was the *alana* and the other children there. Like a turncoat, my friend Soula had started playing with my other friends once she heard the news. I told her that we would come back often to visit Aunt Eleni, but I couldn't really be sure. Yiayia kept reminding me that we would be living next door to Uncle Antonis, Father's older brother and business partner, whose family, his wife and three children, would be next to us on Alexandria Street.

On moving day, I rode in the jalopy, with Father bringing in the last load, mostly his tools, to the new house. That day, I kept my eyes on Soula, who waved goodbye from the *alana* until the jalopy had turned the corner onto the arterial. The rows of one-story houses, yards, the army base, and an occasional car soon took over the view of the horizon, leaving the fading image of my friend behind. Although I felt like crying, I kept my eyes dry. I did not want my father to see me that way. I was his strong daughter.

"You will like the new house. Many fruit trees to climb on!" he joked.

"So what?" I mumbled.

He drove straight into a new two-car garage adjoining the house, turned the engine off and, looking pleased, declared, "It will be nice not to get rained on."

Then we unloaded his tools onto a bench right by a tall window that shed a narrow funnel of light on the counter. My father shut the double garage doors, showed me the side door that led to the garden, and took to arranging his tools in drawers and along the wall. Leaving him to his work, I drifted into the yard with its fruit trees and flower beds with rose bushes, mums, and withered pansies. My new neighborhood had several homes with fenced yards and large gardens, but there was no *alana*. An interior, circular wooden staircase led from the entrance of the building to our second-story apartment. I climbed the stairs and wandered around the rooms, where my father had arranged for the large pieces of furniture to be set up in the apartment ahead of time. My stepmother, wearing an apron and scarf tightly tied over her hair, was mopping one of the two balconies and handed me some cleaning supplies.

"Take them to the kitchen counter," she told me. And, following her instructions, I could see that this house had a marble kitchen counter and a marble sink. Even the bathtub was made of marble; it was sturdy but, I learned later, very cold to lean against when I took a bath.

Drifting then into the bedroom that I would share with Yiayia for the last few years of her life, I found her folding my clothes and placing them in the nightstand next to my new bed. Our room was furnished with her old brass bed, the old armoire, and my mother Nitsa's old walnut vanity and *escabeau*. *How strange,* I thought, *to have Mother's furniture here.*

But my yiayia seemed not to notice. Her gnarled hands were skillfully pairing socks. "Help me fold yours?" She motioned me to sit by her, and I copied her movements. Outside, the summer pizzicato of cicadas punctuated the morning, and the new day filled with busy tasks to take care of.

Ours was an apartment with two balconies, one with a view of the main street and the other facing our yard and my Uncle Antonis's house. My stepmother set out to furnish the house to her liking. Her upright piano occupied one corner of the living room, kitty-corner from my father's heavy oak desk. A couch and table filled the rest of the room. A set of three interior curtained French doors led to the formal dining room with its wide buffet, expanding table, and six chairs. That room was destined to house many celebrations and extended family gatherings, though a couple of other rooms still looked makeshift: my parents' bedroom with basic furniture and the empty reception room that echoed absently and, for the time being, stored odds and ends.

By the end of two weeks, though, there was a full sense of order in the place. I liked helping my stepmother hang the voile curtains on all the windows and line the kitchen shelves with paper. A housecleaning lady started coming every week to help with the home maintenance. Our kitchen was large enough to have a permanent table and chairs for our daily family meals, and my energetic stepmother seemed at her best organizing that new home. Yiayia, too, kept shuffling from room to room, still assisting in meal preparation in the mornings, though mostly spending her time watching the neighborhood life behind half-open shutters. "Your father is home with groceries," she would tell me. "Give him a hand, Sophoula." Without anyone having to tell me, I could see that she was slowing down at a sadly escalating pace.

Even so, I liked being needed, so I would run down the stairs, eager to help him carry bags of groceries and food supplies. Always, my father carried the heavy bags, giving me lighter items to carry up the staircase to the kitchen. "You're a good helper," he would tell me.

A month later, a new set of bedroom furniture was delivered for my parents, soon followed by a full reception room set we would use when we had company. And yes, I could see that our lives there would be permanent now, and ubiquitous. The move to a new home on P. Sindika Street, for instance, also meant changing schools that September. From third through sixth grade, I'd have to go somewhere different from my old friends. Korais, a private elementary school, was considered a feeder school for Anatolia, a gymnasium for middle school and high school, that my older Kouidis cousins were attending, along with many other children of refugee families in Thessaloniki.

On foot, my new school was a half hour away from our house. Each morning, I slid down the two-story banister to our front door and joined a group of noisy children who headed out to Queen Olgas Avenue. Rain or shine, we walked along the paved sidewalk on busy city streets, filing two by two and three by three with fellow students, a small crowd snaking its way toward the school. With our school bags loaded up with books and notebooks that got heavier each year, we chatted, teased, and exchanged assignments and tips. At the end of the day, the same bundle of kids sauntered along, peeling off to our yards and homes. Because the streets were so safe, there was no need for adult supervision back then. And so, I had my independence and my new friends, and life somehow entered into a familiar stride that seemed predictable again, despite its newness.

Still, there were differences. To begin with, those intense days of moving with all that hard work had led to my stepmother needing bed rest because she was pregnant and in danger of losing the baby. The change in our home then was palpable. Everything turned quiet, adults looked worried, and Yiayia took charge of the kitchen again. In time, a healthy baby boy arrived in March 1956, born in the house, for there was not enough time for my stepmother to run to the hospital. He was fussy and blue-eyed with thin blond hair. I heard him crying when I returned home from school that day and watched him changed and swaddled and breastfed every so many hours like clockwork. Soon my stepmother showed me how to help change my precious brother, and later I got to spoon-feed him his freshly ground food. He was above average in height and weight and definitely adored by my whole family. He loved fruit best of all foods, so we soon nicknamed him "fruit-fed boy." Visitors were tempted to and sometimes did pinch his soft pudgy legs and cheeks and would often follow the Greek custom of spitting in his direction, a way of offering protection by saying playfully, "*Ftou, Ftou*! I won't lay an evil eye on him."

He became a well-loved son, a welcome addition to our household. For my part, I turned into a watchful big sister, ten years his senior, hovering over him under my stepmother's tutelage. He was my baby doll brother: noisy, cute, and demanding. Moreover, he needed a lot of extra attention, because he was a finicky eater and required being rocked to sleep. So, when I'd finished putting him down, I would cover him carefully and tiptoe out of my parents' bedroom, hoping he wouldn't wake up.

My new brother loved tossing spoons, plastic cups, or whatever he could reach from the tray of his highchair to the floor, as he broke into gales of laughter.

"What did you do?" I would exclaim, to match his joy.

"Don't encourage him," my stepmother often countered, trying to restrain her amusement.

No one could help loving my new brother, and when he turned one, the extended family gathered to celebrate his baptism. He was named Leonidas, the third one in this generation to be named after our paternal grandfather. And he was strong like our grandfather once he started walking. Leonidas was a busy and unstoppable boy. His thrill of throwing things to the floor took on a new dimension the day he carried his own chamber pot to the balcony. Watching him, I was sure he'd be okay, since Father had fitted the balcony with chicken wire. But oh, Leonidas! With a strength I hadn't expected, he lifted the pot over the railing, tossing it onto the street, narrowly missing an unsuspecting passerby. Like my stepmother before me, I had a hard time keeping a straight face as I came down the stairs to retrieve the pot and apologize to the angry man.

Meanwhile, the new neighborhood was calling me. It did not take long to link up with my cousins next door and the neighborhood kids. That year, we thundered up and down the wooden staircase, rushing out of the house to play on the street and gather in neighboring yards, while my baby brother remained indoors in the playpen that my father had built for him from scratch. The following summer, our whole family, and that of my aunt Ioulia, moved to a rented house by the sea for our summer vacation.

That would be a summer, though, away from my mother, who had to remain in the hot cement walls of her parents' downtown apartment. Those days, then, were pulling me in the stream of my Kouidis family, and the current seemed strong. But equally strong was another bond: I was my mother's only daughter. And there she was, nesting in the back of my mind, in a child's imagination, still wondering how we could be apart.

23 OVER THE ATLANTIC
ON THE WAY TO CHICAGO
November 19, 2015 (11:30 p.m.)

What the adults around me did not realize back then was that the shroud of protective silence had only served to arouse my sense of danger and tendered the first dim flickers of desire to discover new, unknown destinations, a place of my own. The waves of the day's strife could not have escaped me entirely. No longer a child, I *had to* penetrate this silence back when an apprehensive society was waking up to recognize the fact that women had rights. But back in 1953, I could only guess at how aware of these discrepancies people were. And perhaps they weren't aware. Perhaps Greek women in my mother's generation believed that they had no other choice than to grin and bear their philandering husbands and hostile mothers-in-law and keep their children in the dark. It was certainly socially undesirable for a woman to divorce or to remain single. In those years, dowries still belonged to husbands, no matter what. If a woman divorced, how could she possibly support her children?

"Did you know that voting rights were granted to women only as recently as 1952?" Christina, my attorney, had informed me.

In the United States, these rights had been granted to women in 1920. That contrast had to be part of the novelty, charm, and excitement that I experienced when I arrived in America in 1965. Young and free, living on a college campus, I found the new customs and freedoms I'd encountered too good to be true. During my own early days living in America, I remember observing closely my American host family, who had two daughters in their late teens. By my Greek standards, they took a lot of liberties. They would inform their parents when we would come and go without reporting exactly where we went. Even more shockingly, Beth, the oldest daughter, who was my age, was matter of fact about disagreeing openly about Vietnam with her attorney father.

"We just need to end the draft. I lost two more dear friends to Canada."

Johnson was the president at the time, the Beatles ruled culture, and it was the era of "Let's twist again." I was grateful to be living in a climate that gave me greater latitude and plenty of options for friendships, an education, and a career. Also, I felt that American adults considered it acceptable for girls my age to have a boyfriend—something I did not assume in Greece. Given such contrasts, it was still too early in Greece for people to sort out which approach would be best suited for children who got caught in parental separation and divorce. For the most part, I was lucky to stay out of the middle of my parents' conflict. My stepmother's neutrality on the whole subject, her avoidance of entanglements and discussions, was a wise move. Although the custody arrangements were, for some unexplained reason, heavily weighted in my father's favor, I still saw my mother on a regular basis, for holidays and after summer vacations. But my father undoubtedly had the financial burden of raising me, which made sense, as we'd all seen firsthand how the Hadjimichael family had lost so many of their resources. My father accepted the role of raising me, which went more smoothly for me, admittedly, than it might have. In my career, for instance, I often met angry and recalcitrant parents whose desire was primarily to take revenge on their partner in the course of separation and divorce. Children could easily become pawns in fights over custody, visitation, and financial support.

At least I had been spared that. With my parents lovingly bonded to me, there was never a question about staying physically safe and adequately supervised. Still, their silence was my worry stone—as it has been for years. Clearly, I needed to understand more about my parents' marriage: the battlefield between them, and the equally rocky terrain between my mother and Yiayia Sophia, who had been, I was increasingly beginning to realize, a much more complex figure than I had ever realized as a child.

24 WEEKENDS
1956–1962

In so many ways, my new life in the apartment with my father and stepmother was shifting everything I knew. Even on what had otherwise been relaxing weekends, I was now expected to fill my time in ways that I never had before. With a very orthodox yiayia and a very unorthodox father, two clashing adult role models, my growing sense of spiritual life was conflicted. On Sundays, we heard the Resurrection Church bells ringing, calling the faithful to the service; while Yiayia and Father did not go to church, I was expected to show up.

My stepmother was not all that devoted to regular church attendance, but she had been active in Bible study groups with adults. Not only had she saved my life, now she was trying to guide my spirit and my soul. Her hypocrisy made me bristle inside. The good thing was that in the absence of adults from my household, it was easier to skip the service and find my friends on the belfry interior steps. Other neighborhood kids would join up, relishing the delicious pleasure of disobedience.

"Hi, did anyone see you?"

"No, they're all inside."

"Show me your bracelet!"

"Can I borrow it?"

"Were you in the park yesterday? I thought I saw you and your brother."

"Shhh, you're too loud! They may hear us inside."

Then, when the service was over, we would show up at our homes, angelic and innocent. My brother, of course, was still too young for religious expectations, so coming home to find him was a relief. During those afternoons following church, I would look for my baby brother to play with and rock when he took his baby naps. I took to cataloguing his baby words in a notebook that my stepmother kept for a long time in the family annals. I would write out his words phonetically and "translate" their intended meaning. A composite he used in the summer was naming the vehicle that sprayed water on the streets to clean and cool down the neighborhoods, offering relief from the heat. He called it "to bou too lomou," "to bou" being his word for water and "too lomou" being a short phrase for "the street!" And, good-spirited baby that he was, he was delighted every time we laughed at the sounds of the big truck going by.

But even entertainment from my brother wasn't enough to fully quell the pressures that I felt from the rest of our family. On certain Sundays, for instance, more expectations piled on, including confession and communion. The fasting before communion was a pain, especially because my father did not have to suffer it. He ate as he pleased every morning. After all, "He's a working man," as my yiayia used to say.

Still, my family expected good things from me, so for a while, I did try. At first, I took the idea of confession seriously—though my efforts didn't last. By the time I graduated from elementary school, I could no longer see the point. For instance, one week around that time, I made an appointment and met the old, semiretired, burned-out priest with his long white beard and black robes. We sat on empty chairs in the Resurrection Church, surrounded by icons and darkness in the otherwise vacant pews that afternoon as I fessed up to some lies that I had told, or admitted I had been egotistical. Under the glare of all the saints peering out of the frescoes and icons, I told him, "My biggest sin is being a pleaser of men, *anthropareskos*," evoking God.

He looked at me, puzzled, and continued with the final prayer and blessing to conclude the session as if nothing had been said. Offering no guidance, he simply completed the ritual without any attempt to help lead me to correct my ways in metanoia, or shifting my thinking.

What's the point? I thought. Was this man a representative of Christ, who counseled humans in the ways of the church, or wasn't he? Years later, I still wonder if he even listened to what I had confessed, or if this "pleaser of men" expression was familiar to him. But I'll never know, because all he had done was mouth the prescribed prayers to conclude the session.

I had meant to alert him to the fact that I was trying to please my stepmother, going along with her new demands like going to confession, even though they so countered my wishes. Still, I did it because I was caught up in trying to be a Miss Goody Two-Shoes, because I was afraid of the things I heard, like a god of thunder and lighting, one that promised hell for sinners. But beyond those apparent dangers, the church rituals themselves did not speak to me. In the end, it all felt so foreign to me that I preferred to avoid it.

All these strange expectations and inconsistencies were on my mind when I visited Mother the following Saturday. She went to church sometimes, but mainly on social occasions, as for weddings and funerals.

"Do you know what *anthropareskos* means?" I quizzed her, almost certain that she would.

"Of course, a pleaser of men." Unlike my stepmother, she most certainly did. "Where did this come from?"

Pleased with her quick response, I told her the whole vexing story about the priest, the confession, and the pointless session that followed. A smile formed on my mother's lips, one that did not reach her eyes. "Tell the story when your father and stepmother are both in the room." She knew my father well. *Did she miss him?* I wondered. *Why did she never speak of him?* So, I did as she'd suggested, telling my father that same story in my stepmother's presence while Yiayia was napping and we were getting ready for dinner the next day. My father was enjoying a glass of ouzo and some appetizers and seemed in a good mood.

"Have you ever gone to confession, Father?" I stopped slicing bread on the cutting board long enough to ask.

"You should know better than that," he smiled, confirming my suspicion.

I followed my mother's advice, telling him about the previous week's session with the priest, ending on a note of frustration, "I won't go again."

My stepmother was motionless, hearing my blasphemy for the first time. But my father laughed at the priest's deafness, furrowed his eyebrows slightly and snapped at my stepmother, "Enough of this, Evdokia. No more confession nonsense."

I was delighted. My acts of "religious disobedience" had never been so successful and, sensing that more was possible, I started my search for other ways to feed my own spirit within the context of Evdokia's conventional regime. Among other things, these small defiances took on a spiritual bent, as, throughout my adolescence, I had been reading about Eastern religions—Buddhism, Taoism, and Confucianism—and discovering eye-opening things like the poetry of Rumi and Rabindranath Tagore, whom I loved to read over and over again. Tagore's poetic optimism drew me like honey: "Clouds come floating into my life, no longer to carry rain or usher storm, but to add color to my sunset sky."

For years after that, I read translated holy texts and the works of mystics, leafing through *The Three Religions of China* and looking up Asiatic deities and concepts. Because these religions weren't practiced in Greece, they were, for me, filled with beauty and poetry rather than oppressive societal routines. My exposure in this way to the novel cosmos theories was a welcome distraction from the orthodox routines. Best of all, I was lucky in that no one was censoring what I read. My mother, for instance, especially liked to see me explore Eastern and Western thinking and appreciated the poetry and richness in these books. She knew about all these new ideas because we had ample time to discuss them; on weekends and nice days, my mother and I would take walks along the waterfront, which was filled with families and children in the afternoons, before returning to P. Sindika. She liked to walk to the White Tower Park, which had grassy areas defined by well-trimmed boxwood bushes and benches to sit on. We fed eagerly pecking pigeons handfuls of breadcrumbs, listening for their satisfied calls. At other times, I would get a soft drink or a pastry, and we would watch the passersby. "Inhale the sea air; it's iodine," she would say, slowly filling her lungs with the fresh waterfront air, tilting her face toward the sun. I would copy her, taking deep breaths, imagining the kelp as the source of iodine. And, back at my grandparents' home, what I enjoyed best was when Mother and Aunt Marika would break out into song. Learning the words to their favorite tune, "Sweet Dreams, Sweetheart," I'd belt it out along with them.

One song would bring another, and we would harmonize, steeping ourselves in those mellow moments. But even the peace of those afternoons was not without its lessons and learning. For instance, both my mother and her sister had established pen pals in Paris, France, and in Atlanta, Georgia. They'd taken up writing to these people in their teens, and still maintained contact into their middle years.

"A letter from Andrée," my mother announced. She is coming to visit us."

Andrée Coquille was a Parisian teacher whom I'd never met, but about whom I would get regular reports. In the spring of 1962, she stayed with my grandfather's family for three to four days and continued on to Athens by train. Whenever these things happened, the sisters would thrill over it all and talk about Paris for a long time.

"I loved the perfume she brought for you, Marika. Can I borrow it?"

"Yes, if you let me use the scarf you got. Can you imagine shopping with Andrée on the Champs Élysées? Or roaming in Montmartre? Oh, we must visit her sometime!"

There was also Heloise, an African American librarian in Atlanta, who kept corresponding—although less frequently. Whenever letters arrived at the Hadjimichael home, I liked hearing about their updates, and I saved the stamps for my collection. My mother would read them in the living room, pointing out the vocabulary that she thought I should learn. It was a game we liked to play: "Surprise!" "Bonjour!" "Comment ça va?" She would have me trying, correcting my accent.

When it was time to leave, to return to my father's house, my insides grew tight. I could not push away that perennial weight—a dense mass that sat on my chest—of our dashed dreams for a normal family. I sensed that my mother felt it too. Visiting time could only stretch so far. Even my grandfather had started reciting a rhyme for his goodbye:

I am going, leaving you my shadow as consolation
to have and to hold, so that it breaks your heart.

It did break my heart when I heard him. Listening to him made it harder to keep a brave face. I would kiss him and quickly follow Mother to the door to escape my emotions. Then, my mother would accompany me to the bus stop and wait for me to get on the bus. I would board, watching her figure turn into a tiny dot as the bus moved on. My clinging eyes would lose the battle of keeping her with me. Engulfed in the moment, I swallowed my resentment at having to belong to two households. An unfair world demanded that I leave her behind. I wanted to rebel but felt stifled by the demands of the adults who shaped my days. All I had was a half hour of alone time before arriving to P. Sindika to close one chapter and open another. Staying connected to both my mother's and father's families was a force that stayed with me for life, but later in adolescence, the magnet of independence became a strong current, a campus that I had to investigate.

My parents were still curious about each other's separate lives. For a while, they questioned me about the other—at least my father did, when we were alone. My answers were vague and brief, though, because I didn't much like his questioning. "Yes, she is fine!" I would answer tersely, with perhaps just a bit of detail about that day's activities. Back then, I was too young to understand that even after a divorce, after nearly ten years together, we all had ties that would not evaporate. Yet, I did know well that I had a core of my own that burst with life and the desire to be independent of my parents' choices. Father seemed content. Those days, he returned home earlier from work, and I would see him more often before going to bed. Except for my torn feelings about how little I saw my mother, life at that time was good for me too. The extended family assembled at our home for holidays, and Evdokia prepared fine appetizers and whole meals for them. And even on less special occasions, I loved the company of my cousins, those who lived next door and the ones that came to us from other parts of the city. Often enough, we played in our yard with those closer to my age, while the older ones frequently left to be with their friends and go to parties.

Still, my father went on asking after Mother, as if out of habit. One evening in the early 1960s, when I returned from a visit to my grandparents, he stopped his work on the accounting books and asked again, "How is your mother?"

But by then, I'd had enough. "Ask her yourself."

He shrugged. It was the last time he inquired.

My mother, on the other hand, must have had a direct source of updates on the Kouidis family. It was rare that she had questions about them. I suspect that instead she phoned my father's siblings, like my godmother and my father's sister, Ioulia.

This suited me better, as I wished to be left alone; it was difficult having my loyalties challenged. To respond to one of these questions felt like a betrayal. Moreover, some scenes were simply unexpected, and I wish they had never occurred. Like that day on Egypt Street.

25 OVER THE ATLANTIC
ON THE WAY TO CHICAGO
November 20, 2015

In provincial Thessaloniki, secrets are difficult to keep hidden forever, especially when people are seen and talked about. Finally, I could see, the day had come when my mother found out about my father's dalliances. Even there, sitting on a transatlantic plane all those years later, I could still feel her ferocity—and the injustices mounted against her. For years, her words would ring in my ears. "I know what was going on behind my back! You stole my youth," she had thundered before walking away, a woman wronged, yearning for another start in life that was not to be. I followed her with my eyes until she turned the corner, away from Egypt Street, betrayed, torn by anger when I stepped in my father's car. But there had been nothing I could do, so I'd just ridden quietly with my father back home to Yiayia in silence and slammed shut the door to my room once we'd reached the house. Sad and ashamed, I'd cried, bursting with my mother's pain and my own. She and I had never spoken openly with each other about my father's philandering because we were steeped in the culture of silence.

Now a mature adult, settled in my airplane seat, I was finally realizing that her departure had been neither thoughtless nor dismissive. She hadn't abandoned me. Rather, my mother had left our home out of a dire need for self-preservation. She had lived with disapproving family whispers for too long. My mother, like me, was ultimately a free spirit, unwilling to succumb to a culture of submission. Both of us, in our time, had had dreams. She'd hoped to have a husband who respected her, one who was faithful to her and supported her and the family. My dream was to develop soaring wings, strong enough to carry me away to America, where I could shape my own future. My school, our American teachers, movies of the time, and magazines all painted a picture of this magic land that held the shape of my dreams.

I was lucky to actualize my hopes. In my mother's case, her strength had helped her fight for her independence from a husband who had taken her resources and ignored her needs—but it could not truly right all the wrongs. Still, my mother would not yield to a demanding mother-in-law who judged her over cultural clashes. How had I not seen these things before? She was my kin, the woman acting with the determination and perseverance I had emulated. Nitsa was transforming into a woman who would make hard decisions, face challenges, and manage declining resources and the care of a mentally ill sister. So much had been mounted against her, and still she had persevered—seeing me every weekend and still finding time and money to take me to the movie theater from time to time. So no, finally, she was not simply the mother who had abandoned me, leaving without a trace for months until I was allowed to visit her.

Discarding an empty cup in the restroom, I returned to my seat and turned on the overhead light to continue reading when the food cart rolled down the aisle. Shutting down my computer and storing it back in its bag to make room for lunch, I sighed, just like Mother used to, trying to relax before deciding against lunch; I had no appetite. Rather, curled up in my seat, I tried to ignore the petition, my roiling anger, and the world. Many times, I had felt motherly and protective toward the children for whom I had advocated, motivated by anger toward what I saw they were up against. The hope that I might be able to make things right for them was the altruistic beginning that steered me to my social service career. I saw so many things leading parents astray: egos, jealousies, the need to dominate others, money, and addiction to substances. Sometimes, compared to all that, the children simply did not matter.

My years working for child protective services had required a lot of me. In my everyday shoes, grit, scuffs, and often worried steps, I would knock on front doors to investigate complaints of child abuse and neglect. I still ponder the first time that I carried in my arms sweet four-year-old little Carol, welts, cigarette burns, and all. *Breathe deeply*, I'd told myself. That is what my mother had always done when she tried to relax. But that time, it just hadn't been enough. How could it? On that sad day, we'd left Carol's mother smoldering at the front door of the project apartment, where a string of boyfriends had come and gone and hurt her unprotected only daughter. Carol's mother's pupils, almost always dilated, screamed of rage and helplessness. Faced with memories like those, how could I forget my years during those child protective days, when I was committing the unnatural acts of breaking up families to help the children? The real and the unreal world called for me to steel my throbbing heart and take a child away from her home—because of the promise for a better day. Sometimes it worked: a clean home, no boyfriends for a while, and a hopeful day for little Carol.

Each night before I had to take a child away from her home to move her into foster care, I would pace for hours between my bed and the kitchen counter. Was that how Mother had spent the night before the truck had shown up at our house? Had she steeled her heart that morning when I skipped out of the house to play with my *alana* friends? Was she hoping that her attorney and the court would get me back to her? My heart still wants to believe that.

There were more pages that Christina had scanned, waiting for me to read, but I needed a break, time to uncoil my chest, taught with feelings. I took the airline blanket out of its plastic wrap, folded up the tray, asked the flight attendant not to disturb me, and shut my eyes.

26 BLOOD TIES
1959–1963

Family, it is true, is larger than either me or my mother and, throughout my childhood, blood ties and family alliances would shape me in ways that I did not always understand. Those warnings began with the worry that I might be too thin, as I was getting ready for my annual medical exam in the spring of my second year in middle school. The pediatrician thought I should be gaining more weight and ordered a blood test. Father and I walked straight into the back room of a pharmacy, a large and sterile lab, the sort of sparse space with lingering antiseptic odors, tweezers, petri dishes, and a couple of microscopes siting on a metal table. In his white coat, the pharmacist greeted us from his stool, lifting his eyes from a microscope. He did it all—from lab tests to the dispensing of drugs—as most people in his trade still do in Greece. I noticed his gold wire-rimmed glasses. When I smiled in his direction, he nodded back. Then, while chatting with my father, he tied an elastic band around my arm and stuck his needle in my vein. A slight pinch. It was over quickly.

I felt perfectly fine, yet anxious about what a microscope could reveal. *Should I worry?* Already, as a child, I did not like that kind of worrisome attention. A day later, the pharmacy called my stepmother to come by and get the report. "Is your mother back?" my father asked. He had been home all afternoon, leaning over his desk to study ledgers from the store. He had turned toward me when I walked in the room, his bifocals barely balancing on the tip of his nose.

Just then, she came up the steps from her shopping trip with the report and some iron pills for me with the instruction, "Take one pill every day until they run out." Quickly, we set the table, chatting away, and Father joined us in the kitchen. As soon as Evdokia had set the salad bowl in the middle of the table, my father helped himself, got a couple of slices of bread by his plate, and waited for her to serve the main dish.

"I have the blood results. She is fine," Evdokia said, smiling at me.

"Her blood type?"

"It's O."

"She takes after our side of the family," my father answered, pleased, before spooning some eggplant on his plate and passing the dish to Yiayia. He handed me a slice of bread. We both loved dipping into the delicious tomato sauce, flavored with feta cheese, oregano, and onions, that Evdokia had poured over the eggplant dish.

So, blood came in types. I registered the information—but what did it mean? *I must remember to ask my mother for her blood type*, I thought.

"It's B," she answered on my next weekend visit, "Why?"

"Just to know," I lied. It seemed to matter to my father.

Simmering thoughts in the next few days led me to, *I am a full Kouidou. In body and soul.* Did that explain why I lived with my father and not my mother? In a way, I loved being claimed by him— by someone. They say, "blood ties." They say, "Blood is thicker than water." But what was I to think, then, about my mother? I had been told that I had her mouth and nose and Father's eyes—so why hadn't she claimed me?

That inconsistency felt like a schism, a separation that was not right. Schism . . . schizophrenia, that is what my mother's sister, Aunt Marika, suffered from. Maybe it was a good thing not to have the same blood as my mother. Blood ties could mean inheriting stuff— and what did I want? Or not? That O identification influenced me over the length of my lifetime in ways that I did not recognize then, identifying strongly with my Kouidis family.

From time to time on moody teen days, I wondered if I was smart or crazy. The thing is that Aunt Marika did not scare me; I was attuned to her monologues. Was this natural to have no fear? I loved my aunt and was more curious than afraid about her being different. I knew she was smart. Was I like her, then? What kind of puzzle was this? On my visits with Mother, I had witnessed Marika's one-sided dialogues and strange giggles. A couple of times, I had asked about her hallucinations, her inaudible voices, and her questions. That seemed to startle my aunt, but the voices seemed to answer things too. One of the personas she talked with, for instance, had to do with time.

"Clock, where are you coming from?"

"I am in space," she had answered.

"What do you do?"

"I get signals and ring messages," she'd answered again. "The time is soon."

I saw my grandfather's face sinking along with Mother's, who had listened to our exchange in the sunny living room of their apartment. They looked away like no one was talking. Yiayia Athena's face turned to stone. Marika was now giggling, ignoring me, absorbed in conversation with her voices. I could feel the blood draining out of the room; it was no time for interruptions.

Could I be crazy too? It was more than a passing thought. Schizophrenia shows up in families once in four generations. I had read it in my books. But then I had blood type O. What a relief!

During my teens, I'd spent a lot of time reading my books. I had a small collection then, and all it took was daylight or a flashlight under the covers to indulge. There was nothing back then like the touch of printed paper, turning a page, reading a special line. I loved Loudemis, Delta was fun, and I favored plays: Somerset Maugham,

Oscar Wilde, Eugene O'Neal, and Albee. Goethe, Kafka and Sartre . . . the lot of them. Some were family gifts, and a few others came from the library, but either way, they often landed in bed with me, where lovers belong. I bought a handful more with my meager allowance, like the English textbook that compared Freud, Jung, and Adler. It was a perennial short pile that I kept next to my nightstand. When I stayed focused and had finished all my chores, I could manage to read whole chapters. Sometimes I was interrupted to help with errands: "Could you borrow a couple of eggs from your uncle's home?" I complied but bristled.

The good thing is that my books were always there to read and reread. They were not consumed like a drink that enticed me, was slurped up, and finished. They grew to be my steady companions. Even if I had to use a dictionary, I liked discovering what was in their pages. And by the time I wound up in high school—going to Anatolia, one of the best schools around—it was a good thing, because I was about to be exposed to new people and ideas that would ultimately change the course of my life.

In the meantime, I innocently enjoyed getting lost in the pages of books, never imagining what learning might do for my life. Certainly, I had heard about the availability of scholarships abroad after high school and understood that participating in activities mattered to those institutions, but I didn't think much of it. My activities were simply things I was drawn to, like writing and seeing some of my poems published in our high school magazine. In time, they elevated me to be the poetry editor for our school publication. Beyond drama club and choir, it was the activity that I enjoyed most. But then, during my junior year, a new club became available with Mrs. B. as the advisor. She was a rather traditional Greek literature teacher, but the topic, psychology, appealed to me. I managed to talk my buddy Efi into joining, and we showed up for the first meeting. Maybe, I thought, I could get a better understanding of people like my aunt Marika and this blood business.

Most Wednesdays, we assembled in a classroom during an extended lunch break. By then, I had read about the id, ego, and superego, and about archetypes, dreams, and descriptions of psychopathology. It was fascinating material, and these were new concepts for the early sixties in Greece and not yet available for study at the university. Further, I had also purchased another book written in English entitled *Contemporary Psychology*. On my own, I'd read it and struggled through its pages with the help of a dictionary, finding myself especially drawn to the descriptions of schizophrenia, which sounded increasingly like what I saw in my aunt—and those blood lines of ours.

But there in the club, the implications of things were much less significant. Our task at club meetings was to apply the concepts we were learning to movies we saw and books we read. "Did you see Hitchcock's *The Birds*?" And off we would go discussing irrational fears and phobias and sharing our own. We were fascinated by *Vertigo*, Jimmy Stewart's acrophobia and Kim Novak's acting. And of course, as teenagers, we were particularly pleased with ourselves for learning concepts that were almost unavailable throughout the rest of the country. It was like a secret language, something we could see about other people that they had no awareness of. Even things as innocent as romance were not past our notice, and we snickered about our friends who dated. "She sure has an oversized libido!" we'd giggle, or, "Yes, the pleasure principle!"

Having no lack of libido myself, I watched my friends pair up with boyfriends and decided that I had to have my own, albeit an imaginary one. My closest friends were to hear the details of our romance. He was a busy medical student, tall and smart and very sensitive, a fellow who was most thoughtful and brought me flowers or wrote notes. When on vacation, he would mail them to the "poste restante," and I would collect them at the local post office wherever we might be vacationing in the summer. He was also ever so clever in planning our secret rendezvous around my school schedule. On one occasion, when Efi and I were shopping for small items at a kiosk, I pulled her sleeve to get her attention and said excitedly, "There he goes!"

Immediately, she asked me urgently who I meant, surmising that I was talking about my mysterious friend. "Where? Where?"

Leaning toward the street, I pretended to point him out. "There . . ."

"Where?" she scrutinized the street for his motorcycle.

"You just missed him," I answered, getting myself quickly out of trouble.

Recently, in our mature years, Efi has quizzed me about that day. "Did you really have a boyfriend?"

And then I'd had to laugh and fess up to my deception.

"And I was wishing back then," she pouted back playfully, "that my boyfriend was as thoughtful and caring as yours!"

But we did not talk about boyfriend, teen, or family issues in the psychology club. The discussions we had were mostly theoretical. One of my favorites was Adler and his dream analysis. Bringing night fancies and dreads into consciousness was a reasonable way for a person to better understand and extricate their interior. Most members preferred Freud's theories emphasizing sex drives as forces of behavior. Still, our discussions were shallow since we lacked life experience. That was fine at the time, but I did long to know more—not only for myself, but out of care for my aunt Marika, which had me keenly interested in understanding mental health issues and drew me eventually to study psychology and social work in college.

Back then, though, my educational path was shakier. It was a near miss, for instance, the decision about which school I was going to attend for my middle and high school years—or gymnasium, as we called it in Greece. "Education is like a bracelet on your wrist," my mother liked to say, meaning that it was a good investment, so I knew the choice was important. She had graduated from high school, and

then attended Anatolia College to learn more English right before
WWII.

Most of my paternal cousins had attended Anatolia, known as
"College" in the city and equivalent to the Greek gymnasium. When
my mother went there, the school had offered post-secondary education and language courses, but in my day, it had shifted to serving
seventh to twelfth graders and helping students to identify scholarships for university studies. Although Father was a high school drop-
out, never completing high school after fleeing from Turkey when he
was fifteen, he also wanted a good education for me. But he and my
stepmother, Evdokia, did not see eye to eye about where to send me.
Did my mother's opinion matter? I do not believe she was even asked.

"What nonsense and green horses!" Evdokia had said, when
Anatolia came up for me. Uniquely her expression, it was a line that
became widely quoted in my family circles. But, despite our affection
for her turn of phrase, my Kouidis aunts and uncles were bothered
by her objection.

"We send all our children to Anatolia," Aunt Ioulia, Father's sister
and my godmother, insisted, and the extended family had weighed
in—and ultimately prevailed.

Besides activity clubs, what was special about Anatolia was the
American faculty. This was at a time when relations between the US
and post-civil war Greece were strong. With Greek entry into NATO
and American aid pouring in, there was a sense of relief from the
misery of the internal conflicts for everyday people. In the US, the
Vietnam War had begun to escalate, Joan Baez was emerging as a
popular singer alongside Bob Dylan, the FDA had just announced
the availability of a safe birth control pill, and John F. Kennedy had
been elected president. But then everything changed on a single
day: Friday, November 22, 1963. I was still a junior in high school
when we'd sauntered out of the classroom for our morning school
break in the usual cliques, waiting for the next class to start, and

someone who had listened to the *Voice of America* broadcast shared that Kennedy had been assassinated. The news spread around like wildfire to a stunned crowd of students. A hush spread around our Anatolia campus.

That evening, we rushed to turn on the news at our homes and heard about the motorcade, the early confusion of how it happened, and the death of a bright and charismatic politician. It had only been in July of the same year when he stole the hearts of Europeans with his, "*Ich bin ein Berliner.*" It was a message of support to West Berliners during the Cold War era and after Soviet-ruled West Germany had erected the Berlin Wall. "All free men, wherever they may live, are citizens of Berlin, and therefore, as a free man, I take pride in the words '*Ich bin ein Berliner!*'" he proclaimed. His words had rung true to my teenage heart! So did the music we were exposed to. Our typing teacher, a recent arrival from Alaska, played her guitar and sang Pete Seeger and Joan Baez songs during morning gatherings. We hummed their tunes and listened to American records that blared cheeky melodies of the late 1950s. In class, she played Mozart to set the desired rhythm, the speed she wanted us to use in practicing typing. Hers was a cool way to teach us, in contrast to memorizing and reciting, as was required by most of our traditional Greek faculty. Miss Lucas, a tall, elegant teacher of English literature with an East Coast accent, assigned us texts out of two thick volumes of collected works in our junior and senior years and advised the drama club. She was entertaining, too, so I joined the club, taking part in Giraudoux's play, *The Madwoman of Chaillot*, acting in a minor role, that of Dr. Jadin.

Our American teachers, though, rarely mentioned politics or civil rights issues. That wasn't why they had come to Greece. They were after our sun, our beaches, and, for a few of them, our ancient history. Still, when they spoke about life at home, it sounded alluring, progressive, and liberal—quite a contrast to Thessaloniki's provincial, conservative culture. My friends and I became fans of American movies, the Wild West, romance and comedy, fashions and music. It was not so much that the movies and magazines were in English, a language I was studying at the time while still relying on subtitles, as it was the excitement of escaping into other people's worlds, foreign landscapes, and adventures. On the screens of dark movie theaters that I would frequent in my neighborhood and downtown, I discovered there was more out there than my everyday world, and I was thirsty to see and taste it. Glimpses of borrowed *Seventeen* and *Vogue* would cross our hands and stimulate our imaginations.

So it was a fortuitous decision that my family made that September of 1958 to send me to Anatolia, an international school that emphasized the teaching of English and exposed us to teachers from America and routines used in American schools, such as clubs, the selection of class officers, and faculty class advisors—none of which was available in Greek schools. What was most valuable, though, was the fact that this was the place where I first dreamed of moving to another continent and applying for a Fulbright scholarship for my post-secondary studies, unburdened by my family situation—not only my parents' divorce, but also the sadness of my maternal aunt, and finally that complex, aging woman, my yiayia.

By the late 1950s, I had noticed that Yiayia Sophia was slowing down a lot. She had no wind left when we climbed down two flights of stairs each time we went out. I found myself walking down the steps slowly, arm in arm with her, to lend her support. But eventually, even that became too much for her to manage. Although her efforts to remain independent must have become Herculean, she demanded very little from us. She had given up reading, and she never wore glasses but navigated a lot by touch when she moved from room to room. Her favorite activity became sitting by the window with shutters pulled together, watching the street with blurry vision for endless hours. "Sophoula, when you go to the kiosk, look for some licorice for me."

It was our favorite candy, and I would bring it back for her to hide inside her pocket. This act was conspiratorial because she was not supposed to eat sugar.

Still, when it came to my own habits, she was full of warnings for me. "Don't buy gum and don't chew it at night," she would tell me. Total abstinence was impossible, of course, but still, she did what she could to scare me. "You're chewing the bones of the dead!" was certainly a way to ruin my fondness for that indulgence! Despite her slowing down, though, Yiayia was still doing her best to track the kitchen needs of the household with prompts for us: "Remind your father to bring some dill and cucumber for the tzatziki when he goes to the Modiano Market." By early winter of 1959, she had taken to her bed and never got up again. With the start of the school year, I found myself alone in the kitchen. Once it had happened, I missed my childhood companion—despite all of her bossy admonitions— and our tea and toast breakfasts and her ever-watchful eyes.

Once she became bedridden, covered with her pink silk quilt, curled up into a tiny ball in her queen brass bed, my stepmother cared for her for well over a month. Yiayia and I still shared a room, so I could hear her labored breathing and coughing at night.

"Hungry?" I would ask at times, thinking of something to soothe her. "Would you like some broth, Yiayia?" But when I would bring it to her, she would take a sip or two and seal her lips, shaking her head.

We tried what we could to comfort her, sometimes bringing my two-year-old baby brother to come up to her bed and ask in baby talk, "Can I bring you something, Yiayiaka?"

But after a while, she rarely answered us anymore. Curled up in a fetal position, spending long hours asleep, eating little and less frequently, she was leaving us behind in a quiet, weary way. It was hard to see her disappearing, watching signs that were unforgiving and unmistakable. She meant well and tried hard to serve and influence and hold on to life, but her energy was seeping away. My brother and

I would stand in our bedroom, wondering how to soothe her. She had always been like a mother to me, and in her decline, I felt like a helpless child. "It was old age," people said later when she passed away that spring.

And that was my yiayia. She had survived the threat of extermination just before the genocide of Greeks had broken out in Turkey in 1922, and then the trauma of relocation to Thessaloniki. She had experienced, too, becoming a widow, along with its loss of status, but had also seen her children grow with renewed energy and establish themselves in their new home. She had seen me turning thirteen in a stable home—and finally, it was her time to rest. She was my dear old yiayia whom I loved so much, and a much more complex woman than I realized at the time. But it was another, this time unavoidable, abandonment for me and another message to push on, to move ahead and create my own niche in the world.

For days, I heard her footsteps behind me and looked for her shadow, swallowing tears. The vanity mirror was covered with a white sheet for the week after her passing. Her brass bed was soon gone from the corner of our room. I had lost my yiayia and was seeing little, in those days, of my mother. For the first time, I was getting a glimpse of being alone, without either of my mothers to shield me. And yet, I knew I had their strength, blood, and genes to carry on with.

PART III

27 CROSSING THE ATLANTIC
November 20, 2015

"**S**ophoula, Sophoula, sweetie pie, give me a neck rub." My mother's sing-song voice drew me away from the window, where a butterfly had perched on the wrought iron curlicues of the D. Gounary balcony. She turned toward the arm of the couch and leaned on the pillow, a spasm running across her face. "That kink in my neck is not going away."

In slumber, I felt my body moving in her direction. My mother and I had been meeting often in my dreams. In midair, in my plane flying over the Atlantic, she came to me again, this time for a moment, ignoring the swarm of airline passengers crowding me. An instant later, I woke up startled, drying tears after my short nap, stiff in the tight confines of my airplane seat. Coming alert, I stretched my limbs and reached for my computer, still sitting on the tray. Thankfully, it was turned off. The airplane lights had been turned down, and the window blinds were drawn shut; a few people were watching television shows on tiny screens, while others were asleep.

My mother, too, had once been on an airplane like this, leaving behind her apartment balcony with the view of a sometimes calm and other times stormy Thermaikos Gulf. That was years ago, in the mid-1970s, when we had been surrounded by passengers watching movies of the day on screens mounted under overhead compartments. It was a time when travel on airplanes was not as widespread, and a trip that actualized an unspoken dream for me and my mother. By then, I was a married woman, having completed graduate school and been hired for my first professional job at the Oregon State Hospital, an hour away from our home in Portland, Oregon. I was bringing my mother along to my new home where my young wings had carried me to America, to a new and more productive life. It was the year I had managed to cover legal costs for the Greek attorney who obtained a visa and a ticket for my mother allowing her to live with us in the US.

Although my mother, a Leo, read her daily horoscope in the paper, she had, by then, lost her faith in miracles. Life had shown her its harsh side as she passed through it, leaving her hanging in midair like a forgotten rag doll on the clothesline. And while she had never asked me directly to bring her to Oregon, her energetic preparations and shining face as she was packing for the trip told me that it was her dream come true.

The fall that I brought her to America, her friends Anna and Marianthe celebrated with her: "Finally, your time has come to enjoy the good life." Hearing them, my mother's face would light up, her smile blossoming, the best gift she could ever give me. Then her friends would praise me: "Bravo, Sophoula." Brimming with satisfaction, I was proud and happy to finally be providing for her, making things right after the hardship and injustices she had suffered with my father. As the day to travel to the States was approaching, we had gone shopping in Thessaloniki, filling her suitcase with carefully selected summer and winter clothes and gathering her favorite photos, scarves, and cosmetics—all in preparation for this move, which was meant to last for the rest of her life.

It had seemed like a reasonable idea. After all, my mother had always liked my husband, a tall, gentle American fellow who was supportive and willing to have a mother-in-law join us. She called him "my Billy," and he had learned enough Greek to surprise her and make her smile. As we prepared for her trip, I showered her with details about our home life and daily routines, all of which delighted and intrigued her.

"Wait until you see the house, and the large yard," I informed her. "We have a kitty, cars, good jobs. . . . Don't forget your raincoat—it rains a lot! And you will have a room of your own!"

"You are by the sea! A Greek church in Portland! How lucky can you be?" she'd responded, adding an enthusiastic, "Let's go!" Then, she'd wanted to know, "How many hours on the plane?" and "Will we really stop in London?" There was more color to her cheeks then, vigor, and the return of lipstick on her lips. But there were also spells when her voice would falter and drop: "I have to tell Marika when we leave."

"Yes," I admitted, sad, because at that time my aunt Marika was hospitalized in La Bête, the city's public mental hospital, and that was where we had to say our farewells. Heart-wrenching as it was to watch the two sisters when the time came, it seemed as though Marika was the braver and stronger of the two. In the hospital day-room, she shed no tears, but gave me a hard look, almost like a glare, and an admonition: "Take good care of her." Then she'd turned away, drawing her hanky out of her sleeve to deftly dab away a tear, as my mother's chest was heaving with sorrow.

Feeling oddly guilty, I remained on the sidelines, waiting to see whether or not she would hug me goodbye. When she finally did, she held me hard and long, and I leaned into her, whispering, "I will. I love you." Slowly, then, she turned and walked away, leaving us and the smoky dayroom behind. My mother stayed there on a chair by a window for several minutes before we finally started for the bus trip home.

The price of separation—and my guilt and simultaneous pride for giving Nitsa a chance for a new life—whirled inside me then as it does even now. My mother had already said her goodbyes to her parents, both of whom had passed away with broken hearts within a year of my arrival in America in 1966, Athena from a stroke and Constantinos from a heart attack. At the time of their passing, my wise aunt Marika had written to me, "I hold the hope that one day we will meet again because loved ones are not apart while they are living. As times passes, we remain in touch via correspondence, and we are grateful for that." And that is how it was among us—my aunt, mother, and even my stepmother—during many of the years we lived apart. Letters on onion skin paper and aerograms filled the gaps of the distances and the years. Yet, best of all was the time when my mother had no need to correspond with me—the time that she lived with us in the Pacific Northwest.

Goodbyes are never easy. They must be especially hard for butter-flies—and moths—as they are short-lived. The image of the butterfly in my dream—her fluttering monarch wings—came back uninvited. Yet Nitsa's butterfly was deceivingly delicate. My mother was eagerly launching into our new adventure with the determination and will of a woman ready to uproot herself to reunite with her daughter in a distant land. Years earlier, she was a woman who had endured the vagaries of divorce and the chagrin of public scrutiny in the court-rooms of Thessaloniki; now, we were about to make up for lost time, starting on our transcontinental journey to a new world, celebrating our new connection, and optimistic that the best was yet to come. Some forty years later, I was reliving it all in my mind on the plane.

28 THE NAME DAY RUCKUS
September 17, 1962

It was another name day without my mother to celebrate it with me at home. Still, I looked forward to my sixteenth patron saint celebration that came around every September 17th, not knowing that this one would be troubled. Ordinarily, it's a special day, one the Greek Orthodox church has dedicated to St. Sophia for all girls named Sophia to celebrate. Anticipating visitors and excited with the fuss over me, I had started the day in high spirits, as had my stepmother, who had purchased treats for visitors and had gotten the house spanking clean, ready for company.

But one guest was not expected. Near the noon hour when I peered out the window, I was startled to see my tall aunt Marika on our street, looking up at the house and yelling in a coarse voice: "The brothel of Periclis is here! It's a house of prostitution." Between short pauses, there was more: "Come on out if you dare! Where do you keep your whores?" My aunt's words were discordant, reverberating spite. She was loud, upset, and repeating herself. The Furies, vengeful spirits of the underworld, had highjacked her in broad daylight, right outside our house, and she was spewing vicious news in our quiet neighborhood.

In disbelief, I retreated from the balcony. What was she talking about? Moreover, alarmed and embarrassed by the public humiliation, I looked for my stepmother in the reception, hoping my aunt would go away. She was disturbing my celebration—and why? For what? It would take me years to accept what she meant, and the fact that she was the truth teller who, like the ancient Greek chorus, was revealing my father's foibles to my neighbors in angry, vile words. Back then, my aunt was shouting out things that were true, but that we did not want to hear. What had she heard about my father?

Yiayia Sophia knew well that in his youth, my haggard and bedeviled father had loved to chase skirts. He and his young friends, many of them sons and daughters of other refugees, often escaped life's hardships by entertaining themselves in shoreline cafés and dance halls. They walked the neighborhoods in the dusk, serenading under certain balconies. In particular, my father enjoyed singing and playing the mandolin, two breezy talents that were sure to get him the notice of the ladies.

Occasionally, he and his best friend also got up to small bits of mischief, such as by pilfering daisies, mums, or other seasonal bounty from my aunt Eleni's garden. One day, her son caught sight of them in the backyard, each man holding a small bouquet of daisies. "Hello," my cousin greeted them. This was not the first time that they had stolen blossoms from that yard.

"Shh . . . you did not see us," my father winked and counseled him. "This is just a small bundle for our dates tonight." Sworn to secrecy, my cousin kept that confidence for years. After all, my father was his favorite young uncle, and my cousin was getting close to the dating stage himself. Years later, when he told me that story in the comfort of his living room, I noticed that his eyes were smiling. "He was a ladies' man, your father."

I smiled back awkwardly and moved toward the window to look outside. It was already getting late in the afternoon, and it was time to take my leave. "The rush hour traffic is just beginning. I had best hit the road right away, Cousin, or it will take me forever to get home." He protested, paused, and seeing that I kept moving toward the exit, he left the couch and accompanied me to the door. Stepping onto the landing, I called the elevator. I loved my cousin—we had grown up together—but the story he shared distressed me. We exchanged warm goodbyes, and when the elevator arrived, I stepped inside, shutting the door behind me and pressing the button for the lobby. Checking my hair in the mirror, I straightened my part and worried about how many people knew about my father's fondness for women. I hated the thought of being known as the daughter of a philandering man. Other kids did not have to bear such an embarrassment—though perhaps there were others like him. Yes, of course there were.

Another of my cousins remembered a different story that became widely known within the family. My God-fearing yiayia Sophia had stepped out on the stoop to get the milk, carrying an aluminum pan in her hands that morning, when she noticed that the milkman's eyes were fixed next to her shoes. But it was not her shoes that mattered, it was the voodoo doll lying on the top step. I imagine her eyes popping wide. She could not even have greeted him with a "Good morning" that day, her God-fearing instincts repelled by the sight. Flustered, she would have picked up the doll to hide it from public sight, only to read the curse pinned on a note: "Death to Nitsa." But evil, devilish spirits had come into the house with the doll. Totally disgusted, Yiayia went to Aunt Eleni's house, once the milk was boiled and put away. She knocked on my aunt's door, carrying the voodoo doll wrapped up in a newspaper, her blood pressure as high as could be.

"What is this wretched thing?" my aunt exclaimed, when Yiayia revealed the doll with pins through the heart.

It turned out that the "gift" had come from one of my father's shunned girlfriends, someone willing to visit the gypsies for this purchase to get some revenge. Within the hour, my aunt Eleni was leaving her house on a mission. Inside her handbag, still wrapped in newspaper, was the cursed gift. Yiayia Sophia had entrusted it to her daughter, who rushed down 25th of March Street, and when she reached the shoreline, she checked to the right and the left. Seeing no one around, she ditched it in the sea, newspaper and all, and with a sigh of relief she turned around and took the road back home. By then, I had already heard how my grandmother felt about my father's "hussies," an unexpected word to come out of her proper lips. Still, it had taken years before I'd realized that Yiayia Sophia disapproved but had lain the burden for the trouble in the girlfriends' laps. "If they would only leave him alone." I wonder if Yiayia scolded him. I imagine her: lips pursed, her eyes burning as she asked for an explanation.

My father would have earned bragging points from his buddies about successfully trolling the dance halls and cafés of the city. I disliked thinking about that, but it must have been true. Thessaloniki has always been known as a city with lots of entertainment venues and after-hour hangouts. He would have snickered with pride at his friends' comments.

"Did she really get a voodoo doll for you?"

"You have a knack with girls, Pericli."

"Can't they tell when it's over?!"

Despite feeling awkward listening to these stories, I would join my cousins in shallow laughter. In the moment, what else was there to do? Still, I was glad they had kept the details to themselves all these years; they were not fit for a young daughter who adored her father, although fine morsels for the storyteller.

After Yiayia Sophia's passing, I wondered if my father stopped philandering when he remarried. I could never be sure, once I had met the stark truth. My biological mother's unexpected deep sighs of unhappiness had amplified the burden she'd faced during her marriage and explained her silences that took her away from me when I visited her at my grandparents' home. She never mentioned my father's dalliances, but I was witnessing the funeral procession of her dreams for family, life, and happiness. She was drowning in a crescendo of disappointments, realizing that her future looked bleak. Society did not have a place for women of divorce, and she had never been employed. To make matters worse, people wondered about her giving up her child—a question I tried to bury. Still, a weight would crawl into my heart when I caught her staring in the distance, her brown eyes swollen, a pool of dark emotion. My mother needed love and comforting, but I did not know how to soothe her, and I was not about to confront my father. I missed her presence in the house when my name day celebration came around, although she always remembered to have a special treat waiting for me at her place, often a piece of fancy French pastry. In my teens, all I had to give her was a hug, a kiss, and a brave face.

So, on that September 17th of my sixteenth name day, our doorbell rang. It was my aunt Marika, wanting to come upstairs after her outburst. She had never visited us here at the house. Still, I came out to the landing, leaned over the banister, and greeted her with a questioning hello.

I knew that my aunt had always been Mother's close ally. The two sisters shared secrets and were each other's confidantes and supporters. They had shared their joys and troubles with each other because there was no one else. Yiayia Athena was a strict and demanding mother, and her daughters did not always share their lives with her. Their father, my Papous Constantinos, was a traditional man, devoted to his business, his station in life, and deferential to his wife when it came to their daughters. So the sisters were devoted to each other, and, even during the tangled days of her mental illness, my aunt had been there for my mother. Shouting in front of our house about prostitutes was an unexpected way to take up her cause.

That morning, my aunt was not about to go away. "Ah, you are upstairs! Happy name day, Sophoula," she declared in a calm voice, and labored up the two flights of wooden steps. As she turned up toward the top flight, I saw that her eyes were steely hard. She looked past me, examining the interior of the house. Just then, my stepmother joined us from the kitchen, where she had been preparing a tray of treats, and looked at me quizzically, having heard the commotion.

"It's my aunt Marika," I apologized. Did my stepmother know about her mental illness? What might she do, finding my wayward aunt there at her house?

Aunt Marika was well educated, a graduate of the French Lycée in the city, fluent in French, and a liberal thinker. Up until recently, she had been employed by a pharmaceutical and cosmetics company. She was tall and trim, and her sparkly eyes and wide forehead projected an image of intelligence. But that day, her eyes looked wild, stark, and cloudy. In her twenties and thirties, she wore smart-looking suits and fixed her graying, naturally curly hair into waves, an attractive, classic style. Even that day, she was stylish in her suit—and I loved my proud aunt, now a more complicated soul than I had known before. "Shall we let her in?" I'd asked tentatively.

Certainly, my stepmother must have known her story—and quite a story it was. Sometime in the 1950s, Marika had gone to Switzerland for a while and then on to Istanbul, returning home with Turkish souvenirs, brass ashtrays, a model of a catamaran, and other trinkets now displayed around my grandfather's house. Later, I learned that the first trip was for psychiatric treatment, and the second was another doctor's recommendation, who was pressing her to get married and seek a "change of scenery"—all of this because Aunt Marika had been diagnosed with schizophrenia in her thirties, and the family desperately wanted to see her return to her old self. Instead, she'd resigned from work and continued to live with her parents. Although she had previously received plenty of marriage proposals, she had turned them all down, never recovering from the loss of the love of her life, who had suddenly abandoned her for a cabaret girl. Wounded from that jilting, she had lost all interest in relationships and marriage. The family believed that is when she began to crack. My stepmother must have known her story.

"Come in, come in," Evdokia replied, smiling politely, waving her in the door with an exaggerated, nervous welcome. The neighbors and a couple of school friends, already settled in the reception, were chatting away, unaware of the commotion. With quick glances, my stepmother signaled me to show my aunt to the living room.

"This way, Aunt Marika." I motioned her to step through the French doors into the living room.

My aunt, in her early forties, was heavier and stronger than either me or my stepmother. She had dressed up in a gray suit, low heels, and a leather purse. My stepmother, staying calm, followed us a couple of steps behind.

"How are you? Could I get you a glass of water? It is such a hot day."

Aunt Marika examined my stepmother closely before answering, "I came to wish Sophoula a happy name day. Yes, a glass of cold water." She was clutching her purse tightly in her lap. Grateful to observe the exchange of social niceties, I relaxed into a false sense of normalcy and sat down across from her. My aunt took her handkerchief out of her purse and padded her forehead dry, surveying the room.

"Is this Periclis's wife?" Marika inquired.

"Yes, you know I call her 'Mother.'"

"You only have one mother!" she stared me down sternly.

Shifting in my seat, I stared back, pained by her disapproving face. It was not my fault.

"Happy name day," she toasted me again, though she was doing her best to spoil it, and raised the glass, slowly sipping the sweet, homemade cherry liqueur my stepmother had offered her on a tray.

"Thank you, Aunt Marika," I replied automatically, making no attempt to keep the conversation going. My insides felt chilly, my throat dry. I loved my aunt, but I feared, too, that she might hurt my stepmother with another angry outburst. Our reception room guests must have sensed the change. When my stepmother returned to the room, they made excuses and cut their visit short. Relief settled in my chest as I heard their footsteps going down the wooden staircase. My stepmother did not join us right away, and I was glad for that.

Searching my aunt's face, I could see that she was pulsating between two worlds. Staring outside the balcony, she tumbled into streams of that unnerving laughter of hers. I could still hear her harsh voice spitting anger at this house when she was outside, and I could not think of one thing to do. I just had to wait her out.

After more bouts of unexplained giggling, she finally turned to look at me, but it was hard to look back. I was in awe of her, at a loss of how to penetrate through to that other frightening realm. What spirits were exciting her mind, and what swirls of dancing images could elicit such uncontrollable laughter?

"Sophoula," my stepmother chirped after several moments. The air cleared. Thankfully, she had phoned my father, and the two of them had devised a quick plan. Motioning me to the door, she slipped some coins into my hand, whispering, "Take the bus to your grandparents. They need to come and get your aunt."

"Certainly," I nodded. I knew that my grandparents didn't have a phone—but what might happen in my absence?

"We'll be okay," my stepmother reassured me softly, glancing back at my aunt. Then, for Aunt Marika's benefit, she made some loud excuse about sending me out to do some errand, and I left for the bus, my head throbbing. Fortunately, I did not have to wait long, and once I got on the bus, I stood by a window for air. Stop after bus stop went by, and that ride seemed to go on forever. Finally, reaching the hammam, I got off the bus and ran along the narrow sidewalk. I stepped over the stoop and through the doorway, heavy with the news I was about to deliver. Climbing up the steps to my grandparents' apartment, I reported breathlessly my aunt's arrival and crazy behaviors. "She was shouting outside our house; she called it my father's brothel! She came upstairs . . . she is still there . . . we have guests. . . ." Yiayia Athena's face went ashen, and as she imagined the worst that an upset Marika might spit out, she told Papous that she would get his clothes ready.

Alarmed at the news, Papous in turn asked me where Father was. "He is at work, and my stepmother said you should come and get her." He left the room to quickly dress in his gray-striped business suit and vest, and together we ran to catch the bus back to P. Sindika, leaving Yiayia Athena behind, crying silently in the living room with my mother watching us from the door where she stood, frozen.

Still, despite his women's grief, all through that trip across town, my grandfather seemed his normal self: erect, projecting a calm exterior. A heavyset, balding man with white hair and a well-groomed appearance, he exuded a lot of authority around his household. The only thing that gave him away on the bus was how fast he flipped his worry beads while we rode. Wrapped in an adrenalin rush, I looked for the right exit and galloped ahead of Papous to my house to ring the doorbell, warning my stepmother that we were back. Apparently, while I was gone, Aunt Marika had moved into the parlor, quietly visiting with a couple of recent well-wishers. My stepmother met us at the door, shook Papous's hand gratefully, and showed him in, briefly introducing him as "Marika's father."

He greeted everyone in the room, but he did not sit down. Instead, he took his watch out of his vest pocket and made a public showing of checking the time. "It's getting late, Marika. We need to get back home." He spoke in a soft voice, looking directly at her even though she did not acknowledge him, glancing all the while at the guests with pursed lips. "Your mother and sister are waiting for us back at home," he repeated. My aunt continued ignoring him, looking out the window, her forehead furrowed. Carefully, he moved closer and tried to lead her out of the room by taking her arm, but she pushed him back forcefully. My heart was throbbing madly against my ribcage as I watched my grandfather stumble and half fall onto the floor.

We leaned in to help him, but he managed to steady himself, standing up alone and firmly offering his arm to Aunt Marika without another word. Startled by her father's near collapse, my aunt rose from her seat reluctantly and followed him to the front door with no further resistance. I planted myself at the exit briefly until I heard their last footsteps fade away. Then I returned to the reception.

Still, I wonder what had transpired when they returned to their home. Did Papous get her on medications then, or had she stopped taking them? Was she hospitalized? I can only be sure of the family's embarrassment. Not being kept in the loop about how the family dealt with her was not unusual in a household that kept secrets to shield their sense of dignity. In later years, when she was no longer at the house, I learned that she had indeed been hospitalized.

Back then, on my name day, though, with cheerful spirits gone, I found it hard to exchange pleasantries with our remaining visitors. I can hardly remember who came by on that name day, but I thought of my namesake, Yiayia Sophia, no longer alive, who had been spared this embarrassment. It was a topsy-turvy day. Polite, forced smiles, standard wishes, and more visitors did not make it right. Later on, as they left the house, our guests wished me the traditional, "May you live to be a hundred." But all I could think of was an ancient Greek proverb: "Nothing is hidden under the sun." Watching the adults on that day, even though I was worn out and distressed, I appreciated how people who did not know each other collaborated to restore calm to our house. However, I was also slowly resolving to find a way to avoid the burden of their struggles and strife; I craved to be free of these problems and find my own way.

29 CROSSING THE ATLANTIC OCEAN
November 20, 2015

The flight attendants dimmed the lights to encourage us to rest. But not me; I reached for the overhead light switch, determined to keep on reading. My father's attorney had remained relentless. He'd developed more grounds, and I imagined his fierce oratory and purposeful arguments, portraying Mother as a jealous woman, a woman without reason. In the petition, he had written:

> *She caused scenes daily, demanding that he should be back home to wait for her return from visits to her father's family. On a recent occasion when he was gone the whole day, she swore at him and addressed him as follows: "Horrid man, you do not deserve a wife. Stay here and live with your mother." Since then, she abandoned her husband's house and, to date, has been living at her father's home.*

This certainly did not sound like my mother. *Shouting, swearing, threatening?* It did not ring true, but a distressing memory snapped into place of the summer when my mother had taken her furniture and moved out of our house without a goodbye. She'd left her home like a thief, in the days when divorce was just emerging in Greece. As for me, back then, how could I have answered anyone who asked me, "Where are you going?" To my ears and theirs, it sounded so odd to reply, *"To visit my mother."*

Still, in the days that followed after she left, I dripped with questions, drowning in disappointment and loss; I can still picture the truck carrying away my mother and all her furniture. The depth and pain of my confusion lingered on so that, years later on that massive jet crossing over half the globe, I read that petition over again and realized—for the first time—that my mother was the one who had walked away. After ten years of marriage, she had stopped singing her song and had needed to slip out of the cage. A shiver ran down my spine, a lift of joy as I witnessed this new Nitsa, a woman filled with strength and decisiveness. For months, she must have steeled herself in order to reach that moment when she could finally leave. Now, glancing around myself on the plane, accepting a cup of coffee from the flight attendant, I thought, *Look, even airplanes have evacuation plans and a life vest under the seat.*

From the row in front of me traveled a woman's voice: nasal, loud, and irritating. I could see the top of her head, her coarse, short gray hair. She sat next to an old fellow with sparse white hair and hearing aids. He had been quiet but, just then, mumbled something softly, and she stood up to let him leave his seat, towering over him. With unsteady steps, the old man headed for the bathroom, holding onto head rests on either side of the aisle. Tall and hefty, the woman wore a long denim coat, embroidered with white flowers around the seams, a pair of jeans, and Birkenstocks.

When the older fellow returned to his seat, the woman stood up to let him in and looked directly at me, smiling. Nodding and returning the smile, I realized that it was only the quality of her voice that I disliked. I needed to clear my head and abandon my exaggerated, biased response to her. I knew nothing about this woman. I could not have articulated any good reason for my negative reaction. Was it similar to Yiayia Sophia's gut reaction to my mother, unexplained, not reasoned, and yet so powerful that it had ruined a marriage? Are we that fickle in our relationships? I still did not want to believe that.

When the man returned, she picked up the conversation, continuing her soliloquy.

"It was sad. Their marriage fell apart. His wife had a daughter, and they moved away."

She could have been the typist in my court script or the domineering mother-in-law who had set a course to get rid of Nitsa and dissolve her son's marriage. The typist would have recognized the typical mother-in-law story. Yiayia would have been horrified to hear my mother swearing at her son. But had she? Only this time, in the tall lady's story, the child had stayed with her mother. What had they told the court? Did it matter which parent was "right"?

30 THE "COME DOWN" APARTMENT
1960

Years ago, after a long summer vacation when I was fourteen, I set out under a dusky September sky to visit my forty-two-year-old mother. After the bus let me off, I walked on narrow sidewalks that flanked a mound of dirt to the broad, irregular terrain of Navarinou Square. My grandparents' new apartment, where my mother now lived, was downtown on D. Gounary 30, one of several cement high-rises with boxy exteriors. The family had moved there over the summer months, and I couldn't help comparing its stark facade to the art deco lines, wide entryway, and spacious lobby of their previous apartment near the hammam, in Saint Sophia's neighborhood.

The city was dotted with kiosks, conveniently sprinkled along sidewalks, each crowded with edibles, candy, gum, chocolate, newspapers, and magazines. I looked for one in my mother's new neighborhood, on tree-lined Prince Nikolas Street, to find a treat for her, one I could afford on my small allowance. Finally, I settled on a bar of ION almond chocolate, the kind my mother liked best, in order to cheer her up from her perpetual melancholy.

By the time I arrived, she was pacing outside her apartment building, looking worried because of my late arrival. "Did you find it easily?" she wanted to know.

"Yes, of course." I ran up to her. We hugged and kissed, and I placed the bar of chocolate in her hand. "Here, look what I got for you." She looked down to see what I was handing her. I watched her reaction carefully, trying to read her face. It was unusual for her to be waiting for me on the street. Was everything all right?

"Oh, my favorite!" she squealed, excited as I hoped she'd be. "With almonds!" Mother unwrapped the foil and took a bite. "Delicious," she said, smiling and turning toward me. It had been another summer we were kept apart, and this separation would repeat during subsequent summers that I would spend with my father's family away from the city. I wondered how Mother felt about it, not only because it kept me away from her but because a new wife enjoyed vacations on Greek islands she might have liked if she had compromised and stayed with Father. Did she resent him, did she count herself lucky, or a bit of both? She kept up her cheery tone, checking me quickly trying to appraise any change, and finally asked, "Let me look at my fourteen-year-old daughter—so tan! Did you have a good vacation on Skiathos Island?" She was glossing over our separation in her familiar, chatty way. Her eyes shone brightly as she motioned me to twirl around so that she could have a good look.

"It was fantastic, Mother. Koukounaries is a spectacular sandy beach. I wish you could have been there." I choked back further comments. It had been quite a while, I knew, since my mother's family was able to afford a long-distance summer vacation.

You wouldn't have known it, though, to look at her. With a steady smile, she pressed onward, asking, "Did you get a new swimming suit? Your body is changing." As she scrutinized my shape, my cheeks reddened.

"I bought a new one in Skiathos," I answered, noticing her clothes. I wished my mother would not wear this old, faded dress in public. Also, I noticed that she had gained some weight over the summer.

"You will have to tell us all about it. Come. Let's go upstairs." And we sauntered arm in arm to the building.

The entryway to the modest condominium on Number 30 was small but fine, dressed up in white by naturally watermarked ivory marble with an inch-wide black border along the top edge. We climbed a couple of steps and walked to an elevator, shutting a pair of bifold doors behind us. My mother pressed the button, and the elevator rose noisily to the fourth floor. "How old is the building?" I asked, as we stepped off the elevator, my eyes taking a moment to adjust to the dark landing. My mother searched for the light switch, turned it on, and was getting her key ready to unlock the apartment door. But before she could answer me, a short, middle-aged brunette unlocked her door from the apartment next door. In her robe, she looked me over, smiling expectantly at my mother.

"My daughter, Sophoula," my mother indulged her, but she had barely finished when the Hadjimichael apartment door across the landing swung open, and my aunt Marika stepped out with a big grin and a welcoming kiss. "*Tzoutzouki mou*," she said, "my sweetness," and I reached out to hug her. Tucking her handkerchief into her pocket, she held me tightly for a long moment.

"Mrs. Nitsa, I will have the hem done tomorrow if you need your skirt," the neighbor interjected.

"That's fine," my mother cut her short, and we entered the Hadjimichael apartment after my obligatory, "Nice to meet you." She smiled at me approvingly.

Inside the apartment, I walked quickly through the entryway, asking, "Where is Papous?" My mother pointed me past a dark middle room to a living room; beyond it, my grandfather sat in the stuffed armchair, next to the balcony. I rushed to kiss him on both cheeks as he squeezed my shoulder.

"Good morning, Sophoula." My grandfather smiled, dressed in his customary white starched shirt and vested suit. Then he reached for his strand of worry beads and began flipping through them slowly.

Yiayia Athena entered the living room from the kitchen. "Look at our young lady! You have grown taller yet. So fine." She sat down, making room for me on the couch. I rushed to sit by her side, warmed by her dimples and easy smile.

"It's a small apartment," Yiayia said, looking down, "and we are still getting used to it." She sighed. A practical woman, she'd realized that the family needed to reduce expenses and live more modestly. So she'd organized the whole search for and move to their new location. Papous knew that the dwindling family resources and his daughters' everyday needs required a drastic solution—and that had forced him to sell the St. Sophia home. Still, Yiayia Athena was a strong woman who refused to accept defeat. The whole family wanted their stark new place with its dull ochre paint and unadorned walls to be warm, clean, and livable. "Chin up. We can do it!" was Yiayia's motto. Through her sadness, she would make it work. She was good at hiding it, though, and it would take me years to recognize how Yiayia's restrained despair used to fill me with a sense of gloom whenever I visited them.

Looking around, I spotted the imposing Big Ben grandfather clock with its deep-sounding quarter-hour bells that stood against the wall of the windowless middle room. Next to it, the glassed-in bookcase was crammed with the tall volumes of the encyclopedia, *Helios*.

"Where is your bedroom, Mother?" I asked.

"I use the living room couch you are sitting on and make my bed there every night," she answered in a tone that did not allow for questions. "I love being next to this balcony."

I shrank inside. *She didn't even have her own bedroom.* I couldn't imagine sleeping on a couch in my father's house, where I had my own twin walnut bed and vanity. But I remained silent; what could she do? What could I? After a moment, my mother rose to open the glass doors to the balcony and left them ajar for some fresh air. A couple of flowerpots sat outside, signs of my mother's touch. The most pleasant room of the cramped apartment—and the best lit—was the living room. And now that I sat there, I could recall an earlier conversation that I'd heard between my mother and her sister before I left for my summer vacation with my father's family. At the time, the two had just viewed their future home, and they were walking me to the bus at the end of my weekend visit. "We will move out from our beautiful St. Sophia home with its corner turret and wide balcony to this small and dark fourth-floor box!" Aunt Marika had complained. "At least it's in the center of town," she'd added, trying rather unsuccessfully to perk herself up.

"So, how big is it?" I'd asked Mother, surprised to hear about the move.

"A small place," Aunt Marika had answered in a glum voice, "without a soul."

"Where is it?"

That time, my mother had answered, "It's still downtown, in Navarino Square, closer to the bay, and Father has already paid it off."

I knew that area, and it had always seemed fine to me, but what I had not understood clearly was just how much the Hadjimichael family's finances were dwindling because of Papous's retirement and Aunt Marika's resignation from her job due to her mental illness. Their lifestyle was trimming back, and the first time the two sisters saw their new apartment, they had hated it. The odor of shut-up space that had not been aired for weeks especially bothered my mother. She had turned to Aunt Marika to announce, "I want the room with the balcony, and you can have the one right next to mine," with presumption in her tone.

"I know, you got a promise out of Mother," Aunt Marika had replied, sounding resentful.

Yiayia Athena always tried to be fair, but this time she had favored Mother. It was the privilege of the older sister to have first dibs. And so, the best room in the apartment, which doubled as a sitting room, became my favorite too, once I began to visit.

* *

And now it was time to take the not-so-grand tour with my mother. She stood up and motioned me. "Come, I will show you the rest," she said. By the time I visited, my mother was still trying to put a good face on the "box." "We will have to put a carpet over this lino-leum flooring," she explained. "I hate this color." As the years passed, though, the carpet never came.

I heard an annoying, steady hum. "Is that the elevator?"

"Yes, it's going up," she answered and went on, changing the sub-ject, "We put the furniture where Yiayia Athena wanted it."

Yiayia warned her, "I may still have more changes."

"Where is the Tesla?" I asked, recalling all the fine moments of singing along with Mother and my aunt when we listened to the radio.

Yiayia pointed to it on a table next to the couch. "Papous will turn it on to listen to the noontime news," she answered.

Although I was still young, I understood that my mother's Hadjimichael family were proud. Clearly, they still had not come to terms with the smaller space, the noise from the apartment next door, and the rattling elevator. It was painful to witness. And just then, I heard the alarming sound of a fire truck leaving the firehouse diag-onally across from them on Prince Nikolas Street. Running back to the balcony, I craned my neck to look outside, excited and disturbed.

"There must be a fire somewhere, Sophoula. They are on their way," Yiayia suggested reassuringly.

My mother was waiting for me back in the windowless room. As I turned, I recognized the display case that held the family's silver tea service and crystal, humbled now in this dark setting; it cov-ered a wall, with a couch on the other side. Then we moved back to the entryway and opened one of the opaque glass doors to a small kitchen.

"Oh, the floor here is tile. I like the starburst pattern. It's like the tile in our kitchen," I exclaimed, thinking of the elegant patterns at my father's house.

My mother, though, turned toward the balcony that faced the alley, chasing a wry wrinkle from her forehead. "Fresh air, great for getting rid of the cooking odors!" she forced her voice cheerful again, opening the balcony door wide. The kitchen was Yiayia Athena's kingdom. "She likes the white-tiled counter and the clean look," Mother added. On top of the counter rested a propane stove with three heating elements, and across from it was the varnished hutch from the St. Sophia kitchen, which stored dishes, pots, pans, and supplies. Next to the hutch, Yiayia kept her chair.

"I wonder what she cooked for lunch, Mother."

"We will go to the restaurant next door," she replied, "and you can pick out what you like."

Not eat at home? I was surprised and disappointed; Yiayia's meals were the best. "Is Yiayia tired today?"

My mother winked, answering in English, as she sometimes did. "There's still Yiayia's dessert waiting for you," she assured me.

I nodded and replied in that second language that we used together, she and my Aunt Marika, sprinkling in a phrase or two to help keep me in practice: "Yes, thank you." Or, "No, don't worry." It was helpful, I supposed, though there were times, too, when the two sisters took off in English or French in exclusive communication that left the rest of us in the dark. Sometimes, they got as bad as Father and Yiayia, speaking Turkish and concealing their exchanges. "What are you saying?" I'd demand at moments like those, when language was being used more to keep people out than to keep them in.

"Whatever do you mean, child?" one or the other of them might answer sweetly. And it was true; if I tried hard enough, I could usually understand their words. It was the meaning that evaded me. All the same, I liked the cadence and sound of English, like a secret world that was calling to me.

When Aunt Marika came into the living room from the kitchen that day, she spoke in French. "I see they are taking good care of your daughter. She is beginning to develop. Her stepmother dresses her well," she admitted. "I like the dress and shoes she's wearing today."

"I could do a better job," my mother answered, scowling.

As they continued in French, I asked what was going on, and my mother claimed they were discussing which lipstick to wear. But I had heard her use the words *fille* and *robe*.

"Whatever. . ." I flipped her a knowing look, assuring them that I understood the nature of their secrecy, but they ignored me.

As we moved back out of the kitchen, leaving the balcony door ajar, I looked in on a tiny bathroom with barely enough space for a hot water tank and shower. A narrow window with opaque glass opened out to the alley. Back through the entry hall and the middle room was another closed door, which led to my grandparents' bedroom. It was furnished with their large bed, an armoire, and a trunk from the old apartment that held all the family linen and clothing. I peeked into the room but stepped back out just as quickly. How much did I really want to see of my family's new circumstances? Here, everything was so different and so cramped. There were fewer pieces of furniture in this flat, and yet it felt cluttered. I felt the family's loss and the sad atmosphere of the new apartment; I knew, as well, that it was not a place that I would bring my friends. How embarrassed I would feel to expose them to the sorry state of my Hadjimichael family. And, just like that, I understood that, for the remainder of my childhood, it would only be at my father's comfortable home that I would socialize and connect myself with the world.

Still, it was all so astonishing. How had this happened? "Where does Aunt Marika sleep?" I pressed on, still puzzled by the fullness of my family's demise.

"In the middle room," my mother answered curtly, referring to the windowless space at the center of their new home. "Every morning,

I open the balcony doors to bring fresh air into the house." Then, she changed the subject abruptly. "My basil and gardenia flowerpots sit right on the balcony. Come, let's water them. Look, you can see the bay!" she chirped as I followed her out. It was the first time that she had sounded cheery. "Even on dark days like this, I can feel the breeze and see the water," she assured me, though her eyes fixed into the distance.

That was about the time when I began wondering if her marriage had fallen apart because my mother had refused to turn into Cinderella, in the scullery of Yiayia Sophia's world. Even at that early age, I knew that my mother had wanted more for herself—and for me—than household chores. Even in her compromised position, she was showing me the beauty and promise of the sea pregnant with yet unmade adventures in distant lands. I, too, could see the promise it held; that was the initial moment, I can see now, that I had begun dreaming of my escape.

At lunchtime, using one of Yiayia's silver forks, I ate my meatballs with the restaurant mustard and salad on a tray resting on my knees in the living room, draping a cloth napkin on my chest. My grandmother served her famous clear *pelte*, a fruit-flavored gelatin, in a small shallow crystal bowl. "I thought about your dessert in Skiathos," I told her as I scooped the bowl with my spoon until every delicious trace was gone.

Afterward, my mother took the bowl from my hand and carried the dishes to the kitchen. I stood and held my grandmother's wrinkled hand and looked tenderly into her eyes and at her graying hair. My yiayia never sought compliments or thanks, but I knew she was pleased when I said, "Thank you, Yiayia!" Her brown eyes softened, And at the end of the day, Yiayia Athena asked me when I would return for my next visit.

"Can you call me midweek? I will know by then whether it's Saturday or Sunday," I answered, looking at my mother and feeling a tightness in my chest, irritated that I had to be the go-between for my parents. But, as was the case in many households back then, the new Hadjimichael home did not have a phone, and it would be a real trek for my mother to get to the neighborhood pay phone at the kiosk. I wished she would talk to my father directly, but she would not.

"Let's see if we can set a routine for the coming year," Yiayia suggested.

"Talk to your father," my mother advised. And, later on, I would ask him, and he in turn would check with my stepmother before answering the question.

"Will do." I tried to be cheerful, giving in to the necessary evil of belonging to two households, but my heart and my loyalties were torn.

Then, it was time for goodbyes. Papous sent me off with his customary rhyme, with sad eyes and stooped shoulders:

> . . . I leave you my shadow as consolation,
> For you to have and to hold,
> to sear your heart.

I have never been sure if he meant his own shadow or mine. Perhaps he was asking for me to remember him when I was gone, even if it was just carrying his shadow. Maybe he knew that I felt pain for the split of my two families and anger at the tug I felt.

My aunt was the last one to see me off. Her eyes spelled sadness. Softly, she kissed me on both cheeks, "Au revoir, mon amie."

Today, I still wonder if that day was a first glimpse into the price of goodbyes. In time, I came to know it well: my own guilt for my escape to privilege as I abandoned my mother and the Hadjimichael family every time I took the bus back to my thriving and wealthy Kouidis home. All I knew was that I did not want my mother's life.

31 OVER NORTHERN CANADA
November 20, 2015

It had been several hours since the wheels of the Boeing 777 had lifted off the ground in Munich. This was the longest leg of my return trip, a bit over ten hours from takeoff to landing. Thick clouds in the night sky hung outside my window. I checked my watch. We would be in Chicago's O'Hare in another three hours—still a bit of a stretch before landing.

By then, some people were waking up and opening the window blinds as flight attendants rolled carts down the aisles, serving us another meal. Famished, I stored my laptop under the front seat, making room on the tray. Coffee sounded good, and even the cardboard packet with scrambled eggs and hash browns was most welcome. Looking around, I noticed a middle-aged mother across the aisle in the same row. She wore a bright sundress with a long-sleeved red vest over it. Stretching her arms over her head, she began waking up her daughter, who had been leaning on her mother's shoulder up until then. Removing the blue airline blanket, she called softly, "Good morning, sunshine! Wake up, we're getting breakfast." Then she started clearing their trays of coloring books and crayons, depositing them in her large bag stashed beneath the front seat. They were traveling alone and, I don't know why, I had the strange notion that there was no father available, and the woman had custody of her daughter.

What would I have done had I been given a choice—one I was too young to make—when my parents split up? Certainly, I would have followed my mother to my grandparents' home. During my earliest years, we had been part of the fabric of each other's very days. So, why hadn't I gone? Could I have? Had there been a time when I could have run to her to ask about what was happening? Why hadn't I done that? And why hadn't she asked me to come along?

Given all that history, now I wonder, too, whether Yiayia had ever considered moving in with any one of her other five married children. Had my mother ever suggested it? Had my father ever considered hiring some household help for my mother, as he had later on for my stepmother? Whether or not they'd considered such things, they hadn't followed through—which, I was finally beginning to realize, had left my mother suffocating there in a home so repressive that she had to get away just to breathe again. And certainly, it had taken significant strength for a woman like her to take that step. But still, what that step had cost her—and how—continued to haunt every moment of my own journey to unlock that history.

A momentary silence had fallen over my imaginary courtroom. With a sigh of pride and relief, I took a seat in the front row. All eyes now turned to the tall, thin, bespectacled man sitting at the other desk. It was my mother's attorney, soon to be the city's mayor, who'd turned to counter the accusations. He'd stood up, buttoned his coat, and begun: "Your Honors, kindly listen to my client's situation in this unfortunate match. She experienced unprecedented hardship and harsh conditions in her marriage."

It was satisfying to see that my mother had countersued my father, and that a good attorney had defended her case. After all, she had not been a passive woman who would have allowed herself to be trampled by that hostile household. Ten years of marriage she had endured, after all. And, decisive and strong, she was standing up for herself. My eyes moistened. I rubbed my cheek mechanically and quickly wiped a tear; how I wished I could turn the clock back and give her a hug just then.

Without delay, her attorney had elaborated the core arguments, presenting an embattled, emotionally abused woman who had suffered in a family with unreasonable expectations. During most of those ten married years, he explained, she had lived in a culture new to her and insulting to her sensibilities. "We strongly object to the picture presented thus far and offer the following, Your Honors. Several witnesses can substantiate our descriptions to satisfy the court as to the accuracy of these statements." The next allegation read:

The husband treated his wife in a shabby and crude manner soon after the wedding, calling her uneducated and ill-mannered. He abandoned her all day, returning to their home at midnight, never offering a reason or accounting for his absences.

In disbelief, I stopped reading and got up from my aisle seat, agitated. *Who was my father calling uneducated? My mother had graduated from high school and spoke English and French! My father himself was an eighth-grade drop-out.* Aunt Marika would have raged if she'd read that part of the petition—a thought that made me smile. "Sheer deception!" she might have exclaimed in disgust. Perhaps Father really felt inferior to Mother, but whether he did or whether this was simply an attorney's exaggeration for the court, what I knew for myself was that, like Mother and Aunt Marika, I prized education and certainly later would invest a lot of energy in pursuing post-secondary degrees.

"He must have been having an affair, Nitsa," my aunt would conclude for the hundredth time. But since that was all supposition, Mother's attorney had not been able to list it in the petition. Still, I remembered that Father would often return home at midnight and I would occasionally awaken to the sounds of his dying car engine.

On the court document, my mother's attorney had listed new grounds:

Furthermore, he never allowed his wife to visit her relatives,
requiring that she get his explicit permission. Eight months
before the petition was filed, he prohibited her from visiting
her relatives at all, claiming that they had not delivered the
full agreed upon dowry as promised.

The words formed an odd, dark kaleidoscope, its prisms performing a bizarre dance in front of my eyes. Had my father really exerted such unreasonable controls over my mother? Had he presumed that much authority over her? If so, it turns out that my stoic mother had been a determined woman who could demand respect and set limits even if it led to divorce—aided, of course, by my aunt Marika. In my mind's eye, I could imagine the sisters' intense conversations: "What is he talking about, Nitsa?" Marika would have asked. "More lies. I cannot believe that my father would not deliver on his promise of your dowry."

"Our father's handshake is as good as gold," my mother would have agreed. "But this household follows a different bible. It is a rotten man's world, Marika. Our father was never that way." Then she might have added the bitter truth: "Our mother has always run our household. I never had a chance to run mine."

In the company of that raging history, the flight to the States seemed endless. Parched for a drink, I logged off my computer, leery that a stranger might read my document, and walked to the rear of the plane for more water. A tall flight attendant in a blue uniform smiled and handed me another cup, which I gulped down gratefully before returning wearily to my seat.

The overhead light was still on, so I opened the next attachment, wondering if my parents had been a mismatched pair from the beginning. Had there been good years, romantic times? Would their marriage have survived had Yiayia Sophia not lived with us? Was there any way that my mother would have tolerated my father's dalliances?

At one point, I'd hoped to learn more about those questions during the days that my mother had lived with me and my husband in the United States, but she had always maintained a silence about my father. In my mind's eye, I could still see her locking the door decisively to the empty D. Gounary apartment as we carried her suitcase and bag down the elevator to the cab that had taken us to Thessaloniki's airport. Many hours later, when we'd finally landed in Portland, Oregon, after an exhausting long haul with stopovers in both London and New York, we'd piled our suitcases into a taxi to take us home. Near the house, my mother had quipped in English, "Why do people drive monster cars?" And we'd laughed with relief. It was true that European cars were much smaller than oversized American ones.

"You haven't seen anything yet," I'd promised, replying in Greek. Outdoing myself and her expectations was my charge, and my husband was all for that. "But first," I'd told her, "it's time for a good night's sleep."

Once we arrived home, our large yard and kitty welcomed us, and we'd settled my mother in her own room. In those days, my husband and I were renting a house across from a grade school and next to a nursing home in a working-class neighborhood of northwest Portland. Homes were one- and two-story structures made of wood, and most had yards, a stark change from the multi-story cement row of condominiums where my mother had lived with Marika, before my poor aunt was hospitalized. Her comments reminded me of the kinds of differences I had noticed decades earlier upon my arrival in America: signs of a new language, a new land, and a cultural shift. I wondered how my mother would take to it, though mostly I looked forward to the days ahead when we would develop our daily routines for the months and years to come. But after a few months, it was clear that my hopes would not materialize.

32 LA BÊTE
1964

Even as a child, I knew I had my own set of wings like Nike, the Greek goddess of victory. I believed the universe conspired to my benefit. Now in high school, I would test those wings. I would strike out on my own to make sense of my broken world.

When I visited my mother on a Sunday in 1964, the spring of my junior year, my beloved aunt Marika's absence screamed at me. In the previous few years, I had lost my paternal grandmother, Yiayia Sophia, and I was not, I decided, about to lose track of my aunt's whereabouts, even though my mother assured me that she would return soon. In my maternal grandparents' living room, I insisted, "When did her doctors order her to the hospital?"

My mother seemed reluctant to share much; she was sullen, her lips pursed tight. "They know best," she answered, resigned. I cringed and pressed her with more questions. My aunt was hospitalized again at La Bête, the mental hospital in nearby Stavroupolis, the City of the Cross, and my mother had visited her the day before. "Marika still needs more time there," she assured me.

Well, I thought to myself, *then I need to see her.* My mother did not need to know of my plan to visit her; she shared very little about my aunt's condition anyway. A lonely girl and a member of my school's psychology club, I was doubly drawn to my aunt's case. If this kind of fate could befall her, what might it mean for me—a girl as well, and her blood relation? How had my aunt gotten there in the first place? Was she really so sick? Or were there other influences that had caused her undoing? Perhaps some of the same influences that had unraveled my mother's life? Whatever the reasons, I had to see Marika, so on Monday, I sought out my good friend Efi at school. A practical and playful classmate, she was my size, with shoulder-length hair and expressive brown eyes. Efi was curious and dependable, and I loved partnering with her in adventure. Often, we explored our cityscape, sometimes setting out on missions that we did not wish our parents to know about. In the schoolyard during morning break, I asked, "Do you remember my aunt Marika?" reminding her that she had heard me talk about my aunt's visit on my name day celebration.

"That must have been an ugly scene," Efi empathized, recalling my descriptions of my aunt arriving outside my father's house, shouting about my father's philandering and calling our home a brothel. "How is she?"

"She is at La Bête, the mental hospital, for the third time. She was agitated again, and my grandparents sent her there to recover." I spoke in a subdued, low voice so that other kids wouldn't hear us.

"What did she do this time?" asked Efi.

"My mother told me yesterday that my aunt became convinced that her own father wanted to harm her. My grandfather felt he was in danger. She was gone when I visited Mother on Sunday." Efi blanched, listening, and I hated having to admit it to her. What had become, after all, of the women in my family? And how had it all come to this?

"I hope she comes home soon." Efi tried to be sympathetic. She was one of only a couple of friends who had met my aunt the time she had come with me to the Hadjimichael home on one of my weekend visits.

"I think about her. I want to visit her at La Bête," my voice waxed earnest. "Would you come with me?"

Efi nodded slowly. My aunt exhibited a frightening set of behaviors, but also compelling. Along with me in the psychology club at

Anatolia, Efi had been present for our recent discussion of mental hospitals and the progress that medicine had made in treating mental illnesses. Our study interests could suffice as an excuse if we needed one. Still, we skipped classes quietly that morning, and, guessing that the adults still might disapprove of our behavior, we kept it a secret.

"Let's take the eleven o'clock bus from the terminal," I suggested. My mother had let me know which bus she took to visit the hospital, never suspecting that I would soon set out on my own. I was nervous; my stomach clenched. This was not just a visit to see Aunt Marika. We were going to encounter a whole hospital filled with people who suffered from various mental illnesses. It was reassuring to have Efi along; I needed her support. But what would she think of my aunt? And what state would Aunt Marika be in when we saw her?

We traveled for more than an hour to a neighboring town, Stavroupolis, the City of the Cross, where Zeitenlik, a military cemetery, is the last home to more than twenty thousand World War I French, British, Serbian, and Russian soldiers. The bus rattled each time we went over the deep potholes of the rural road. Once we got off, we walked through an unguarded gate into a yard surrounded by wrought-iron fencing and park-like grounds. That was the entrance to La Bête.

People said that the French Army had once used the area to house their horses in the early part of the twentieth century. That is how the hospital was named "La Bête," which translates to "the beast," a place for stupid beasts. This was the hospital that housed my aunt, who herself was no animal. "It's odd to walk into a well-fenced area with an open gate," I noted, nervously. The long, narrow, off-white building ahead of us needed some fresh paint. Formal boxwood bushes edged the pathway. The soil was dry, the grass yellowing from a rainless spring. We moved along the paved path slowly.

My aunt's illness had come about gradually. Toward the beginning, the family believed that a betrayal by her beloved had broken the dam of her fragile sanity, spilling her over into a netherworld. She had been abandoned by the love of her life, a long-term relationship, just as she expected to be married to him. That was when the first signs of illness emerged.

"What next?" Efi wanted to know.

We noticed a man who looked to be in his thirties sitting on a bench. He was short, clean-shaven, with attractive hazel eyes, wearing a summery short-sleeved shirt and jeans.

"How can we find a patient on the floor? Do we just walk in?"

"Who are you looking for?" inquired the man, slowly puffing on his cigarette. I told him my aunt's name.

He shrugged. "There are so many people here. I don't know her." He suggested that the social worker could help us and pointed to her office inside the lobby.

"Are there visiting hours? Is it okay to go straight in?" I continued. I had made no inquiries ahead of time and had no prior experience with hospital routines, and neither had Efi.

"Go right ahead. You can visit up until four o'clock," he answered.

"And what are you doing here?" Efi asked him.

"I'm a patient—and a painter," he said in the same breath. His blue eyes shone with pleasure for the inquiry. And indeed, we noticed his long paint-smudged fingers.

"What do you paint?" I asked carefully.

"Here, I'll show you." He rose, put out his cigarette in an ashtray, and led us to his easel. His paints and brushes were set on the cement sidewalk next to the hospital building. He took a large canvas resting against the building and placed it on the easel for easier viewing. The figures on the canvas were a clearly drawn pair of angels looking out toward the horizon line with hollow eyes. He had portrayed the figures using a palette of delicate, pale oils. He was no amateur. Efi and I exchanged a look, both of us disturbed by the angels' dark, hollow gaze. Did they represent death? *More like the haunting hallucinations of a man*, I thought, chilled but intrigued, *who is both intelligent and talented*. We thanked him and quickened our footsteps, heading to the lobby.

"I did not expect to meet a 'normal crazy person' here," Efi confided.

We walked up marble steps to enter a large, empty hall painted in institutional ochre, a color that I have come to dislike. Our shoes echoed hard against the cement floor. I knocked on the social worker's door, and she answered. She was in her fifties, with pinched, expressionless features, dressed in a chocolate brown suit and flat shoes.

"We are here to visit my aunt, Marika Hadjimichael; and, if you have time, we would love a hospital tour." I wondered if I was being too demanding. After all, Efi and I were mere schoolgirls, members of the psychology club. Would she quickly get rid of us?

The woman must have had spare time because she answered all of our questions and mentioned a few of the treatments, explaining that electroshock was useful in treating depression, for example, but they were now using psychotropic medications instead, and that was a huge improvement. The medications helped reduce the number of lobotomies, even for violent, psychotic people, she explained. At the sound of "lobotomies," I feared for my aunt. This place had its dangers.

After several more minutes, we followed the social worker's invitation and started walking down the long bare corridors on a quick walking tour. We would end up in "recreation," the woman promised, where we could visit with my aunt. "At La Bête we use occupational therapy." The social worker spoke slowly, in a monotone, as we kept peppering her with questions. "Mostly, that means gardening and raising crops. That keeps patients engaged in activities. They function better when they are busy."

We never saw the garden because it was in a distant corner of the large property, and she did not have enough time to take us there. She had already given a long tour for just two high school kids. So we moved along, coming to a doorway where we got a view of an open room with a dozen bathtubs lined up in two rows. Ceiling fixtures with a couple of flickering neon tubes blinking unevenly shed a pale light in the large room. A couple of naked women lay silent in the tubs. We peered in from the doorway, embarrassed by the intimacy of this scene. At least the women seemed peaceful, but it was surreal to see them so exposed and vulnerable in a barren, military-like setting. A small table piled high with folded white robes rested by the far wall. An employee in her starched white staff coat stood by, silently overseeing the room. She seemed stiff, intimidating, and she ignored me and Efi, barely nodding at the social worker when we arrived, rooted to the cement floor in the back of the room. The social worker spoke to us quietly, explaining that they had capacity for a thousand patients and used the tubs to "calm them down." We had no questions. I was glad to move on, away from that indignity.

Next, we visited the large dayroom, where a man stood eerily still by the wall. I had only read about that type of schizophrenia and recognized the symptoms of catatonia from my reading. It was as if he were made of wax and would remain so in the years to come. He stood expressionless, the pupils of his eyes still. What might be roiling inside him that had him so frozen in time? Occasional cries and shrill sounds wafted out of patients' rooms, where three and four in a room shared space along the long antiseptic-smelling corridor. My heart was beating louder, startled and overwhelmed by the sounds of human suffering.

Then I spotted my aunt. She sat by a window, clutching her ever-present hankie and gazing outside. Her eyes seemed larger than I remembered: piercing, fixed on something invisible. When she noticed me and Efi, she let out an unusually high-pitched giggle, a sound that I recognized, for I had heard that laughter at my grand-parents' home, but inside, I cringed.

"Hello, Aunt Marika," I walked toward her, hugging her and kissing her on both cheeks, expecting a warm welcome. She barely responded, remaining seated. What was wrong? That was so unlike her. As she sat there before me, Marika was a dispirited shadow of herself. My bright and fun-loving aunt, who used to smother me with treats and love, was absent. Dressed in a green buttoned-down gown, she looked every bit like a patient. I was shocked.

Efi stayed by the entrance to the dayroom door to give us privacy, watching the overall activity. Around a long wooden table, some patients were using hospital supplies to roll their own cigarettes. Ashtrays were full, and the heavy acrid smell of cigarettes filled the room.

"Shall we take a walk outside for a bit, Aunt Marika?" I asked, getting close enough to rest my hand on the back of her chair. I was getting ready to help her get up, wishing to see her more energized, hoping to connect with her away from everyone else.

"I don't feel like it," she answered blankly. "It's close to lunchtime." Her gaze filtered distractedly off into the distance. This was no way to be. I hated the passivity I saw in her and could not accept the change. Why was she this way? I tried to find reasons. Maybe we had come too early for a visit, I thought. Perhaps there could be a better time when Marika would not be so preoccupied with her daily routines. If so, I would come back. It was important; I needed her to really *see* me.

Around then, a couple of nurses in white uniforms and caps showed up to dispense medications. As I watched, it was eerie and a little surprising to see them ask patients to open their mouths wide after swallowing their pills. Too often, they told me afterward, some of those patients "cheeked" their medications and spit them back out later. But there at La Bête, patients had little choice about how to act, and so, my aunt's spirit had been clipped by her demons and the staff at that beast of a hospital. I watched Marika dutifully swallow her Thorazine pills, an antipsychotic drug that, I later learned, had the side effect of photosensitivity, the result being risk of sunburn. Realizing that we could not have our walk—or any privacy in that place—I handed her a small package of Oreo cookies. Accepting them, she waved me away: "Go on, go to your friend." And that was all.

"Goodbye, Aunt Marika," was all I could muster.

She did let me give her a quick peck on the cheek, but she would remain ever remote, mired in hallucinations, a wounded soul. Backing away, I walked across the room, weaving between the long tables to meet my friend Efi. For all the effort that it had taken to get there, ours had been a painfully short visit with my Aunt Marika.

"Leaving already?" Efi asked, surprised.

"She's tired—not in the mood for a visit. At least, not today."

We fell silent.

"Not much different than a well-run summer camp." Even I could hear the note of wryness to my voice.

Efi laughed, "Hardly."

"Thanks for coming with me," I offered, grateful.

As we left the grounds to wait for the bus, Efi commented, "Did you notice? I didn't see any other visitors today."

"Not a happy place to visit. I hate seeing my aunt here." *Could pain,* I wondered, *lead to insanity?* What shapes the way that we respond to it, anyway? Why would my aunt, always such a strong and intelligent woman, allow an unfaithful boyfriend to overtake her psyche? All those years ago, I was naïve enough to imagine that it had been a willful decision on her part.

Whatever the reason, though, that visit had upset me deeply. I had admired my sophisticated and well-educated aunt before her illness, but now I was chilled by the misery of that hospital, a cold institution that functioned as a mere holding tank. My aunt was remote, unresponsive, and unable to recognize my efforts to find her. She had pushed me away. Worse yet, I was leaving her behind in the smoky dayroom of La Bête, surrounded by strangers, her wings clipped.

So, it was with both guilt and relief that I returned to the bus stop, and my ordinary life. But that day, as it turned out, was not at all ordinary. Hours later, I still couldn't shake off the impact of that visit. Even years thereafter, it would linger on as an indelible memory in my adult life. As an impressionable teen, I had for the first time witnessed a hospital filled with lost souls living in the confines of custodial care. Witnessing the kind of living my aunt was subjected to upset and repelled me. I rebelled at the passivity and secretly wished to drive my own life, to plow my own path and remain independent.

For Efi, the visit was jarring too. The painter, the tubs, and the institutional austerity lingered in her mind. "Did you notice those burly attendants? They could have been wrestlers," she whispered on the bus ride home.

"Do those patients actually feel safe?" I gripped her hand. "They do lobotomies in there!"

"Yeah, and that social worker didn't show us where they use electroshock with patients," Efi mused. "I wonder how they do that?" Her curiosity horrified me. At least, as far as I knew, my aunt hadn't been subjected to that.

"It's such a terrible waste, Aunt Marika in La Bête," I moaned. "You should have seen her before—such a bright, smart, and loving woman. She was my favorite aunt, and my mother's best friend!" I hated to see my independent aunt confined in a hospital and the two sisters split apart. Both of them had seen their lives turn sour and both on account of men.

That evening at home, my thoughts kept returning to my aunt. Did she feel trapped in that place, or did she find relief living there? In later years, I have come to believe that the latter was true. There, she didn't need to censor her delusions and hallucinations and battle the waves of furies when they overtook her and threatened her family. Whenever the meds leveled her enough, she could return to my grandparents' home, a kinder place for her to lead her life.

Over time, I realized that after at-home periods of failing to take her pills, my aunt Marika would hear voices and become delusional. Each time, she would be readmitted to the hospital, a chronic patient, to be medicated and stabilized again. And finally, that was where she ended her life after a fall that had broken her hip. Painfully, I'd learned about it too long after the fact to attend her funeral. By then, she'd outlived my mother, who had looked after her when she was discharged from the hospital and returned to the D. Gounary apartment after my grandparents' passing.

Still, as she aged, my aunt's bright and limber soul had become hostage to delusions and hallucinations. Eventually, she was diagnosed as paranoid schizophrenic. Observing the galaxy of her visions and voices—possessive, demonic, and demanding—lured me to a career in social services, where I continued to explore the song of the Maenads with little fear, and mostly with a desire to help. Although I was never able to go back to visit her again, this was my aunt Marika's gift to me and to the children and families that I later helped through my child welfare work. I, too, had faced family loss, helplessness, and pain and had struggled to watch loved ones deteriorate. In my work, I recognized clipped wings: a mirror of my own long-ago loss, of Marika, and the distance between us that would never close.

33 FLYING OVER CANADA
November 20, 2015

We had experienced a brief time of turbulence that kept us buckled into our seats, but the clock kept ticking, bringing us closer to our destination. By then, Thessaloniki seemed like light years away from North America, and we would be landing at O'Hare in Chicago in another couple of hours before ending that interminable trip with yet another flight to Seattle. Feeling confined, I removed my seat belt, adjusting my seat and leaning it back to settle into renegotiating the truths and falsehoods of what my parents' legal petition had suggested.

Even after all that, the court document held still more surprises. At first, I was puzzled by what I read about the dowry argument. But then, I'd recalled eavesdropping on my father, sitting at his desk at home, explaining to Yiayia Sophia in frustration that he would fight for my custody, "all the way up to the Supreme Court if that is necessary." At that time, all that I'd made of that remark was to understand that I was a very prized child, one who deserved the attention of a very high power. But I had no idea what the word "custody" meant or why the Supreme Court would have any interest in me.

Eventually, back on the plane, I decided that fighting for full custody was actually a sly legal maneuver on my father's behalf to avoid paying child support. Winning my custody, I realized, had likely freed my father from certain financial obligations to Mother when it came time to discuss a final settlement.

First, though, back in the courtroom, as my mother's attorney had proceeded to lay out more arguments, so, too, the tension of my history mounted. Indeed, he was a savvy lawyer who must have deciphered my father's strategy and responded, doing his best to protect Nitsa:

The husband had the audacity to brag in public, in front of friends and relatives, that he could easily find a better educated and richer wife. He told third parties freely that "the woman disgusted him." Living with her and giving her his name was no longer possible.

Sadly, by then, the social status scales had tipped in the opposite direction. My mother's family's decline had allowed my father, a rising businessman, to claim superiority, despite the fact that it was her own dowry that had funded his accomplishments. But even so, during that low ebb in her family's finances, with her parents' support, my mother was able to defend herself, in spite of the shift in fortunes.

And by then, of course, my parents no longer valued the good, early years that they had together: the shared family, friends, and the daughter that they had raised. No, during that legal battle, I imagine that my mother's thoughts were the same as my own. "He took my dowry," she must have thought. "That had suited him well to build his riches. Now, he is parading like a peacock as an eligible groom. Well," I can imagine my mother scoffing, "he can go get another wife, for all I care. I am done. All I want is my child and my dignity back."

Shivering, I reached for the blanket I had stored under the front seat and covered my body, sitting still for a minute, waiting for warmth to return to my legs. For a moment, I thought about the strong women who had mothered me as I was growing up in Greece; two of them had never met each other, my mother and stepmother. Those mothers had been born six years apart. The older one had carried me in her belly and, even though we were separated, she was my life-long angel, while the other came to know me as the nine-year-old daughter of her new husband. One had been born and home-grown in Thessaloniki, and the other had wandered all over Greece with her military family. Their relationships to my father were so different, and so were their choices in life. I owed them both my life path and well-being. And then, there was Yiayia Sophia, a woman more complex than I had realized.

It was plain that communication had ceased to exist in our family home long before the divorce proceedings themselves had begun, and Yiayia had played a part in that dynamic. What had developed in the absence of dialogue was an insufferable situation that had dragged on because of the ten-year marriage requirement. Even all those years later, I could barely tolerate reading any longer; and yet, I could not stop, either. Her attorney wrote the last allegation:

> *Since December, he demanded that she stop taking care of her child, as his mother was now in charge of her. Creating scenes and incidents in the neighborhood against his wife, he forced her to abandon her husband's home and move in with her father's family.*

This document portrayed my yiayia as a dominant figure: possessive, demanding, and interfering in my bond with Mother. By then, it was February of 1953, three months after the petition had first been filed, and Yiayia was claiming me as her own daughter. A naïve and vulnerable six-year-old, I had, back then, been eager to accept her love, craving the security that every child needs. Betwixt and between once more, I stared at the document, feeling deceived. My unconditional love for Yiayia was, for the first time, utterly shaken. She had stolen me from my mother.

But perhaps it should have been no surprise. Now, as an adult, I know the dynamic all too well, having witnessed it time after time in my child protection work: grandmothers who claim their grandchildren for their own and take them away from their mothers. When a parent is abusive or neglectful of a child, families often burst in through anger and passion, and the courts sometimes order placements with grandparents who offer a safe and familiar environment. The important difference in my case was that I had a loving and nurturing mother.

As I know well, it is often a good choice to place children with family instead of in the "stranger care" of a foster home, but it does not always work out. In the aftermath of losing a mother, and amid the complex and often toxic relationships between parents and grandparents, it is often the children who pay the price. Quarrels and mistrust add tension to family relationships that shows up during visits and in court hearings when attorneys argue each party's point of view, upsetting children who live with the consequences of family strife. My grandmother's possessiveness, then, was out of misguided love.

Squeezed in the tight seat of a 777, I had been surrounded by passengers at a time when all I craved was privacy; I had been transported to the shadow years of my early history and was left with much to absorb. The petition left no further doubt that our home had been embattled. Caught up in the acrimony, I was struggling to sort what was true and what was exaggeration—or a flat-out lie.

34 TURNS OF FORTUNE
1964–1965

ate in the winter of 1964, a large envelope with the Fulbright Foundation logo arrived at our P. Sindika house. By then, it had been years since I'd first started dreaming of the possibility of traveling to the United States—somewhere far away from my mother and father's disagreements and the quiet shame of their divorce. Studying the English language since fourth grade, and being taught some subjects—literature, biology, and health science—in English in later grades by American teachers at Anatolia, participating in several school activities (psychology club, choir, drama club), and being the class president for a couple of years were credentials that I hoped would count when I was considering study abroad.

Months before, on the advice of one of my teachers, I had applied for a scholarship that would do just that: take me away from Greece for a time, just long enough, I hoped, to get my own bearings in life. Would the organization accept my application? Did I have enough qualifications to earn a scholarship? Or would all my effort be for naught? Now, the mailman was waiving me down to deliver the letter directly into my hands. Grasping it there at the entrance to our building, I could barely stop my fingers from trembling. Bursting with excitement, I sliced it open with my index finger and read the short cover letter in one breath.

"We are pleased to inform you . . ."

Two flights of stairs later, and very out of breath, I found my stepmother, who was cleaning lentils in the kitchen. "I am in!" I squealed, delighted. Together, we plunged through the enclosures, spreading them out on the kitchen table. There were more forms to fill out, and then I came across one that would cause me trouble.

"Nothing is simple." I shook my head. Because I was still a minor, I would need my father's consent. "Do you think he'll give it to me?"

But my stepmother just watched me quietly, setting a warm hand over mine.

That evening, when he returned home, I rushed my father through my good news, handing him the form with a grin. *Maybe if I showed him how exciting this was, he'd sign the consent without question.* My father did listen quietly, but then he frowned, taking the paper from me. "Too tired now. I will look at it later," he answered, locking it in the top drawer of his desk. Then, confused and dejected, I watched him leave the room.

For days thereafter, each time I pressed him for his signature, he replied with his slippery, well-worn words, "We'll see." Although he supported a good education, he was also true to his upbringing, wishing to keep his daughter near. And why? Did he also think of me as the son who might succeed him some day?

The consent form languished in his desk untouched for weeks; over time, I was getting more and more desperate, as I felt my dream to study abroad slipping away. I couldn't check on the form because my father always kept that desk drawer locked. Instead, from time to time, I'd ask my stepmother: "Did he sign it?"

And she would tell me, "Not yet."

"He's impossible!" I'd fume, turn around and walk away upset and mumbling under my breath, "Who does he think he is? I don't know what to do with him anymore!" He was getting in the way of my future, dithering, when it was clear to me what he should do. He knew about all my efforts to go to America and certainly had no right to stop me this late in the process.

Although perhaps he meant well, my father's passivity did not feel like a loving act. For a man who grew up in a culture that kept women at home, safe and taken care of, and gave them dowries to marry them off, the question of international studies was not an easy decision. On the day that his response was due in the mail, I brought it up again, pleading this time, "Come on, Father."

The paper had been retrieved from his desk. It stared at us bald-faced from the table.

"Please," I begged again. "I promise to make you proud."

Finally, I saw him pick up the document, holding it gingerly in his hands. He didn't look at all convinced. *Was he toying with me?* My stepmother stepped closer to him. I held my breath, watching them. "I hope it's the right decision," he muttered finally, picking up a pen to sign the document.

"Of course, it is," my stepmother assured him. "Give the girl a chance."

What a lovely surprise! And so unexpected. Apparently, my stepmother was on my side. She had, after all, shared her disappointment about having to give up her hope to study mathematics at the university because World War II had broken out and disrupted her dream. So now, I could have a bit of that dream, and I imagined that she must have done something behind the scenes to help convince my father. And why not? They had their son, my ten-year-old brother, who would one day be old enough to step into the family business. As for me, I was a girl—and I was headed to America!

Elated, I threw my arms around Father's neck and winked appreciatively at my stepmother. Then, I gathered the paperwork quickly and bolted for the post office. Queuing up, I did my best to wait calmly before handing the manila envelope to the clerk who weighed, stamped, and tossed it in a bin. Then it was off to the Fulbright Foundation in Athens, certified. The following week, a new list of "to-dos" came back from the Foundation, with another set of instructions. With renewed zeal, I made appointments and filled out more paperwork to meet the student visa requirements for the US: a physical exam, an X-ray, and more forms from the American Embassy. This was really going to happen!

Furthermore, good fortune had smiled upon me that last spring when our Anatolia dean of women introduced me to an American couple from Portland, Oregon. I'd met them when they were taking an Anatolia campus tour. I couldn't wait to tell my stepmother about Dr. Nevin and his wife whom I had met during my junior year. "They visited our campus, and I met them. He is a minister!" I knew my stepmother would especially appreciate that, as even heretic churches were better than nothing. John was a Presbyterian minister, tall, lean, and bespectacled, and was originally from Scotland. His wife, Gertrude, was a heavyset woman, with a quiet and kind disposition. The couple had generously offered me room and board while I came to study in the States at Lewis and Clark College. "They have an extra bedroom for me to use because their kids are grown and have moved out of their house," I said. I never knew if this introduction was a coincidence or planned by our dean.

And so, as things became more and more concrete, my excitement was building. I told the Nevinses that Joanna, my friend, had already graduated from Anatolia and was attending Whitman College. "Is that very far from Portland?"

"It's in the northern part of the neighboring state, in Washington," the man answered kindly, examining me through silver-rimmed glasses. His two children were grown and now it was just the two of them, he explained. They had plenty of room for me. Would this really work out?

Leafing through school catalogues at the British Council Library, I searched for and located Lewis and Clark, and selected a couple of other institutions on the East Coast to list on my Fulbright application. There were lots of forms to fill out and helpful advisors to interpret the questions I had to answer. Then it was time to wait and hope and watch the mailman closely when he delivered our mail. It took so long, I started telling myself it might not happen, but it finally came together. That offer from the Nevins, along with a Fulbright grant and the admission acceptance letter from Lewis and Clark College, was the last assurance that I would be going to the States. Life was good and scary, filled with the promise and fears of the unknown. In my own mind, I was already in Oregon. It was early spring of 1965. I was in my senior year of high school and I would soon be getting ready to leave Greece.

35 THE ACCIDENT
1965

On a spring afternoon, coming home from school, I noticed that a car was parked by our front door, and a couple of men from the Ladadika were making their way to our door. And then—horror!—I saw it: They were lifting my father's limp body into the house.

"This way. Careful. One more floor!" I heard them say, and I got closer, trying to sort out what had happened to him. My father looked helpless; his face was pale. Was he really so helpless? That was not at all like him. But he seemed alert; he was groaning, as though in pain.

"What happened?" My question hung in the air unanswered as the men struggled to carry him up the stairwell. I followed behind, watching my stepmother guiding them through the house. Even as they laid him in bed, pain escaped his lips. He must have been having spasms. I felt my stomach churn with acid.

Once they had laid him in bed, the men moved out of the bedroom and told us that a row of heavy coffee sacks had fallen on him, taking him down to the warehouse floor. The injury was bad; he couldn't move on his own and became dependent on the women around him for help. All night long, I could hear him whimpering. It was a fitful sleep that night for the whole household. The next morning my stepmother ordered me, "Go to the pharmacy and get some pain pills."

For the next few weeks, a thick sense of chaos hovered over the household. Father was paralyzed from the waist down. I was shell-shocked. The family was rudderless. All week, I could hear his muffled moans, and I stood by his door, ready to help—to bring water, a pillow, anything, hoping he would soon get up. Would he ever walk? Was his back broken? Finally, a doctor came to the house and recommended hospitalization. So my father was moved into a bare hospital room, where he lay on a metal bed, looking uncomfortable. But at least he was not in pain, drugged as he was.

As for us, back at home, my brother and I hovered in the care of our cleaning woman, anxious for news from my stepmother when she returned from her hospital visits in the evenings. A couple of times on weekends I went along with her, bringing flowers to my father's room, though mostly feeling helpless as I sat by his bed asking him if there was anything he wanted. "Just take me back home," he'd answer with barely a smile. I wanted to cry. Despite all the things that happened in our family, my father and I always had a special kinship. Always, I hungered for his support and confidence in me, and I was torn apart by that turn of events. It was a trying time.

As I worked to finish all the tests and scheduled appointments for my student visa, I began to reconsider my options. Up until that time, I had been exuberant about leaving. But could I now? Was this really a time when I could leave my family behind? Could I leave them, even though it was just for a while, until I earned my college degree in America? Was there something wrong with me, that I still felt excited about the prospect of leaving home? My teenaged heart had already unlatched the door to a new home, and freedom. It was hard to give that up.

Finally, when I heard that my father would be coming home to continue with treatment, I began to feel hopeful; maybe it would all work out. He would be all right, and I could go on with my plan. But then, the doctor was not willing to give us a prognosis. Faced with the stress of my father's possible paralysis and my upcoming finals at school, my own stress worsened. I began experiencing headaches and seesawing emotions.

One day, I walked into the living room to see a remarkable sight:

My father was lying flat with his legs suspended and counterbalanced by a cylindrical weight. He could hardly move, though at least that contraption eliminated muscle spasms., He looked uncomfortable a lot of the time. Everything had become complicated: his eating, drinking, changing into fresh drawstring pajamas. Even his basic hygiene routines required assistance. Occasionally, a physical therapist would show up, and we kids had to be mindful, though we still hovered in the living room. My father was rarely bothered, and my stepmother did police our activities, sending us outside to play. The days moved ever so haltingly.

Several weeks went by with little change. On one particular evening, my family was all gathered in the living room. As I was getting ready to settle down for the night, my father said to me, "Open the balcony door a tad and come sit by me."

It felt strange to have my father ask me for a favor. It was not his habit. Still, I crossed the living room and opened the balcony door a crack. The curtain swayed gently, as if giving life to a ghostly presence. Then I settled in the chair next to his bed and waited.

"The worst-case scenario is that I remain paralyzed," he said wanly.

"But, Father, you will get better. It's only a matter of time," I protested, unwilling to admit that it had occurred to me too.

"You may have to forget America," he answered, looking grim. His words dripped with danger about his future, and mine. I had a shrinking feeling inside.

Listening in, my stepmother handed him a glass of water and a straw to sip with. "You *are* getting better," she reminded him. "The physical therapist says he can see it." Her voice was emphatic; we all wanted him to get well.

The next time he brought it up, I paused and asked, "So, what would you have me do, Father?" realizing that I might need to act in his stead, and it would be best to find out what he had in mind.

"I would start you in the office," he paused, explaining how I'd have to begin taking my role in the family business. "Your uncle will help you too." But, as he spoke, I felt my hopes withering into the pit of my acidic stomach. *My adventure! America! What might happen to it all?* I much preferred to go after the adventure of America and desperately hung onto hope.

But my father had been thinking about different priorities: work, and how he could keep the family business running. Still, I didn't see how it would work. How could I really help? I didn't have the skills that he had acquired: his intimate knowledge of coffee; the roasting, grinding, and packaging process; and his familiarity with his clientele. My father had trained his clerks and personally took care of so much, together with his brother, who was his business partner, that it was hard to think about replacing him. How could he trust me to do all of this? But then, too, it pleased me that my father trusted me. What more could that mean for me as his daughter? Or as a woman? Would my life, miraculously, turn out differently from my aunt's or Mother's? My own father, somehow, had a hand in all of this. Whatever happened—my going to America, or my becoming a woman running a business—it all seemed to rest on him.

There must have been more discussions between my father and stepmother because when the subject came up again, my stepmother declared unexpectedly, "I will work in the office every day, if we have to." My father remained silent. I felt relief—and gratitude toward my stepmother. Whether or not it was even possible to manage with a young son and a paralyzed husband at home, what mattered to me just then was that my road oversees was still open. Realistic or not, I was grateful to hear her offer, even though I believed that it must have been convenient for her to see me go. If she could manage even a part of all that, I would certainly be on my way to Oregon for the years it took to complete my education. Settling in the United States was not an impossibility; my stepmother had to have known that. Once, my stepmother had spoken about an uncle John, someone related to her, who had settled in Texas and had never returned to Greece. Maybe I could find him, she had suggested. Perhaps it was hard to know if all that had a bearing on her support; but, with her willingness to work in the business, my chances to study abroad were improving.

Dreaming, wondering, and planning—we'd all spent several trepidatious weeks that way. Then, unexpectedly, one afternoon my father joked, "Don't forget to bring my suit and tie from the cleaners, Sophoula. I will soon need it."

Maybe it was just humor, but that, I thought, was a good sign. Over the next month, he started sitting up more on his own. Yes, I thought, maybe I can go. I had, after all, been keeping up my preparations through it all, despite my other lingering sense of guilt: my mother. The lead weight of worry for also abandoning her was likewise stealing my excitement. By then, it was almost August. My father was coming along well, and I was on one of my last visits with my mother. That afternoon, we took the familiar road to the park by the White Tower. I tried telling her about attending a college orientation program in the US.

"It's in a town they call Eugene, on a university campus. We will stay at the dorms. I've never stayed in dorms." I could hear the flatness in my own voice.

Was I ready to close the door on eighteen years of growing up in Greece, to leave behind those I loved, and to open a window to a world that was foreign and unknown? I was certainly willing although I wished I could leave Thessaloniki without guilt. Maybe I was heartless deep-down inside, but I was also stubbornly sticking to my goal to study abroad.

My mother listened to my descriptions, though she soon shifted to her advice-giving mode. "Remember, be careful about who your new friends will be," she said, resigned to my leaving. "I know you will. And do write to me often."

I promised her I would write every week. After all, that was my last visit with my Hadjimichael family before my departure to the States. My grandfather's goodbye verses turned out to be prophetic.

I am going, leaving you my shadow as consolation
to have and to hold, so that it breaks your heart.

Little did I know that I would never see him or my grandmother Athena alive again.

Before leaving the D. Gounary apartment, my mother and I decided to go look for a photographer, one with an old, quaint box camera that sat on a tall wooden tripod. That morning we again strolled down to the park by the White Tower, where outdoor photographers in white lab coats looked for passersby and tourists most every day. The photographer was older, tall, and trim, and a man of few words. He suggested that we pose for him seated on a bench. My mother agreed and asked me to take my glasses off. "I want a clear view of your eyes."

As the photographer lifted the lens cap for a few seconds and quickly covered the lens again, we sat as still as could be. A few minutes later, he reached from the rear of the camera inside the box through a black sleeve. We watched him silently. Then he dunked the photographic paper in chemicals stored in the drawer inside the box and showed us our images: sad, gloomy expressions that we would hold onto long after my departure.

My mother asked for two pictures and handed me one. I would carry it in my suitcase and keep it by my bed in America. It would be how I saluted my mother's melancholy image for the next three years. Because yes, in the end, I would go. By the time school finals were over, my father was up and walking on his own again after three months of treatments. My departure was set for mid-August of 1965.

I was untethered, slated to reach the opposite end of the globe traveling on the ocean liner *Queen Anna Maria* to New York, and then flying on to Oregon. Though I was sometimes forlorn and still living with unanswered questions about my divorced parents, I was excited, ready for the adventure of a lifetime, heading into the unknown.

36 LANDING IN CHICAGO
November 20, 2015 (2:00 p.m.)

Finally, we were about to land at O'Hare. Quickly, I searched my purse for my passport and boarding pass for the final flight to Seattle and placed them in my coat pocket. Already, it had been a very long, exhausting trip. I would still need to clear customs and find the gate for Seattle, but the best part was that I would be able to stretch my legs in the wide hallways and escalators of the airport.

As I waited, I returned once again to my imaginary courtroom where the judges were still deliberating. They had reviewed and signed off on the petition to indicate the court's acceptance. There was not much more left to read in that document other than a list of witnesses. I vaguely recognized a couple of names, but there were more that were unknown to me. Apparently, the court had not been satisfied with testimony because of contradictions and inconsistencies among the witnesses. The judges had responded by setting another hearing, requiring the presence of four witnesses and my parents, in person this time, for further questioning. I was quite sure that neither Periclis nor Nitsa would have relished the thought of exposing their differences in a public hearing. To the best of my knowledge, that hearing never took place. (At least, Christina had been unable to locate any other court documents.) If so, it seemed like an unusual way to pursue the dissolution of marriage, a deviation from the ordinary route that would have kept the judicial system involved to the end. Just then, I was realizing that, when my own marriage had not worked out, in a way, my husband and I had made the same kind of choice: one that avoided a public display of our differences by choosing to engage in mediation.

My thoughts were interrupted by the voice of a flight attendant that came on the loudspeaker to deliver landing announcements to O'Hare: "For your own safety, please fasten your seat belts and remain seated until the plane has landed."

I adjusted my watch to the local time and turned off the overhead light, smiling at the word "safety." It did not suit me on this flight; I had endured enough inner turbulence and was eager for the bumpy flight to end. When the wheels touched down, I had already shut off my computer. At last, we were on the ground, and I began collecting my belongings.

On the crowded plane, I lined up in the aisles, ready to exit, and we all soon poured out of the Boeing 777 to join a stream of anonymous crowds at the airport and wait to clear customs. Pulling my carry-on, I clenched the laptop case under my armpit and looked for my gate. Navigating through the documents that Christina had sent had kept me preoccupied. I looked at my watch; it was nearly three o'clock, and this stopover was barely an hour and a half long. Thankfully, customs had cleared us quickly, and, past the metal detector, I put my shoes back on, rushing through escalators and corridors and under fluorescent lights, asking security for directions and following signs to my gate. The departures board had shown that my flight was boarding. It was a tight timeline, pressing on me to nearly run, though it did help me to set aside the tight and gripping mix of emotions that I had been carrying in my chest for several hours.

As I made my way through the hustle of the airport, I turned my mind back to Yiayia Sophia, my perplexing grandmother, who was the riddle that I still needed to understand better. She had been a daughter, wife, and mother, a strong woman who had managed to survive the challenge of a jealous husband who relocated his family from Constantinople to the distant Cappadocia in Southeast Turkey.

Then, again in Greece, she saw her family start from scratch and slowly gain its foothold. All of life's uncertainties would have made her a person who clung to the precious past and the known. She was the matriarch of the Kouidis family and naturally partial to her youngest son, my father. It probably was the culture of her upbringing, her era, that was tolerant and even accepting of things like men's dalliances.

By the time I reached my Seattle gate, it was four o'clock, and I was the last to board. Down the aisle, I was self-conscious of all the eyes fixed on me as I searched for my seat and settled down as best I could for the last leg of my trip home. It was a quieter flight that evening, the passengers tired and subdued, the airplane lights dimmed, and flight attendant activity sparse. We had four and a half hours to go before reaching our destination. Laboring to stay awake, my thoughts meandered to my mother and her short-lived stay in the States.

Nitsa was leaving behind a patriarchal society that had challenged and harmed her in the insidious ways that shaped the turn of events when our family broke up. I experienced that influence growing up but perceived it more clearly after living in the US for a number of years. The move to the Pacific Northwest came too late in my mother's life to give her a full flavor of the American experience. In her time, of course, her Greek husband was entitled to a dowry by law, and a woman belonged in the house and especially in the kitchen. Society was skeptical and suspicious of divorced women, and the economic consequences of her divorce were catastrophic for her and the Hadjimichael family, changing their social status entirely. In retrospect, this injustice was hurtful but also fascinating. I realized that this type of social structure broke down my Hadjimichael family and left my mother vulnerable and unprepared to support herself, seek employment, or have some basic resources to live as an adult. Quite a turn of fortune for her and other women caught in similar circumstances.

Today, even in a more progressive country like the US, the influence of patriarchy justifies in the minds of some several inequities: unequal wages, male dominance in the board rooms, sexual harassment of female employees, and domestic violence that often results in the breakdown of families, to name a few of the symptoms. Change comes slowly, but American women are aware and demanding social and legislative change. For my mother, coming to a new continent and moving to a new culture could not alleviate the wounds of her past, but her arrival gave her a chance to experience living in a gentler world.

In spite of my enthusiasm, it was not easy for her to leave Thessaloniki. She had never been abroad and was about to move in with a daughter whom she had only experienced directly for short visits throughout most of our lives. Also, we had decided to move her in with me and my young marriage to an American husband, who, although good-natured and accepting of the arrangement, needed my time and attention as well. Bill was a kind, mild man, a social worker by profession, and ten years older. I could still picture him sitting patiently in his corduroy slacks and white button-down shirt in our living room, straining to follow my mother and me speaking in Greek—often about people he didn't know. Most of the time, my mother would talk about her aunts and other relatives, people whom I didn't know very well either, but most often she would bring up my aunt Marika.

"I worry about her," she would tell me. "When they release her home, she can't be by herself." Even with—and perhaps because of— the challenges that they had faced, my mother and her schizophrenic sister had remained close. Their letters traveled slowly, not quite filling the gap of everyday access and contact. Still, having my mother there had its good points. I worried about Aunt Marika, too, but I liked hearing my mother's thoughts about her life in Greece, and I loved the daily patter of ordinary Greek conversations inhabiting my home.

Nevertheless, during her six months there with us, my mother was often frustrated with the new ways of managing everyday tasks. "I need a couple of eggs from the grocery. Do you have to drive me? Isn't anything closer?"

The distances were long and public transportation was not within walking distance, like it was for her in Thessaloniki.

"What bus do I take to go to the park?"

"It's almost easier to walk there, if you must," I would answer. "Wait until Sunday, and we can all go together. Make a list."

"How do I pay the bus driver?" she would persist. "I can't even get some fruit from the grocery store without needing to get in the car, and have you drive me."

Despite these frustrations, though, she was glad to see that my husband and I were getting along well, and she said she liked him. All throughout her visit, she continued calling him "my Billy," and was relieved to see me content—something that seemed important for her to witness firsthand. But the workdays were long. Home alone, she was getting restless. So we tried to make conversation; we tried to get by. "What did you do all day, Mom?" I would ask when I got home. But before we returned from work, she started taking off on long walks, even in the dusk through empty city streets. That's when I would have to scold: "This isn't Greece. It's not safe, Mother."

"You don't expect me to stay locked up in the house all day!" she would grimace and look away. It became a sore subject. "Trust me," she would demand. "I am not a child." Her sensibilities, based on the safe neighborhoods of Thessaloniki, held no alarms.

"Stop it, Mother. Call a friend, watch TV, read. Don't roam." But Bill's and my protective warnings fell on deaf ears. Sometimes, we returned to an empty house, no note, the front door unlocked. That was infuriating for all of us.

Eventually, she shared with me that she was having trouble sleeping. The days were long with us gone at work. She was lonely and

restless, and the experiment of having her live with us was not working as I had hoped. The few hours at the Greek church each Sunday
did not give her enough contact with community to satisfy her, and
she was reluctant to make new friends. She missed her own people in
Thessaloniki. "If I were home," she would say, "I would be going to a
movie, the park by the White Tower, or for a visit to friends."

Moreover, I found out that she still was no cook. "What are you
making for dinner?" she would inquire.

"Chicken and potatoes in the oven. The chicken is ready to bake.
It's in the refrigerator. Can you start it?"

"I will turn the oven on before you get home," she'd promise,
though that left all the responsibility to me, a discovery that I confess
did not work for me. Although I could cope with the meal preparation with my husband's help, I came to resent it and reconsidered
Yiayia Sophia's reign in the kitchen. I wondered then if it was by
choice or because of necessity. My mother's spirits began to flag. Her
life in America was not what either of us had hoped.

One evening, I woke up in the middle of the night to find her
sitting alone in the living room. She was dressed, forlorn, homesick,
and spoke of her apartment, her family, her friends. I realized that
I had failed to give her the right conditions to adjust, caught up as I
had been with work and my spouse. She was a woman in her fifties;
change came slowly. She wanted to return to Thessaloniki, and I was
getting upset. "Can't you try a little longer? It gets easier with time,
Mother. We are figuring it out. It's like knowing your American shoe
and dress sizes here. It just takes time."

But my mother was clear in her decision. A decisive woman once
more, she was taking a stance, recognizing what was the best choice
for her. "I worry about Marika and my empty apartment, Sophoula.
It's best to go back!"

And she was right—for me too. Sadly, it really was not the best
time for me to try integrating her into my life, just as I was launching

a marriage and a career in my new home. Culture shock devoured our chances to build what was turning out to be my rescue fantasy. In truth, six months later, when we decided that it was best for her to return to Thessaloniki, I felt not only regret, but also relief. Much later, I realized that our opportunity to get to know each other better and to build a real family life was forever gone. I had not been enough to support her, and I was about to lose my mother for the second time.

The distance that had shielded me from a challenging family situation, taking me away from the people I loved, had won. Unexpectedly, the road had forked for me and my mother, and I finally accepted her decision. Once more, our lives were lived across the globe, and our communication was confined to correspondence and the precious days when I vacationed in Greece.

37 AMERICA, AMERICA
1965

On the evening of my last day in Thessaloniki, I could hardly sleep. It was 1965, I was eighteen years old, and America was calling me. The minute I opened my eyes on a day dripping with rainbows, the July dawn broke in sharply. It was a morning filled with a quickened rush of preparations for the long trip to America, wrapping up days of excitement, last-minute chores, and emotionally taxing goodbyes. My eyes opened, I stretched my arms and kicked off the warm bed sheets, brushing away the morning cobwebs and the weight of the hours. I jumped into the clothes that I had laid out the night before, pulled the curtains aside, and opened my bedroom window to gaze out at the brightening lapis sky.

For a moment, I watched a flock of blackbirds scamper into the skyline, gliding toward the sea in frenzied excitement. An odd mix of euphoria and urgency overtook me at the sight of four suitcases lined up on the floor, already locked, the keys on a ring by my bedside. The night before, my father had inked my initials in large block caps on each of the suitcase lids with a permanent ink marker from the warehouse. "To make them easy to find," he'd told me. He always had good, practical ideas. I could not afford to lose track of them. After all, they held all my portable life belongings, each item chosen carefully for the college years ahead: clothes, shoes, books, my harmonica, a handful of photos, an assortment of the necessary and the prized. Packed and locked, they were lined up on the floor under my bedroom window.

I had to find my soothing pocket companion, still missing from my luggage. Searching in my nightstand, I looked for my soft, worn rabbit foot that mother had given me long ago. Soft and tattered from all the years of carrying it in my pockets, I was almost sure I had kept it there, likely on the bottom shelf. It was time to surface it again. Shuffling through abandoned tops and underwear, I finally found it, hidden under a handful of paired socks.

Just in time, I thought.

Unlocking a suitcase, I carefully tucked it in the middle, folding it inside my soft flannel nightgown. In America, I would again carry it in my pockets, my soothing companion in the far reaches of the Pacific Northwest. But just then, I shut the lid, turned the tiny metal key that hung on the lock for the last time, and placed the set in my wallet. Then one by one, I carried all four suitcases to the front door. My parents and my brother were already sitting around the kitchen table. I could hear my stepmother talking to my father in a low voice, and I joined them.

"Good morning," I greeted them, as I had done most days of my life. My voice sounded strained, though, pressed by an awareness that I would soon be absent from that very house. Still, I took my seat next to my brother and asked him, "Did you finish your milk?" He was, after all, my finicky sibling.

"I saved you some toast," he replied, tilting his cup to show me it was empty, his eyes wide and bewildered. At ten years of age, he barely understood that I would be gone for at least two years.

As for my stepmother, she had been up early and had made our break-fast. Father was in the kitchen in his robe, feigning reading last night's newspaper, and watching us quietly out of the corner of his eye. She poured me a cup of tea. I downed it, ate the toast quickly, and took the dishes to the sink. Just then, I heard the alarm that I had set the night before to ring at nine o'clock. So we were out of time, and I was eager to get on our way. I looked at my father, but I couldn't read his mood.

Getting to his feet, he gave me a fleeting smile. "Sophoula, here is an envelope with some dollars I gathered. Keep it safe in your wallet. For what extras you need on your trip."

I stuffed it into my purse unopened and gave him a quick, shy hug. I could always count on my father to make provisions.

Following my brother then, we moved to where I had lined up my suitcases. He picked one up and groaned. "What did you stash in here? Your books?" and he set it down quickly.

"Only those you are too young to read!" I laughed. My thick, trusty *Oxford Learner's Dictionary*, a couple of English school texts, and my favorite Greek novels were packed in it—Loudemis, Kazantzakis— and a poetry anthology by Tagore.

My stepmother was all dressed and ready to go when my brother handed me a chocolate bar. "It's your favorite," he said knowingly. I kissed him quickly on both cheeks and stuffed it in my purse. Last goodbyes were too intense to hold inside. Grabbing my coat saved me from prolonging the moment. This was the hour that would put miles and oceans and, yes, years of separation between me and my family. All that dizzy awareness was getting in the way of the sheer excitement and joy for the adventure that lay ahead of me.

Then my father was calling for a cab. I took one suitcase and, balancing off the banister, carried it to the street with my brother behind me.

"Stay here. I will be back for the rest," I instructed.

After three more trips carrying the bags down two flights each of the wooden staircase, I returned panting upstairs for the last time. Then I held my brother by his hand and looked for our father. He was standing by the front door, looking somber. He was not supposed to lift anything because of his back problems, nor was he one to be effusive. Placing his reading glasses in his pocket, he opened his arms for an awkward goodbye hug. I tucked right in.

"Write us as soon as you get to America." Could I detect a tiny break in his voice?

"I will," I promised, squeezing him softly and smothering my own emotions so no tears would escape. Father was not one for silly outbursts. My stepmother, who had come down to meet the taxi, and the cab driver were arranging my suitcases in the trunk. Following her, I ran down the steps for the last time, took my seat, and we were off, leaving my father and brother behind. They moved to the balcony and waved as we slipped away.

So, the adventure was beginning. My stepmother joined me in my excitement, offering words of advice: "Be careful, be kind, write often. . . ." She went on and on. But most of all, I remained grateful to her for her last-minute intervention that had convinced my father to sign the consent document that would release me to the world.

She accompanied me on the train all the way to Athens. The days that followed moved along fast. There was shopping and more relatives to say goodbye to, and then my stepmother saw me off to the Port of Piraeus and watched me board the ocean liner *Queen Anna Maria* that would sail for fourteen days and nights on the high seas to reach New York City. *New York,* I mused, *I am really doing it.* I'd jumped into the journey to America with the fervor of youth, ready for adventure, excited, eager to find out what the future held. The date was the 24th of July, 1965. It was crisply stamped in the center of my passport, inside a square stamp marked "Passport Control, Piraeus, Exit" in dark blue ink.

After two weeks at sea, we approached Ellis Island in New York Harbor. The morning air was cool, and there was a strong breeze slowly clearing the fog, sending shivers down my back. As we pulled in, I wore my windbreaker and remained on deck. The vast, dark ocean appeared like a seascape, defined by a harbor, now visible on the horizon. Seagulls glided above us, circling in the air and checking out the ship's decks. One of the crew members had told me that about this time we would be coming in full view of the Statue of Liberty,

"The Lady," as I referred to her. I was one of a handful of passengers who were on the front deck eager to see her. I especially wanted to see the seven rays of her crown representing the seven continents, a suitable symbol at this time, when I was relocating from Europe to North America.

I became one of the hundreds of thousands of travelers, immigrants, and refugees who have viewed the Statue of Liberty upon entering New York by boat since 1886. Feeling humble, proud, and inspired, I searched the horizon. Suddenly, the Statue of Liberty appeared out of the morning fog. As we approached the harbor, she grew in size, as did my sense of awe. I stayed on deck, transfixed by the sight of her, partly because of her imposing size, and partly due to my own amazement that I had truly arrived in the United States of America. She gazed in the distance and seemed to be welcoming me, a young woman to the young continent. I stayed on deck as long as I could. She was the promise of a new life, and I was just a few hours away from disembarking at my future home. Then, off the boat and onto land, with my four suitcases in a cab, I headed to the airport.

It was a leap of considerable distance—a separation, my emancipation, and an adventure. But was this flight from a broken childhood (and from a society structured to support patriarchy) an escape, or was it a journey to seek opportunities and new beginnings? Flight can be such an uplifting enterprise. It raises hope and opens new horizons. Flight can also be running away, an escape from misery that pulls one down into further depths of hopelessness and isolation. For me, this was an opening, a time when a dream was fulfilled, when the gods were nodding with a smile. My wings had carried me into the first page of a new chapter. It was my time to show what I was made of and receive what this world had to offer me.

38 ARRIVING IN SEATTLE
November 20, 2015 (10:30 p.m.)

It had been half a century since I had first come to America, and plenty had been buried in Greece, left smoldering all this while in the old country. In a short time, I would be landing in Seattle, back to my year-round home, winding down a chapter of this odyssey. It was time to abandon the family courtroom, the disputes, the guesses, and the revelations that had dominated my thoughts like a swarm of dark, winged companions.

The last announcements about local weather, connecting flights, and luggage location were wrapping up. The hum of landing gear getting ready for touchdown and the night lights of the airport signaled the end of the journey. My neighbors were wrestling with their belongings and looking out the window at the city blocks, the red lights on the side of the runway. When we landed, I joined them in an applause. Then, standing up, I took out my dark blue coat from the overhead bin, wrapping my scarf around my neck—its pink colors for childhood dreams, gray for the bay of a city that I had left behind less than twenty-four hours ago, and red for life's blood. It was a cold November night in Seattle.

Everyone around me was preparing to leave, collecting their books and computers, making calls, and gathering their belongings. I gathered my stuff on my lap and waited for my turn. Soon I would be walking in the empty corridors of the airport with my rushing fellow travelers. We came down a level on the escalator to pick up our luggage from the carousel and headed out, each to our own destination.

As for me, I was relieved to be back in the Pacific Norwest, and even in my exhausted state from the long and arduous journey, I knew that I would be sorting through and reconsidering the uncovered story, one that was all mine, for some time. This cargo held precious contents and deserved some time to settle in, a calmer mind and recurring deliberation. For now, I could relax, stepping onto terra firma, enjoying the rush of being home and momentarily leaving behind Thessaloniki's footprint. How much distance, after all, might I need to absorb all I had learned in recent years? Miles, decades, the gentle space from one heart to the next? And so, regaining my bearings in Seattle's rainy night, carting my visible and invisible luggage, I flagged a cab to take me home.

EPILOGUE: SEATTLE, WASHINGTON, USA
December 2018

In my post-retirement trips to my birthplace, I eventually blasted an opening into a past that I had set aside, but only temporarily, while I lived in America. Relatives, friends, and acquaintances have helped me to rebuild and to fill in the landscape of my childhood as much as possible. My parents' divorce application divulged new information and birthed sizzling memories that altered the canvas of a past I had locked and guarded for a long time. All fragments of memory and search continued swirling in my mind, and I finally came to realize that people's relationships continue to evolve even after death.

It took time for me to absorb the new information and reconsider the past. I had to process my childhood years over again. Overcome by shock, surprise, and anger, I settled into a revised picture of the past, enlightened with life experiences and my accumulated years. My hair is gray, like Mother's was in her mature years, and she is still teaching me life's lessons, showing me that every story has many sides. I have learned that a critical element in human relationships is to seek a balance, not dominance.

Money reigns just as much as the ego. Consider that the court costs were paid by my father, 27000 drachmas, a significant amount for its day. The older generation had a saying that "the big fish eats the small one." People draw their power from money and the influence they hold from their social circle, and they assist and promote each other's interests. The times permitted it, but these kinds of sins and battles are not the responsibility of one person. The times, the

271

inequality between the sexes, and the financial wealth of each family involved played a role in the development of this story. Who took part—and how they managed—is not exactly clear, but that is what happened, and it fits the era in which it unfolded. That was how society functioned then—not unlike today. Nitsa's life burned down in that pyre, and when she lay down to rest, she joined her contemporaries, a pauper in a common grave. Earth to earth, ashes to ashes, and dust to dust.

Today, three years after that 2015 Thanksgiving, I know that my parents' love for me was rich and generous, and I view my childhood with a greater understanding of their actions. For their time and their own histories, they gave me the best they had, trying to protect me and offer me as carefree a childhood as they possibly could. In the intervening years, the distance that had shielded me from a difficult family situation had also distanced me from the people I have loved best. What I ultimately needed was to build my own path with what I had earned and been given. I am grateful that my efforts in recent years have filled in unknown pieces about the past, and I continue to roam and rekindle fond memories of the past in the familiar cobblestones of Thessaloniki, the city I was born in and love. The place has finally yielded some of its secrets.

Greece has always called me back, even after my mother and father passed away. My parents' absence from the land of my birth gave me permission and the freedom to search and learn more about my family, who we were and how we behaved. I no longer risked wounding them by digging into the past. My ties to Thessaloniki remain continuous and vital; I return often and maintain contacts with family and friends.

Now that the riddles are finally dissolving, I savor a better understanding of the past. The shoulds, woulds, and musts of that time are fading, and my people are no longer mythical or definitively drawn; they are softer, gentler, and so much more human, like me. I know that their silence has not been there just to hold secrets; it has rather been a shield for them from what was too painful to remember and share.

The jagged edges of a broken mirror I unearthed have lost their sharpness. It is time to release my young years to the past and seek the fullness of days in my mature years. As I turn bygones to the past, I believe that there is good awaiting us in life, and we ought to have it.

ACKNOWLEDGMENTS

To my literary mentors and writing community near and far—Sandra Hartley, Seena, Jean Gilbertson, Renée E. D'Aoust, Brenda S. Peterson and Salish Writers, Hugo House and its instructors, Theo Nestor and Susan Meyers, and the feedback groups I joined—I owe a heartfelt thanks for showing, teaching, reviewing, and encouraging my work to be more grounded and authentic. To my family, classmates, and friends, I am indebted for shared memories and support as I worked on this project.

You are and will remain my special, heartfelt companions on this journey.

sophiakouidougiles.com

Eleni and her daughter, Sophia. Photo by Studio ΦΩΤΟ.

ABOUT THE AUTHOR

© Yuen Lui Studio

Sophia Kouidou-Giles was born in Thessaloniki, Greece, and university educated in the United States. She holds a bachelor's degree in psychology and a master's in social work. In her over thirty-year child welfare career in the Pacific Northwest, she has served as a practitioner, educator, researcher, and administrator. Kouidou-Giles has published articles in Greek and English professional journals with a focus on services to abused and neglected children. Her poetry chapbook, *Transitions and Passages,* received recognition in a juried competition by the Contemporary Quilt Art Association. *Return to Thessaloniki*/Επιστροφή Στη Θεσσαλονίκη was published by Tyrfi Publications in Greece in June 2019 in the Greek language.

SELECTED TITLES FROM SHE WRITES PRESS

She Writes Press is an independent publishing company founded to serve women writers everywhere. Visit us at www.shewritespress.com.

The Butterfly Groove: A Mother's Mystery, A Daughter's Journey by Jessica Barraco. $16.95, 978-1-63152-800-2

In an attempt to solve the mystery of her deceased mother's life, Jessica Barraco retraces the older woman's steps nearly forty years earlier—and finds herself along the way.

At the Narrow Waist of the World: A Memoir by Marlena Maduro Baraf $16.95, 978-1-63152-588-9

In this lush and vivid coming-of-age memoir about a mother's mental illness and the healing power of a loving Jewish and Hispanic extended family, young Marlena must pull away from her mother, leave her Panama home, and navigate the transition to an American world.

Veronica's Grave: A Daughter's Memoir by Barbara Bracht Donsky $16.95, 978-1-63152-074-7

A loss and coming-of-age story that follows young Barbara Bracht as she struggles to comprehend the sudden disappearance and death of her mother and cope with a blue-collar father intent upon erasing her mother's memory.

I'm the One Who Got Away: A Memoir by Andrea Jarrell $16.95, 978-1-63152-260-4

When Andrea Jarrell was a girl, her mother often told her of their escape from Jarrell's dangerous, cunning father as if it was a bedtime story. Here, Jarrell reveals the complicated legacy she inherited from her mother—and shares a life-affirming story of having the courage to become both safe enough and vulnerable enough to love and be loved.

Songs My Mother Taught Me: A Story in Progress by Eva Izsak $16.95, 978-1-63152-551-3

After years of trying to escape her heritage through constant movement around the globe, middle-aged Eva finds herself in a poor suburb of Tel Aviv, nursing her dying mother in the house she grew up in—and is forced to face the ghosts of the past and belatedly cut the umbilical cord that has had an all-consuming grip on her for more than five decades.